Forever Suspect

Forever Suspect

Racialized Surveillance of Muslim
Americans in the War on Terror

SAHER SELOD

Rutgers University Press

New Brunswick, Camden, and Newark, New Jersey, and London

Library of Congress Cataloging in Publication Number: 2017054953

A British Cataloging-in-Publication record for this book is available from the British Library.

∞ The paper used in this publication meets the requirements of the American National
Standard for Information Sciences—Permanence of Paper for Printed Library Materials,
ANSI Z39.48-1992.

www.rutgersuniversitypress.org

Manufactured in the United States of America.

For my parents, my husband, and my daughter

Contents

Forever Suspect

Introduction

Racialized Surveillance in the War on Terror

I vividly remember the morning of 9/11. I was working at the *Chicago Reader*, a weekly alternative paper, compiling movie and theater listings. That morning, a coworker and friend called me as I was heading out to work and asked me if I was going to stay home that day. When I asked why, he told me to turn on the television. I remember seeing endless footage of the planes hitting the World Trade Center and the towers collapsing. I also recall my friend begging me to come to his house where he felt he could keep me safe. At the time, I lived alone in a condo in a young, predominantly white, professional neighborhood. This friend was worried for my safety because I am a Pakistani Muslim American. Within hours of the attacks, the identities of the perpetrators were revealed: all Muslim. Even though the terrorists came from Saudi Arabia, the United Arab Emirates, Egypt, and Lebanon, my friend feared I would be associated with these men because of a shared religious identity. I called my editor that morning, who told me I could stay home if I needed to but that the paper would still come out on deadline. I knew no one else could do my job, so I decided to go into work. As I was riding in a cab heading downtown, I was confronted with the eerie sight of swarms of people trying to catch cabs and buses in the opposite direction. When I got to work, the silence there was chilling. The only sound was a television brought into the break room that droned on all day. I heard Peter Jennings, a Canadian American television reporter for ABC, urging Americans to refrain from expressing their anger toward Muslims or Middle Easterners. While it brought some comfort to hear him say this, it also instilled fear in me because I knew Muslims would have to brace themselves for the impending backlash.

For weeks after the attack, I felt a range of emotions: I cried as I watched the victims' families grieving on television for the loss of their loved ones; I hated the attackers for the innocent lives they took; I resented them for the lasting impact this assault would have on the lives of many blameless people who would be forced to unjustly accept responsibility for the attack. And I was scared. I was scared for many reasons. I was terrified there would be another attack. I was afraid of how strangers would treat me if they knew I was a Muslim. For a while, I refrained from making eye contact with strangers on the street out of a fear of seeing any anger and hatred toward me because I am not white and am often questioned about my status as an American. I was also fearful of what my friends' responses would be to the attacks. Although the majority of the people I know have always been open-minded about religious difference, I knew any suppressed religious bigotry would surface after a terrorist attack of this scope. I found myself anxious about the safety of my parents, who live in Texas. My mother wears the hijab, and both my parents are extremely active members of the mosque in the town they live in. I knew the mosque would be a target for anti-Muslim anger, and I worried they could be in danger. What I experienced for the next few years after that horrific day was what piqued my interest in the experiences of Muslim Americans.

The fears I had immediately after September 11th in many ways have come to fruition. Anytime there is another terrorist attack, I worry that the response from the public and the government will be worse than the last one. The experiences of Muslim Americans have in many ways gotten worse in the fifteen years since 9/11. That date set in motion a series of laws and policies that would forever change the American way of life I once knew.

For the Muslim Americans who remember life before 9/11, that event brought a new type of contestation and questioning of their national identity because of their religion. South Asian Muslim immigrants and their offspring have historically been denied complete access to an American identity (Kibria 1998; Purkayastha 2005; Dhingra 2007), but because the association of Islam with terror has been structured into laws and policies that dealt with national security after 9/11, their experiences changed.

Of course, it would be a mistake to assume Muslims' experiences since 9/11 have been universal. Factors such as gender, skin tone, and accent also play a crucial role in how Muslim Americans experience everyday life in a nation engaged in the War on Terror.

My father was one of the thousands of Muslim Americans who had to endure questions from the FBI about his patriotism and loyalty to the United States. Shortly after the attacks, my father was deboarding a plane after a work trip to Dubai, where he attended a medical conference. As he exited the plane,

TSA agents stopped him and escorted him to a private room where he was interrogated about his travels. This was an experience he had not encountered prior to 9/11. The agents knew information about my father's travel, such as what he bought while he was there. This made my dad feel that he was being watched and monitored by the government. My father is a practicing and devout Muslim who has always been proud of his status as an American citizen. Like so many other migrant Muslims, he moved to the United States in hope of a better life for himself and his family. For my father, becoming a citizen was a choice that he took so much pride in. But as the years have passed since 9/11, it has become increasingly apparent that because my father is a Muslim, he is vulnerable to being seen as un-American and a potential threat to national security. A few weeks after 9/11, my father began wearing an American flag pin on his coat lapel, something he still wears, in case anyone might question his loyalty to the United States.

The hijab, a headscarf many Muslim women wear to demonstrate their religiosity, marks my mother instantly as a Muslim in the public's eye. Shortly after 9/11, a gas station attendant approached my mother while she was filling up her car with gas. My parents put a sticker of the American flag on all of their cars after the terrorist attacks to show that they too were patriotic citizens. The attendant pointed to the sticker and said, "That isn't going to save you." He continued to verbally accost her because she is Muslim. My mother quickly fled the gas station, fearing for her safety. She was not used to strange men verbally accosting her in public spaces. These incidents are just a few of the many encounters my parents have had with the government and their fellow private citizens over the last fifteen years.

As I show in this book, there has been a steady rise in anti-Muslim sentiments over the past decade and a half, a trend that has reached even the highest levels of government and public discourse. While campaigning during the presidential election in 2016, Republican candidate Donald Trump espoused some of the most vitriolic anti-Muslim rhetoric to date, arguing for banning Muslims from coming to the United States and forcing Muslim Americans to wear ID cards—ideas that were met with support from many Americans. While Trump's rhetoric was overtly anti-Muslim, it was nothing new. State-led surveillance of Muslims in America has been institutionalized in the years since 9/11. This surveillance is neither arbitrary nor colorblind but is racially motivated, rooted in the concept of the racialized Muslim identity as a potential terrorist.

This book is the product of scholarly research inspired by what I saw happening in Muslim communities after 9/11. There were a series of questions I wanted to answer: Were Muslim Americans encountering racism, or was it religious discrimination? Was it because of their phenotype—such as skin tone? Or was it due to other factors, like ethnic identity? Were Arabs targeted more intensely than other Muslims? Through interviews with Muslim Americans, I found my parents' experiences were not isolated incidents but a part of a new narrative unfolding in American society. After spending hours talking with Muslim American men and women, I discovered South Asian and Arab Muslim Americans were encountering increased surveillance as a result of their religious identity. Their daily lives have been greatly impacted by the War on Terror and the social construction of the Muslim as a terrorist. As a result, their pre- and post-9/11 experiences are drastically different, reflecting how their religious identity intersects with their races and ethnicities to reposition them in the U.S. racial hierarchy.

In *Forever Suspect*, I share the stories of Muslim American men and women, detailing what it is like to be Muslim in contemporary America, and situate Muslim American men's and women's experiences within a sociopolitical context of surveillance society. The participants I interviewed were largely professional and strongly middle- to upper-middle-class men and women. Their stories highlight how socioeconomic status does not protect one from racialization within the context of war. While much of the scholarship on September 11th highlights the global motivations and consequences of the War on Terror (Razack 2008; Maira 2009; Kibria 2011; Rana 2011; Kumar 2012), *Forever Suspect* is a part of a growing trend in scholarship on Muslims (Cainkar 2009; Bayoumi 2015; Maira 2016; Love 2017; Maghbouleh 2017) that uncovers where the intersections of race, gender, and religion occur for Muslim Americans in the context of this war, which is also being waged domestically in the United States.

In the decade after 9/11, the approach to law and order in the United States changed drastically with surveillance being a necessary and supported tactic in a society hyperconcerned with preventing another terrorist attack. *Surveillance* is the observation and monitoring of behaviors and actions that are deemed suspicious. The domestic and international War on Terror legitimizes the political and economic need for increased surveillance, resulting in the corporatization and federalization of surveillance. In other words, surveillance has become big business in the United States, where companies profit from surveillance technologies and tools, such as maintaining databases of information on the general public and then selling them to the government for purposes of security. A surveillance society can only survive as long as there is a need to monitor and observe bodies that threaten security. The War on Terror created conditions where Muslim bodies are racialized, justifying the need for their surveillance. But surveillance does not impact Muslim men and women in the same way; rather, surveillance is gendered, highlighting how racialization is also gendered. *Forever Suspect* shines a spotlight on how the experiences of Muslim American men and women in the War on Terror are highly influenced by their interwoven religious, racial, and gender identities.

Muslim Stereotypes: Muslim Men as Terrorists and Muslim Women as Cultural Threats

Any time there is a terrorist attack or a Muslim commits violence in either Europe or the United States, Muslim Americans must brace themselves for an impending backlash as well as the potential for more draconian policies that will further limit their civil rights and liberties. But Muslim men and Muslim women are not impacted in a uniform fashion by the growing anti-Muslim sentiments in America and Europe. Stereotypes of Muslim men and Muslim women are guided by gender. Muslim men are deemed to be a threat to national security because they have been cast as terrorists, or at the very least as having terrorist tendencies that could be "activated" at any moment. Muslim women, particularly those who wear visible religious signifiers like the hijab, are seen as both imperiled and abused by Muslim men and in need of saving while they are simultaneously treated as a cultural aberration and threat to American core values. In the next section, I uncover the history of the stereotypes that have come to define Muslim men and women.

Muslim Men: Clash of the Civilizations and the Making of a Terrorist

The idea that Islam is inherently antimodern has been a construct in the making for more than two centuries. In 1978, Edward Said published *Orientalism*, where he examined cultural representations of the East—which included parts of Asia, North Africa, and the Middle East—in literature and showed how Western scholarship constructed knowledge about these regions, which he called "Orientalism." Said argued that this knowledge was used to support an imperialist agenda, pointing to the ways in which foreign policy was influenced by Western scholarship that produced an understanding of the Middle East as savage, untamed, and uncivilized. These cultural images painted Arab and Muslim men as barbaric by showing Arab women in subservient and hypersexualized roles, such as in a harem. These Orientalist images have always been gendered, with men depicted as having innate violent tendencies toward their own women. The portrait of men as inherently abusive was used to justify the conquest and colonization of Asia, Africa, and the Middle East on the grounds that it would benefit from a civilizing hand (Said 2014). While Said's work centers on the nineteenth and twentieth centuries, Orientalist agendas have continued throughout the twentieth century and into the beginning of the twenty-first. In 1990, Bernard Lewis, a historian who specializes in Islam, wrote an article titled "The Roots of Muslim Rage" for the *Atlantic* magazine, in which he argued that Islam inherently lends itself to fundamentalism and violence, something that Lewis does not believe is characteristic of Western Judeo-Christian societies. He uses the term *clash of the civilizations* to describe this tension between Islamic and Western values, where Islam inspires opposition to modernization and religious secularism. An oft-overlooked detail is that for Lewis, this Muslim rage is gendered: "The third—the last straw—was the challenge to his mastery in his own house, from emancipated women and rebellious children. It was too much to endure, and the outbreak of rage against these alien, infidel, and incomprehensible forces that had subverted his dominance, disrupted his society, and finally violated the sanctuary of his home was inevitable. It was also natural that this rage should be directed primarily against the millennial enemy and should draw its strength from ancient beliefs and loyalties" (Lewis 1990: 49). Lewis characterizes Muslim violence and barbarism as male, and the rising anger in Muslim men is partially triggered by gains in gender equity for Muslim women. Lewis's thesis contributes to the construction of Muslim men as violent and inherently misogynistic and Muslim women as subsequently oppressed and abused. Furthermore, Lewis attributes this tendency toward brutality as part of a culture within Islam itself:

> There is something in the religious culture of Islam which inspired, in
> even the humblest peasant or peddler, a dignity and a courtesy toward others
> never exceeded and rarely equaled in other civilizations. And yet, in moments of
> upheaval and disruption, when the deeper passions are stirred, this dignity and
> courtesy toward others can give way to an explosive mixture of rage and hatred
> which impels even the government of an ancient and civilized country—even
> the spokesman of a great spiritual and ethical religion—to espouse kidnapping
> and assassination, and try to find, in the life of their Prophet, approval and
> indeed precedent for such actions. (Lewis 1990: 59)

Here Lewis's argument reflects what Kundnani (2012) sees as a movement by scholars and the state to reduce an understanding of terrorism to the concept of radicalization, which is motivated by psychological and theological reasons rather than structural issues such as those caused by war and military intervention.

Samuel Huntington, a political scientist at Harvard, also wrote about the incompatibility of Islam and the West. In his seminal article, "The Clash of the Civilizations" (1993) published in *Foreign Affairs*, Huntington argued that the next major global conflict would be Islam versus the West. Like Lewis, Huntington reduced this clash to cultural differences between Islam and Western societies, further perpetuating the idea that Islamic societies are inherently antimodern and anti-Western. Not only were Lewis and Huntington writing for an academic audience; they also reached the ears of state authorities and were highly influential in American foreign policy. In the 1970s, Huntington served as the coordinator of security planning for the National Security Council under President Carter's administration. In 2006, at the World Affairs

Council of Philadelphia luncheon honoring Bernard Lewis, Vice President Dick Cheney gave a speech where he praised Lewis for his expertise on the Middle East. He and former President George W. Bush had met several times with Lewis, revealing his influence on foreign policy. Cheney said of Lewis, "In 1990, he wrote 'The Roots of Muslim Rage,' which anticipated the terrorism of that decade. And in this new century, his wisdom is sought daily by policymakers, diplomats, fellow academics, and the news media."[1] Huntington and Lewis's scholarship influenced America's interventionist foreign policy, which has relied heavily on the creation of the terrorist. In this construction, the Islamic threat to Western society is inherently masculine. These concepts of Muslim rage and Islamic barbarity contribute to the notion that the terrorist is both Muslim and male, which can be seen in his subjugation of Muslim women. The casting of Muslim men as backward, antimodern, violent, and filled with rage initially fueled American aspirations for a military presence in the Middle East (Kumar 2012).

In *Disciplining Terror: How Experts Invented "Terrorism"* Lisa Stampnitzky chronicles how terrorism experts and the field of studies on the subject helped to produce new definitions around terrorism, aiding in sustaining the War on Terror. She describes how political violence was once described as insurgency but later came to be defined as terrorism through the development of terrorism experts and terrorism studies. The U.S. government had a role in the creation of this field through federal funding and federal agency conferences on terror and terrorism. Early terrorism experts identified the Soviet Union as the main supporter of terrorists due to the Cold War and simmering tensions between the United States and the Soviet Union. At that time, terrorism was characterized as having a political motive or a clearly defined agenda. But in the 1980s, the Islamic world replaced the Soviet Union as the next major threat to the West. Influenced by the clash of the civilizations theses by scholars like Lewis and Huntington, this "new terrorism" was characterized as irrational and without political motives (Stampnitzky 2013). The American public was not provided with any political motivations for the bombing of the World Trade Center in 1993, which only confirmed the supposed irrationality of Islamic terrorism. This only added to the perspective that the goal of such events is to bring destruction and fear to Western democracy and civilization. The events of 9/11 provided the right opportunity for myth to become reality. Muslims who committed acts of terror were reduced to people who hated freedom and democracy. The underlying political or economic factors, like sanctions placed on countries like Iran, that are motivators for terror were ignored. The equation of Islam with terror, and more specifically of Muslim men with terrorists, seemed plausible given that it was Muslim men who were the perpetrators of the attacks on 9/11. Even though terrorism has been on the decline while mass shootings, which have been typically perpetrated by white men, have increased over the last decade, any terrorist attack by a Muslim solidifies the belief that Muslim men are terrorists and should be surveilled.

The War on Terror, preceded by Orientalism and the clash of the civilizations, has had the effect of racializing Muslim bodies. According to Rana, the current racialization of Muslims as terrorists is the product of newer racial meanings built upon older forms of racism. In a post-9/11 society, the state perpetuates a fear of terrorism within the public sphere in order to justify increased focus and spending on national security. This anxiety of Muslim terrorists produces a state of panic in the American public. Rana states, "'The Muslim' emerged as a category of race that was policed through narratives of migration, diaspora, criminality, and terror" (2011: 66). Another characteristic of the Muslim terrorist is that he is also a "global Muslim," stripped of individuality based on nationality and culture. In the media, a Saudi Muslim is barely distinguishable from a Pakistani Muslim, as both simply invoke a fear of terrorism due to their religious identity. Similarly, the association of terror with Muslim bodies strips Muslim Americans of their American identity. Their racialized religious identity as a terrorist transforms their bodies into enemies of the state who must be policed and surveilled because they may commit acts of terror against the American people.

For Rana, this Muslim terrorist identity is also clearly gendered in that it is not applied to Muslim women in the same way that it blankets Muslim men's bodies. However, Muslim women are certainly caught up in this construction of Muslim men as potential terrorists. According to Rana, "Boundary making through gendered frameworks is enacted through notions of racialized masculinity and patriarchy and the concept of racialized Muslims. In both concepts, it is women who are made vulnerable in the active practices of racializing Muslims via assumptions about Islamic patriarchy and narratives of the victimization of the imperiled Muslim woman by the dangerous Muslim man (Razack 2008)" (Rana 2011: 169). In the chapters that follow, I show how Muslim American men have been placed on terrorist watchlists and on lists in U.S. airports because they have been racialized as terrorists. They are surveilled by the government and their fellow citizens in unique ways because of this association with terror. Muslim women who wear the hijab have also come to symbolize the threat of terror but are also constructed as antimodern and anti-Western.

Muslim Women: Imperiled and Unwanted in America

Scholars have noted a history of categorizing Muslim women as imperiled and in need of saving (Ahmed 1992; Razack 2008; Abu-Lughod 2013). Ahmed argues that in the nineteenth century, Western understandings of Islam centered on the oppression of Muslim women. This narrative of the oppressed Muslim woman became popular during a colonial era where theories of race and culture were created to justify European imperialism. Ahmed refers to the use of feminism to support colonialism as *colonial feminism*. Victorian men argued that European feminism could save Muslim women from barbaric Muslim men, which justified colonialism of Muslim societies, including India and sub-Saharan Africa (Ahmed 1992). The presence of gender segregation and the hijab became telltale signs of women's oppression rather than being understood as a religious or cultural practice. The equation of the hijab and the burqa with oppression ignores the agency that many Muslim women employ by choosing to wear the hijab. Ahmed (1992) and Abu-Lughod (2013) interrogate the idea that Muslim women who cover their hair in countries like Egypt and Morocco are oppressed, arguing that covering is a sign of class in these countries and has made women's mobility and participation in society and the workforce more accessible. In other words, wearing the hijab and the burqa empowers many women living in Muslim-majority societies, something that is completely ignored by the West, including feminists and academics who continue to equate the hijab and the burqa with women's subjugation. While there are certainly cases in which Muslim women have been oppressed and abused, this narrative obscures the larger structural reasons for their subjugation, such as war, political strife, economic instability, low literacy, and high mortality rates.

The colonial feminism of the nineteenth century resurfaced after 9/11 in order to help garner support for the invasion of Muslim countries. In her book *Do Muslim Women Need Saving?* (2013), Lila Abu-Lughod describes how, in the 1990s, white American feminism shifted its focus from domestic issues women faced in the United States to the abuses of women in the Global South. These feminists became hyperconcerned with issues faced by women in Africa and the Middle East such as female genital cutting, honor killings, and being forced to wear the hijab. The invasion of Afghanistan immediately after 9/11 employed much of the rhetoric used in previous imperialist agendas to justify military intervention by the United States, and women's liberation from the Taliban was an ideological tool used to justify war (Hirschkind and Mahmood 2002). A report by the U.S. State Department titled "The Taliban's War against Women" chronicles these abuses: "[The Taliban] restricted access to medical care for women, brutally enforced a restrictive dress code, and limited the ability of women to move about the city" (U.S. Department of State 2001).[2] The prevalence of such rhetoric downplayed other possible economic motivations for war by the United States, and oversimplified what life was like for Muslim women living in these societies.

Hirschkind and Mahmood show that the Taliban's restrictive policies toward women impacted those living in urban areas more than those residing in rural ones, because the lives of women living in rural areas were already in line with these policies. They also note the majority of people in Afghanistan reside in rural areas, and there has always been some flexibility in the dress code. Rural women who work in wheat fields alongside men rarely wear the burqa and are not reprimanded (Hirschkind and Mahmood 2002). Furthermore, if one were to review the history of Afghanistan, one could see how U.S. foreign policy aided in the rise of the Taliban. The United States was responsible for arming conservative Islamic groups to fight against the Soviet Union in the Cold War, devoting aid to the most violent and extremist groups because they were viewed as strong fighters against the Soviet army (Hirschkind and Mahmood 2002). Yet the impact of imperialism and colonialism on Muslim societies, including the oppression of Muslim women, becomes considerably less visible when cultural practices such as religion are held solely to blame.

While Muslim women abroad have been constructed as in need of saving, the narratives that surround Muslim women's bodies in the United States are more complicated, constantly shifting depending on the agenda of the state. Muslim women in the United States who wear the hijab represent an invasion of Islam in the United States. Cainkar (2009) shows in her study how Muslim women who wear the hijab encounter hostility and stares because they represent a violation of the moral fabric of American society. As my interviews suggest, Muslim American women are simultaneously treated as if they are oppressed and as a danger to society for offending Western values. Since 9/11, Muslim men and women are six to nine times more likely to experience anti-Muslim violence (Abdelkader 2016).

A report published by the Bridge Initiative at Georgetown University titled "When Islamophobia Turns Violent: The 2016 Presidential Elections" chronicled anti-Muslim violence and vandalism in relation to anti-Muslim rhetoric perpetuated by Republican presidential candidate Donald Trump (Abdelkader 2016). The report found that while Muslim men were more likely to be victims of physical abuse than Muslim women, Muslim women who wear the hijab were subjected to increased violence such as being threatened or having their hijabs forcibly removed. For example, on November 19, 2015, three sixth-grade boys at a school in the Bronx attacked a twelve-year-old girl and tried to rip off her hijab (Rao 2015). The following December, a man approached a Muslim woman while on a flight from Chicago to Albuquerque and yelled at her to remove her hijab. The thirty-seven-year-old white male screamed at the passenger, "Take it off! This is America!" When she refused to do so, he yanked the hijab off of her head (Gibb 2016). In an interview on December 11, 2015, on National Public Radio (NPR), two Muslim women who wear the hijab discussed how their lives had become more difficult since the terrorist attacks because they wear the hijab. On the NPR show *Morning Edition*, Shahzia Rahman discussed her experience after the terrorist attack in San Bernardino, where a Pakistani American man and his wife shot and killed fourteen of his coworkers at a Department of Public Health Christmas party.

One of the women described her husband's fear for her safety because she wears the hijab; he even encouraged her to take it off:

> And I have to say the biggest impact that has been for my family because they very much are fearful for my safety. My husband on a daily basis sends me stories of women in hijab who have been attacked, whether it's being thrown in front of a train, whether it's having your face smashed in with a beer mug. And especially having two young children with me most of the time, he is very much scared for me and my safety. (Rahman 2015)

The other interviewee suggested that Muslim women could disguise the hijab by wearing a baseball cap over it. Within the context of the United States, women who wear the hijab are treated as unwelcome because they are seen to represent an "enemy within" who has managed to infiltrate American borders. Because the hijab symbolizes Islam to the American public, Muslim women who wear it have become open targets for those who view Muslims as the enemy, enduring the anger the public has toward terrorism.

Muslim women are also implicated in the clash of civilizations because by wearing religious signifiers, they symbolize an imagined cultural conflict between the West and Islam. Wearing the hijab is seen as a transgression of the cultural values of the West, a form of cultural terrorism. By wearing the hijab, Muslim women are assumed to support misogyny and antifeminist values that are viewed as inherently un-American. The demand to take off the hijab followed by the statement "This is America!" is evidence of the way mainstream society interprets a piece of clothing that Muslim women choose to wear out of religious piety, marking Muslim women as anti-Western and antimodern. This interpretation of the hijab and the increasing subjugation of Muslim American women by their fellow American citizens reveal a contradiction in two prominent ideologies about Muslim women: Muslim women abroad need to be saved through military intervention, while Muslim women in America are a cultural aberration to American values. My research shows that Muslim American women are indeed in need of protection—but rather from the hostility and racism of American men and women. In the following chapters, I chronicle how Muslim American men and women are increasingly becoming targets because of a new era marked by hypersurveillance.

The Rise in Surveillance Societies

Surveillance is the monitoring of certain populations for the purposes of managing or controlling them (Lyon 2003). Some argue surveillance is an inevitable consequence of modernity (Giddens 1990), and it is justified as one of the tools that keeps society safe from criminal behavior.

In the late eighteenth century, philosopher Jeremy Bentham designed a prison structure that would allow for constant surveillance of prisoners. Bentham labeled this semicircular prison structure the *panopticon*. It allowed for the control of prisoners because guards were able to constantly watch them and prisoners were aware they were constantly being watched (Lyon 1994). In *Discipline and Punish*, Foucault built on Bentham's panopticon and developed the concept of *panopticism*, which is the process wherein certain populations are subjected to constant surveillance and discipline, highlighting relationships of power in society: "The Panopticon is a marvelous machine which, whatever use one may wish to put it, produces homogenous effects of power" (1995: 202). For Foucault, the structure of the prison is no longer physically necessary for social control because individuals are aware of their visibility and internalize their own subjection: "He who is subjected to a field of visibility, and who knows it, assumes responsibility for the constraints of power; he makes them play spontaneously upon himself; he inscribes in himself the power relation in which he simultaneously plays both roles; he becomes the principle of his own subjection" (1995: 203). The power of surveillance is not just in the state's ability to surveil but in the self-surveillance of a society's population.

A surveillance society consists of separate systems that work together to make up a surveillant assemblage (Haggerty and Ericson 2000). Surveillant assemblages consist of laws, policies, technologies, and actions by both the state and private citizens. Because of the technological advances that characterize contemporary societies, surveillance has transformed significantly, leading to an increased interest in the scholarship of it (Deleuze 1992; Lyon 2001; Marx and Muschert 2007). Surveillance technologies—such as computerized lists of personal data on individuals and body scanners at airports—have been integrated into the social geography of the United States. Agents of the state no longer need to be present to surveil; technology allows for constant surveillance. Cameras are located in public spaces—such as on the street, in stores, and at traffic lights—to monitor criminal behavior and activity. But surveillance is not colorblind nor completely reliant on technology. The heightened presence of cameras and police in certain neighborhoods, the random stops and searches of black drivers, and the monitoring of Muslim communities reflects just some of the ways the state and citizens participate in surveillance that is directed at people of color. In other words, populations experience differential surveillance based on their racial, ethnic, religious, and gendered identities. Consequently, surveillance reinforces inequality (Haggerty and Ericson 2000), and the War on Terror institutionalized policies and perpetuated a rhetoric that resulted in the hypersurveillance of Muslims in America.

The War on Terror and the Surveillance of Muslim Americans

The use of the phrase *the War on Terror* has a history that dates back to Ronald Reagan's presidency (Arquilla 2012).[3] After the 1983 bombing of a marine barracks in Lebanon where more than two hundred American soldiers were killed, Reagan used the phrase *war on terrorism* to describe his initiatives to prevent such attacks from occurring again. The Reagan administration's war on terrorism provided the key components of the War on Terror such as preemptive strikes, treating terrorism as a form of warfare rather than a criminal act, creating associations between states and terrorism, and justifying regime changes in the Middle East because of the threat of terror (Toaldo 2012). Almost twenty years later, George W. Bush used the term to define the U.S. foreign policy after the 9/11 terrorist attacks that killed more than three thousand Americans. Days after, Congress passed the Authorization for the Use of Military Action against Terrorists, which gave the United States permission to use military force both abroad and domestically in order to protect American citizens from another terrorist attack (Kundnani 2014). This allowed the state to engage in military invasions of both Iraq and Afghanistan if it meant protecting America from another terrorist attack. Not only was the War on Terror global in its scope, but it included domestic policies as well. One of these policies, the Uniting and Strengthening America by Providing Appropriate Tools Required to Intercept and Obstruct Terrorism Act (USA PATRIOT Act) of 2001, increased the state's capacity to surveil its population domestically (Lyon 2003).

The PATRIOT Act provides the state with the authority to conduct secret searches on American citizens, monitor telephone and email exchanges, and collect bank and credit card records. It increased the capacity of the American government to spy on its citizenry without showing reasonable suspicion of the individuals they are monitoring. The government's demand for increased surveillance in the name of national security brought with it the need for new surveillance tools and technologies. Surveillance became a billion-dollar industry, resulting in the government expanding its relationship with companies in the surveillance business. The attacks on 9/11 created lucrative business opportunities for companies involved in surveillance technologies or data collection. Technological advances expanded surveillance to include compiling and mining electronic data on individuals, and companies involved in automated surveillance were able to secure multimillion-dollar government contracts. Companies like ChoicePoint, a data aggregation firm (now owned by Reed Elsevier), had been selling personal and private information on citizens to the government for use as intelligence since 1997 (O'Harrow 2005). In 2002, Unisys was awarded a one-billion-dollar contract to maintain their technological infrastructure used for surveillance and safety (Hoover 2009).

In addition to data collection, new technologies were also created for surveillance, such as body scanners to be used at airports. Beginning in 2008, the Transportation Security Administration (TSA) purchased baggage screening tools and body scanners from companies like Rapiscan Systems, owned by OSI System Inc. (Grabell 2012).[4] The surveillance industry is a product of this blossoming relationship between the state and corporations, developed in a political climate where national security had become one of its priorities.

The U.S. government, which I often refer to in this book as simply *the state*, did not need to force surveillance upon the entire society; rather, a population anxious about another terrorist attack welcomed security and surveillance. Public support for surveillance is vital to the maintenance of a surveillance society, and the constant threat of terror provides the ideological justification for surveilling Muslim Americans. American citizens not only support this surveillance but also participate in it with encouragement by the state. At airports, in buses, on subway trains, and at sporting events, announcements continually remind citizens that safety is a top priority.

But are Americans really in any more danger than they were prior to the attacks on 9/11? A recent study of terrorist attacks in the United States from 1970 to 2011 reveals that terrorism in the United States is actually on the decline. In the year 1970, 470 terrorist attacks were recorded, while the ten-year span between 2001 and 2011 had only 207 such attacks (Lafree et al. 2012). What did increase, however, was the number of casualties, with the 9/11 attacks resulting in the highest death toll of any single terrorist incident in the United States.

While the numbers show that terrorism is on the decline, Americans are still fearful that another terrorist attack like the one that took place on September 11th could happen again, even though other types of violence—such as gun violence by non-Muslims—has been on the rise. Between 2000 and 2013, the FBI reported there were 160 mass killings in the United States (U.S. Department of Justice 2013).[5] In 2012, James Eagan Holmes went to a movie theater in Aurora, Colorado, and shot and killed seventeen people and injured seventy more. Later that year, Adam Lanza shot and killed twenty children and six adults at Sandy Hook Elementary school.[6] These shootings have not resulted in public announcements about safety and security at malls, restaurants, movie theaters, or schools. Furthermore, policy shifts on mental health issues or gun control did not occur in haste in the aftermath of these shootings, and the mass shootings did not result in increased surveillance of individuals who buy and own guns. But Muslims who had nothing to do with the terrorist attacks on September 11th found themselves under intense scrutiny by the state and their fellow citizens after the attacks.

State Surveillance in the War on Terror

State surveillance of Muslims in the War on Terror involves the unjustified monitoring of the bodies of Americans who are by and large law-abiding citizens. Immediately after 9/11, the FBI detained and interrogated thousands of Muslims living in the United States (Hing 2006; Cainkar 2009). In the years since, state surveillance of Muslim noncitizens and Muslim Americans has for the most part been conducted under a cloud of secrecy. However, in 2013, Edward Snowden, a former CIA employee, leaked tens of thousands of classified National Security Administration (NSA) documents to journalists Glenn Greenwald, Laura Poitras, and Ewen MacAskill, revealing the far-reaching nature of state surveillance. These documents uncovered a mass surveillance operation initiated by the United States. According to the documents, prominent Muslim American leaders such as Nihad Awad, the executive director for the Council on American Islamic Relations, were under surveillance by the U.S. government and had their emails monitored by the FBI. Faisal Gill, a Republican party operative, was also one of the names on the list. Even though President George W. Bush had appointed Gill as a policy director for the Department of Homeland Security, he was not immune from surveillance by the government. None of these Muslim American leaders have a criminal record nor has their surveillance resulted in their arrest, but their Muslim identity was enough to raise suspicion and justify their surveillance. Glenn Greenwald and Murtaza Hussain wrote in the *Intercept* about the documents:

> Given that the government's justifications for subjecting [Faisal] Gill and the other U.S. citizens to surveillance remain classified, it is impossible to know why their emails were monitored, or the extent of the surveillance. It is also unclear under what legal authority it was conducted, whether the men were formally targeted under FISA warrants, and what, if anything, authorities found that permitted them to continue spying on the men for prolonged periods of time. But the five individuals share one thing in common: Like many if not most of the people listed in the NSA spreadsheet, they are of Muslim heritage. (Greenwald and Hussain 2014)

The Snowden leaks uncovered that state-led surveillance was not colorblind but rather based on religious identity. Class privilege, service to the government, and party affiliation could not protect Muslim Americans from state surveillance or being cast as suspicious. These leaks provided concrete proof that Muslim Americans were being unfairly targeted by the state.

There is also evidence that state-led surveillance of Muslims is gendered and targets Muslim men specifically. The National Entry-Exit Registration System (NSEERS) is a good example of a state-led surveillance initiative that specifically targeted Muslim men and illustrates how the state conflates gender, religion, and national identities to determine who is a threat to national security. NSEERS was initiated in September 2002 and retired in April 2011. For almost nine years, noncitizen men from twenty-five specified nations were fingerprinted, photographed and interrogated at ports of entry to the United States. Furthermore, noncitizen men over the age of sixteen who lived in the United States prior to September 10, 2002, were required to register with an immigration office. Of the twenty-five nations specified by the program, twenty-four are Muslim-majority countries, with North Korea being the sole exception. These nations each have their own unique history and culture, yet twenty-four of the twenty-five share one thing in common: Islam is the state religion. The fact that there were known terrorists from countries like England (Richard Reid, known as the "shoe bomber") and the terrorist attacks that occurred in Spain, France, and Germany at the time NSEERS was policy and yet these countries were not on the list reflects the state's bias toward Muslim-majority nations (Bayoumi 2006).

Another way the state surveils Muslim men is through the use of terrorist databases. The PATRIOT Act increased funding for the FBI's Terrorist Screening Center, which compiles the Terrorist Screening Database. This database consists of names of individuals who are suspected of terrorist activity. How names are placed on this list is unclear because of the secrecy that shrouds these lists, but there is speculation that it includes more than six hundred thousand names and that there is an overpopulation of Arab names on it (Scahill and Devereaux 2014). The overwhelming majority of those who are on these lists are innocent people, many of whom are American citizens and have no ties to terrorism. According to an article published in the *Intercept*, "Of the 680,000 people caught up in the government's Terrorist Screening Database—a watchlist of 'known or suspected terrorists' that is shared with local law enforcement agencies, private contractors, and foreign governments—more than 40 percent are described by the government as having 'no recognized terrorist group affiliation'" (Scahill and Devereaux 2014).

One space where state-led surveillance of Muslim bodies is overwhelmingly obvious is in U.S. airports. Muslim experiences in airports reveal the interplay of technologies coupled with practices by state agents that rely on religious, ethnic, and gendered cues. TSA uses lists such as the Secondary Security Screening Selection List and the No-Fly List—derived from the FBI's Terrorist Screening Database and the National Counterterrorism Center's Terrorist Identities Datamart Environment (TIDE)—to surveil Muslim passengers in airports. According to the TSA website, the No-Fly List contains approximately one hundred thousand names, while TIDE contains roughly one million names (Handeyside 2014). Passengers who find themselves on these lists either are prevented from flying (the No-Fly List) or have to endure several layers of additional security simply because they have Muslim names. The majority of the Muslim men I interviewed told me they were on some list at airports. The Muslim women I interviewed told me they were not on a TSA list like Muslim men, indicating that the state targets mostly men for surveillance through these terrorist databases. However, Muslim women who wear the hijab were subjected to profiling by TSA agents. The women I spoke to told me they were repeatedly stopped and had their bodies and personal belongings searched at the airport security line by TSA agents. The encounters of Muslim American men and women when "flying while Muslim" are described in detail in chapter 2.

The surveillance of mosques is another example of how state-led surveillance unfairly targets Muslims. In 2002, the New York Police Department engaged in a massive surveillance program of Muslims in the area. According to the American Civil Liberties Union (ACLU), "NYPD's Intelligence Division has singled out Muslim religious and community leaders, mosques, student associations, organizations, businesses, and individuals for pervasive surveillance that is discriminatory and not conducted against institutions or individuals belonging to any other religious faith, or the public at large" (American Civil Liberties Union n.d.[a]). NYPD surveillance included mosques within a one-hundred-mile radius of New York, extending into neighboring states like Pennsylvania, Connecticut, and New Jersey. There were several complaints that claimed the surveillance program was unconstitutional. For example, in 2012, eight Muslim individuals and local businesses brought a lawsuit against the city of New York for discriminatory surveillance practices. In *Hassan v. City of New York*, the plaintiffs claimed their civil rights were violated because they were observed and monitored by the NYPD solely because of their religious identity rather than for participating in any criminal behavior. Judge William Martini dismissed this case, stating in his decision, "The more likely explanation for the surveillance was a desire to locate budding terrorist conspiracies. The most obvious reason for so concluding is that surveillance of the Muslim community began just after the attacks of September 11, 2001. The police could not have monitored New Jersey for Muslim terrorist activities without monitoring the Muslim community itself" (Pilkington 2014).

This ruling reinforces the acceptance of the association of Islam with terrorism. It legitimizes the idea that it is necessary to treat Muslims with suspicion in order to uncover terrorist plots and threats. In June 2013, the ACLU along with other organizations filed *Raza v. City of New York* arguing that the NYPD surveillance program violated the Fourteenth Amendment's Equal Protection Clause and the First Amendment's right to exercise religion freely and mandate that the government act with neutrality toward all religions (New York Civil Liberties Union 2013). In January 2016, the NYPD agreed to a settlement in this case, promising to reform their practices, including barring profiling based on religion, race, and ethnicity. While these reforms represent movement toward protecting Muslim populations from civil rights abuses, the rhetoric in America continues to encourage the surveillance of Muslims, especially after someone who is identified as Muslim commits a mass shooting or act of terror. Donald Trump called for the banning of Muslims from America after the terrorist attacks in Paris in December 2015, where the Islamic State (ISIS or ISIL) claimed responsibility for the killing of 130 French citizens. This blanketed accusation of all Muslims reveals how the state participates in justifying the surveillance of individuals based on their ethnic, racial, or religious identities.

Citizen Surveillance in the War on Terror

Another component of a surveillance society is state-sponsored encouragement of Americans to participate in it, giving citizens a sense of control over terrorism prevention. The "If You See Something, Say Something" campaign encourages Americans to participate in citizen surveillance. Citizens are integrated into the security state as de facto agents when they are repeatedly asked by the government to monitor their surroundings to keep America safe. The following statement on the Department of Homeland Security (DHS) website exemplifies how the state instigates public participation in surveillance: "Prompt and detailed reporting of suspicious activities can help prevent violent crimes or terrorist attacks. If you see suspicious activity, please report it to your local police department. Local law enforcement officers can respond quickly. Once they assess the situation, they can obtain additional support" (Department of Homeland Security 2008). There are no descriptions of the behaviors that constitute "suspicious activities" related to terrorism, yet the state invites citizens to take part in surveillance to curtail it. Government agencies specify "suspicious items" as unattended bags in public spaces, but the public is rarely provided with specific guidelines regarding suspicious behaviors. There is an instructional video on the DHS website associated with the campaign that warns the public not to profile based on religion, race, and gender, yet its description of distrustful behaviors is vague—the video showed individuals dressed in black with ski masks or hoodies leaving a white van or running away from a black backpack.[7]

Without more concrete information of what constitutes terrorist activities, Americans must rely on their own perceptions of what "suspicious behaviors" are in order to be able to identify someone as a potential terrorist, and the removal of men and women from flights because they wear the hijab or speak Arabic because their fellow passengers profile them exemplifies this citizen surveillance. In May 2016, the *Washington Post* reported an incident where a woman wrote a note to an American Airlines' flight attendant about the suspicious behavior of the passenger sitting next to her. The passenger had dark curly hair and olive skin according to the article in the *Washington Post* (Rampell 2016). He was writing something that appeared suspicious to the passenger, like it was a code of some sort. After removing the suspicious passenger from the plane, the airline discovered that Guido Menzio, the man who was removed, is an Italian award-winning Ivy League mathematician who was simply writing out a mathematical formula on a piece of paper. The unrecognizable math, mistaken for code or Arabic, and perhaps his appearance cast his body as suspicious to his fellow passenger. The reasons a citizen might suspect his or her fellow passenger are not called into question but instead are taken seriously by the state. The prevalent stereotype of a terrorist as someone with a Middle Eastern ethnicity and Islamic religious affiliation makes it easy for private citizens to profile Muslims. Because Muslim Americans fit the description of a terrorist in the minds of the American public, their bodies are subjected to hypersurveillance.

Private citizens also participate in surveilling Muslim women for offending American cultural values when they wear the hijab in public. They are often told to "go back home" by their fellow citizens, an act that contests their claim to an American identity. Muslim women have to defend wearing the hijab to strangers who feel empowered to approach them and question them about their American values. They often have to explain to people that wearing the hijab is a *choice*—rather than something forced upon them—in order to dismiss the assumption that they are oppressed by their faith (Gjelten 2016). Chapter 2 delves into the stories of Muslim American women and the types of interactions they encountered with friends and strangers because they publicly display their Islamic faith through wearing the hijab. They told me stories of how they were treated as oppressed and antifeminist because the hijab is understood as a religious tool that silences Muslim women. The surveillance of Muslim women's bodies in public represents how the clash of civilizations between the West and Islam has seeped into the American public's consciousness. As a result, private citizens surveil Muslim women who wear the hijab for transgressing what they think are American cultural values.

Self-Surveillance in the War on Terror

In addition to state surveillance and citizen surveillance, Muslim Americans are participating in self-surveillance. While some of this is a response to the surveillance they encounter, the state has also encouraged this practice. In 2014, President Obama unveiled a new program by the Department of Homeland Security called Countering Violent Extremism (CVE). The DHS website outlines the scope of the program, which includes understanding violent extremism, supporting communities that might be vulnerable to extremist ideologies, helping these communities to resist recruitment, and assisting local law enforcement in their efforts to prevent another terrorist attack in the United States.[8] This program encourages Muslim Americans to surveil members of their own communities who may appear suspicious and report them to the government. Obama encouraged Muslim Americans to participate in self-policing after two young Muslim men were arrested in California for conspiring to help the Islamic State (Reid 2015). Boston was also a site selected to partake in the CVE program in part due to recent terrorist activities, including the Boston Marathon bombing (Bender 2015). In addition to asking citizens to surveil members of their communities, the federal government has also asked state organizations to participate in the program. The Executive Office of Health and Human Services (EOHHS) in Massachusetts recently agreed to collaborate with the CVE by encouraging health and social service workers to profile their clients for "radicalization" and "extremism." CVE has been met with protest by several civil rights advocacy groups (Nguyen 2015). Community members felt this request was unfair because members of other religious communities are not asked to participate in these types of self-policing. The ACLU of Massachusetts, the Muslim Justice League, and former FBI agent Michael Germain have all argued that this program does not weed out extremism but instead simply perpetuates stereotypes of Muslims, subjecting them to racial profiling (American Civil Liberties Union of Massachusetts n.d.). According to Germain, who is now a fellow for the Brennan Center for Justice at New York University School of Law, right-wing antigovernment groups commit the majority of politically motivated violent acts in the United States, not Muslims: "Focusing almost exclusively on Muslims, he added, 'reinforces the false perception that extremist violence is primarily a Muslim problem when the facts show that is not true'" (Bender 2015).

Muslim American men and women are aware of their hypersurveillance by both the state and their fellow citizens. Because gender plays a significant role in how they are surveilled, the ways in which they self-surveil reflect their unique experiences. Chapter 4 examines the impact that surveillance has on Muslim American men and women and calls into question how citizenship in the United States is racialized, wherein some citizens are protected by the state and others are criminalized. This book shows how the racialization of Muslims occurs through the institutionalization of policies that target Muslims, which is maintained via the actions of individuals. The state, private citizens, and Muslims themselves all contribute to the hypersurveillance of Muslims.

Public Support for Surveillance

One might wonder where the outrage is for these surveillance programs initiated by the state that clearly target Muslim populations in the United States. The overt anti-Muslim rhetoric espoused by Donald Trump during the 2016 presidential election campaign has led to the public's awareness of the surveillance of Muslims in the United States. When he said he would register Muslims during his campaign, he was met with outrage from a large segment of the American public. However, in the years before Trump, the American public had not protested the surveillance of Muslims that had been ongoing under both the Bush and Obama administrations. According to a 2010 Gallup Poll survey, 71 percent of Americans supported profiling individuals who fit a terrorist profile based on age, gender, and ethnicity (Jones 2010). While this profile of a terrorist did not mention religion, another poll conducted by Quinnipiac University in 2012 found that 58 percent of registered New Yorkers felt that the NYPD had done nothing wrong to Muslims, even after it had been criticized for its extensive surveillance of Muslims (Boyette 2012). According to the survey, 54 percent of respondents claimed they held a positive view of Islam and 65 percent said mainstream Islam was a religion of peace, yet 58 percent still felt surveilling Muslims was an acceptable practice. Another survey conducted by Zogby Analytics revealed a decline in positive attitudes toward Muslims from 35 percent in 2010 to 27 percent in 2014 (Siddiqui 2014). In the midst of the political rhetoric espoused by Donald Trump to ban Muslims from entering the United States on the heels of the terrorist attacks in Paris, San Bernardino, and Brussels, a YouGov survey found that 51 percent of Americans agreed with this ban (Moore 2016). These statistics confirm that the majority of the public supports the state's surveillance efforts to protect America from another terrorist attack, even if it means unjustly profiling innocent law-abiding American citizens.

Racialization of Muslim Americans in the War on Terror

Studying the surveillance of Muslim Americans enables an understanding of how their religious identity undergoes racialization. *Racialization* is a theoretical framework that has been increasingly used to explain the fluidity and malleability of racial identity. After the passage of the Immigration and Nationality Act of 1965, the United States became a more racially and ethnically diverse nation, as it brought an influx of immigrants from Asia, Africa, and the Middle East. This new and dynamic ethnic, racial, and religious landscape is best understood through theories of racialization, which Michael Omi and Howard Winant define as "the extension of racial meaning to a previously racially unclassified relationship, social practice, or group" (Omi and Winant 2015: 111). The term has been used to describe the complex manner in which racial-ethnic groups like Mexican Americans or Japanese Americans experience race in the United States (Golash-Boza 2006; Vasquez 2010; Tsuda 2014). Whereas Latinx are racialized as "illegals" in the United States and thus treated like criminals who maybe in the United States without proper documentation, other racial-ethnic groups such as Japanese Americans experience a different kind of racialization, like *racial foreignization*, where they struggle for inclusion in racial citizenship (Tsuda 2014). Asian Americans may experience economic mobility, but it is in their exclusion from social aspects of citizenship (like being viewed as a member of society) that their racialization is apparent. Kibria (2003), Purkayastha (2005), and Dhingra (2012) interrogate how Asian and South Asian Americans may have access to social and economic mobility but at the same time experience racism. Racialization allows scholars to accurately capture the myriad of ways groups experience marginalization. The use of this concept also permits scholars to uncover the various spaces where racial experiences occur and to contextualize these experiences.

Racialization is rooted in relationships of power that are institutionalized. Racializing bodies serves those who wield power in society and therefore is constantly changing and mutating based on the interests of those in power. This explains why some groups of people are vilified at one point in time over another. For example, the belief that Syrians are potential terrorists and dangerous to Western nations is perpetuated when the government wants to limit Syrian refugees from entering the United States at a time when millions of Syrians have been forced out of their country due to internal wars and political conflicts. However, as I describe in chapter 1, Syrians were once treated like white ethnics in the United States partially because of their skin tone. Is this current manifestation of their racialization based on physical appearance or visual cues, or are they racialized based on religious and national and ethnic identities? In order to understand how Syrians are racialized currently, racialization cannot be limited to just skin tone or biological differences. While Omi and Winant's definition of racialization is important and a major contribution to expanding scholarship on race, it is still tied to phenotypes, limiting an analysis of other cultural attributes that also racialize individuals. They state, "We provide a concept of racialization to emphasize how the phenomic, the corporeal dimensions of human bodies, acquire meaning in social life" (2015: 109), then go on to posit that

> despite the problematic nature of racial categorization, it should be apparent that there is a crucial and non-reducible *visual dimension* to the definition and understanding of racial categories. Bodies are visually read and narrated in ways that draw upon an ensemble of symbolic meanings and associations. Corporeal distinctions are common, they become essentialized. Perceived differences in skin color, physical build, hair texture, the structure of cheek bones, the shape of the nose, or the presence/absence of an epicanthic fold are understood as the manifestations of more profound differences that are situated *within* racially identified persons: differences in such qualities as intelligence, athletic ability, temperament, and sexuality, among other traits. (Omi and Winant 2015: 111)

This understanding of race and racialization is unduly dependent on physical cues. While the visual dimension does indeed inspire racialization, I found Muslim American experience it even when they are racially visible as white. Therefore, for me to use the concept of racialization to understand how Muslim bodies acquire racial meanings, I provide a newer, updated definition of the term employing other factors that allow for bodies to be understood as racial. I define it as "the process by which bodies become racial in their lived realities because of biological and/or cultural traits as a result of the intersection and cooperation between ideologies, policies, laws, and social interactions that results in the denial of equal treatment in society." This definition allows scholars to examine racialization as interactional—between societal institutions and individuals.

There is also room to understand that race is not simply about skin tone; culture can also race bodies. Garner and Selod argue, "The process of racialization entails ascribing sets of characteristics viewed as inherent to members of a group because of their physical or cultural traits. These are not limited to skin tone or pigmentation, but include a myriad of attributes including cultural traits such as language, clothing, and religious practices" (2015: 4). This targeting of cultural attributes and practices as racialized markers of difference is especially salient in the case of Muslims in America. Furthermore, culture is often gendered. For us to truly uncover how bodies acquire racial meaning, it is important to understand how the process of racialization is gendered and has gendered consequences. For example, religious practices, such as gender segregation in mosques, are treated as evidence of the misogyny of Muslim men rather than understood within the context of religious doctrine. An article published in the *Telegraph* titled "Gender Segregation: The Truth about Muslim Women 'Forced' to Sit Away from Men" critiques the practice of gender segregation of Muslims in mosques and at public events (Sanghani 2015). Similarly, the practice of wearing the hijab is understood as a Muslim woman being submissive and a Muslim man being oppressive. One can look at the media coverage of the Islamic State in Iraq and Syria (ISIS), an Islamic militant group in Syria and Iraq, to see how constructions are created that associate Islam with terror and misogyny (Susskind 2014). A *New York Times* article titled "ISIS Enshrines a Theology of Rape" exemplifies how the media emphasizes Islam as a religion of terror and sexual violence when very little information about ISIS is provided except that they are religious zealots, sexual predators, and irrational killers (Callimachi 2015).

Because there are very few countering representations of Muslims as normal, law-abiding, patriotic American citizens, the dominant narrative of Muslims as terrorists, misogynists, and sexual predators who are antifeminist and anti-American is definitive. These cultural practices are seen as essentialized, inherent characteristics of Muslim bodies. For many Muslims, these labels are applied when they are identified as Muslim through visual clues like skin tone and clothing or nonvisual clues like having a Muslim name. Religious clothing that has acquired racial meaning racializes bodies in a similar way to skin tone. The hijab signifies foreignness and provokes the assumption that those who wear these symbols are "others" who are not American and not white. The hijab symbolizes a threat to Western feminist ideals and is associated with the forced submission of Muslim women to Muslim men (Razack 2008). But for Muslim men and women who do not wear religious signifiers, their Muslim names also racialize them even if they are phenotypically white. Therefore, it is important to examine all the ways that racialization occurs, particular those that are not inspired by phenotypes. Furthermore, we must begin to examine gendered forms of racialization rather than relying on the notion that every body is racialized equally and uniformly.

Forever Suspect expands on theoretical concepts such as racialization by including cultural traits and gender as central to understanding how racism operates both structurally and through social interactions, and I uncover the ways in which Muslim Americans experience racialization in their everyday lives. It is a complicated process that works in different ways for different people or groups. One of the ways the process of racialization occurs is through the gendered surveillance of their bodies: Muslim American women are watched by their fellow citizens and monitored for transgressing "Western" cultural norms, while Muslim American men are carefully observed for their potential to commit terror.

Racialized Surveillance and Gendered Consequences

Surveillance is not random, arbitrary, or colorblind; therefore I use the term *racialized surveillance*, which I define as "the monitoring of select bodies by relying on racial cues," to describe the type of surveillance racialized groups face in the United States. There is a history in the United States of the government purposely targeting black and brown bodies as threats to society who require vigilant monitoring. In a racialized society, some bodies go through intense scrutiny, while others do not.

Surveilling black bodies results in their hyperincarceration, highlighting how surveillance is racialized and targets specific characteristics like skin tone (Wacquant 2014), so the racialized surveillance of black bodies is reflected in their rates of incarceration in comparison to whites, particularly when it comes to drug use, despite the fact that both populations commit crimes at roughly the same rate (Alexander 2012). Racialized surveillance can also be seen in the passage of Arizona's Support Our Law Enforcement and Safe Neighborhood Act (also known as SB 1070). This policy encouraged the surveillance of Latinx in Arizona by local law enforcement as well as employers, making it legal for law enforcement to request documents from individuals they suspected of being undocumented. SB 1070 legitimated racial profiling, as law enforcement are encouraged to stop and search individuals who fit the profile of someone who may not be documented or who looks Latinx. For African Americans and Latinx, surveillance can have dire consequences, such as incarceration and deportation (Golash-Boza 2012; Brayne 2014). Brayne (2014) found that individuals who have been stopped by the police participate in *system avoidance*—where they avoid surveilling institutions that collect and share personal data, such as the labor force, hospitals, or educational institutions—showing how a surveillance society maintains social stratification and inequality.

Racialized surveillance is gendered and has gendered consequences—not only for Muslims but for other populations as well. For Latinx individuals in the United States, immigration laws impact women differently than they do men (Salcido and Menjívar 2012; Golash-Boza and Hondagneu-Sotelo 2013). For example, SB 1070 and the hypersurveillance of undocumented immigrants has resulted in Latinx women avoiding interactions with surveilling institutions such as hospitals or law enforcement, even if they are in need of medical care or are victims of domestic abuse, out of a fear of being deported (Golash-Boza 2012).

Generally speaking, there is a history of scrutinizing women of color's bodies for deviation from cultural norms, while men of color are surveilled for being dangerous and violent. In the mid-1970s, black women began to be vilified as welfare queens who extorted government resources instead of trying to secure work. The Personal Responsibility and Work Opportunity Reconciliatory Act of 1996 (PRWORA) greatly reformed welfare by requiring recipients to find employment in exchange for limited assistance from the state. This policy reflected the prominent racial attitude that black women were abusing the welfare system and having multiple children out of wedlock, ignoring the structural issues that low income black women encountered that prevented them from gaining access to decent health care and employment that pays a livable wage. The impact of the cultural stereotype of black women as lazy, gaming the government, and having multiple children out of wedlock resulted in a reduction in social services that were meant to offset the inequity they experienced due to centuries of institutionalized racism. These stereotypes are also reflected in citizen surveillance of black bodies: black children are more likely than white children to be reported to social services and placed into foster care, a statistic that is directly informed by the notion that black women are unfit mothers and the "welfare queen" stereotype (Roberts 2004).[9] The chapters that follow uncover the intersections of race/ethnicity, gender, and religion via the surveillance of Muslim American bodies.

Study Participants

The Muslim Americans interviewed in this study reflect the broader demographics of South Asians and Arabs in the United States, which are detailed in chapter 1. I met with college students, doctors, lawyers, computer scientists, schoolteachers, and stay-at-home mothers in the Chicago and Dallas/ Fort Worth areas at coffee shops, at their places of employment, and in their homes. The majority of them were professionals and had at least a bachelor's degree. Many of the South Asian Muslims I interviewed lived in highly affluent suburbs of Chicago—their homes were often multistory brick houses with perfectly manicured lawns. They told me they lived out in the suburbs because they wanted to live in a safe neighborhood and provide their children with a strong education. Unlike African Americans, second-generation South Asian Muslim Americans and their immigrant parents were not prevented from buying houses in the suburbs of Chicago through discriminatory housing practices (Prashad 2001). Because their parents migrated with professional degrees, the children of these immigrants of the late 1960s tended to also be professionals and experienced economic upwardly mobility. They were able to access societal resources, such as jobs and neighborhoods, because their racial identity allowed them access into white spaces. However, not all the individuals I interviewed lived in these beautiful suburban homes. Many of the Arab American Muslims I interviewed lived in a small community adjacent to Chicago that has a large Arab presence dating back to early migrations of Arabs to Chicago in the late nineteenth century. This neighborhood was not as affluent as the suburban one where many of the South Asian Muslims resided. It can be characterized as a middle-class neighborhood, revealing a difference in the socioeconomic status of the Arab and South Asian Muslim Americans I interviewed.

Roughly three-fourths of the participants were born in the United States to immigrant parents who migrated after the passage of the Immigration and Nationality Act of 1965. The American-born Muslims tended to be younger than the naturalized citizens I talked to. They ranged in age from their early twenties to midthirties. The majority of them were in high school when 9/11 happened, so they were able to talk about their experiences in school after the terrorist attacks. All the South Asian Muslim American participants born in the United States attended schools that were predominantly white and Christian. They told me they were of only a few Muslims or South Asians who attended their high schools, as did the Arab Muslim Americans who grew up in smaller Midwestern towns. For those who grew up and lived in the Arab neighborhood near Chicago, there was a larger Muslim and Arab presence in the public high schools they attended.

The naturalized citizens migrated to the United States for different reasons. Only the Palestinian migrants who participated in this study came to America in order to escape political turmoil. The other Arab and South Asian participants migrated for economic opportunities. Some came to the United States as young children and others as young adults. Most of the naturalized citizens I talked to were in their late thirties and older. Immigrant Muslim Americans I interviewed reflected on how much they cherished their status as American citizens. They took pride in the fact that they considered their "home" the United States as opposed to their country of origin. Immigrant South Asian and Arab Muslim Americans were quick to remind me in the interviews that regardless of what their experiences were like since 9/11, they still valued the freedoms and opportunities afforded them in the United States compared to the countries that they migrated from. In other words, they wanted me to know first and foremost they were loyal and proud American citizens. This echoed the findings of a Pew Research Center survey (2011) that most Muslims are satisfied with their lives in the United States, which is detailed in chapter 1.

The majority of the men and women I interviewed told me they mostly socialized with other Muslims. A handful of the younger, American-born Muslims in Chicago said they socialized with an ethnically diverse group of Muslims. Many of the younger American-born Muslims from Chicago were involved with an organization called the Inner-City Muslim Action Network (IMAN). The mission of the organization is to address inner-city issues such as violence, poverty, and the destruction of Chicago's urban neighborhoods. This organization is multiracial and multiethnic, bringing together Arab, South Asian, African, and African American Muslims together. While the Muslims involved with this organization tended to have a diverse group of Muslim friends, the majority of the Muslim Americans interviewed tended to associate with Muslims who shared their racial or ethnic heritage.

A common narrative that came up in the interviews with American-born Muslims was that when they were younger, they tended to socialize more with non-Muslims. This was because many of them went to schools where there were virtually no other Muslims. Many of them told me that once they got to college, they met more Muslims and they began to socialize with this group more exclusively. Nadine Naber (2005) found that a Muslim identity became more prominent for youth while in college, partially due to the need to respond to their increasingly racialized identity as Arab and Muslim after 9/11. Many of the second-generation Muslim Americans I interviewed told me stories of how they met other Muslims like themselves in college, which in turn strengthened this identity for them. Some of the women I interviewed explained to me that they started to wear the hijab in college because of the increased importance of their religious identity.

The interviews also revealed that South Asian and Arab men and women, regardless of their status as Americans, were surveilled by both the state and their fellow citizens because of their religious identity. South Asian and Arab Muslim Americans had similar experiences to one another because of the way their religious identity was interpreted. Their ethnicity as South Asian or Arab intersected with their Muslim identity and gender in salient ways that impacted social interactions in their everyday lives because it had made them a target for surveillance.

Book Outline

In chapter 1, I detail the migration history of South Asian and Arab Muslims to America using survey data, and I show how South Asian and Arab Muslim Americans are distinct communities who share many of the characteristics of ordinary American citizens. I also uncover how these communities' experiences were once guided by their ethnicities and now are being defined more by their religion. As a result, Arab Muslims and South Asian Muslims, who are classified differently racially, are sharing racial experiences because their religious identity racializes them in similar ways.

Chapter 2 focuses on state-led surveillance and examines Muslim American men's and women's experiences flying after 9/11. I show how state-led surveillance is racially motivated and further racializes Muslim bodies by presenting them as a threat to national security, a concept that has been referred to as "flying while Muslim." In this chapter, I uncover how the racialization of Muslims through their surveillance is institutionalized via TSA policies and practices, cementing the ideological construction of Muslims as terrorists. Muslim men are on government lists, which results in their hypersurveillance at airports, while Muslim women who wear the hijab are publicly racially profiled by TSA agents.

Chapter 3 uncovers the important role private citizens play in maintaining a surveillance society in the War on Terror through my interviews with Muslim Americans about their daily lives and their interactions with private citizens. Muslim women who wear the hijab experience racialization through these interactions and are treated as an affront to Western culture due to their religious dress. Private citizens constantly watch and monitor them for signs of transgressing Western cultural norms. As a result, Muslim American women who wear the hijab have been yelled at to "go back home" by strangers they encounter in public spaces. By contrast, Muslim men are surveilled as a potential threat to national security by acquaintances at work and school.

In chapter 4, I uncover how Muslim Americans self-surveil and participate in their own self-censure because of their hypersurveillance by both the state and their fellow citizens. Muslim women who wear the hijab participate in both a form of self-discipline and a rearticulation of what it means to be Muslim and American by altering their dress (such as by wearing brightly colored hijabs) and controlling their behavior in public spaces. They are cognizant of their surveillance and try to mitigate the gaze on their bodies by appearing less timid and oppressed. Muslim men feel they cannot discuss religion or politics because they fear being associated with terrorism and silenced themselves as a result.

In chapter 5, I examine how the racialization of Muslim Americans results in a new position for South Asians and Arabs on the racial hierarchy. Racialized as a threat to both cultural values and national security, South Asian and Arab Muslim Americans are stripped of their status as Americans and made to feel like foreigners in their own country. Thus I reiterate how religion intersects with race, ethnicity, and gender in pushing Arabs and South Asians further down the racial hierarchy. I conclude this book with a discussion of the implications of surveillance, the racialization of Muslim Americans, and the tenuous nature of their future in America.

At the time that I conducted the interviews for this book, numerous pundits put forth the idea that the United States had finally realized a "postracial" era with the election of Barack Obama. But the experiences of Muslim American men and women directly challenge the notion that a colorblind society has been attained. Instead, America's social and political climate continues to shift, along with its boundaries. Immigration policies in America's post-9/11 society have become more draconian as a result of being absorbed under the Department of Homeland Security. American borders have tightened, allowing fewer immigrants from certain countries, including those from Muslim-majority countries. Within the borders, Muslim Americans are excluded from citizenship as they are watched and monitored because they are seen as violent and dangerous to America. As I write this book, President Trump has signed Executive Order 13769, attempting to limit the migration of individuals to the United States from six Muslim-majority countries. *Forever Suspect* shows how racial identities are constructed over time and are continuously shifting and changing. By examining the experiences of ordinary, law-abiding Muslim Americans, our understanding of who experiences racism is turned on its head. In the chapters that follow, readers are asked to think about race not just as a black-and-white issue but as one that brings to light religion, as well as how it impacts immigrant groups and their children, who now also comprise the American landscape.

1

Moving from South Asian and Arab Identities to a Muslim Identity

South Asians and Arabs in the United States share a long history that dates back as early as the eighteenth century. In this book, I show how Arab and South Asian Muslim experiences are beginning to mirror one another due to their religious identity, so it is important to note that their histories and experiences of inclusion and exclusion in the United States have never been uniform. By examining their unique patterns of migration within different time periods, I reveal how Arabs and South Asians have come to occupy different locations on the racial hierarchy. For example, Arab Christians who migrated to the United States in the late nineteenth century were treated in a similar fashion as white ethnics, whereas South Asian migrants were not afforded this status. An examination of the histories and experiences of South Asians and Arabs over time in the United States enables an understanding of where they currently exist on the racial hierarchy today and how religion guided their inclusion and exclusion from whiteness.

South Asians in the United States

South Asians are individuals from India, Pakistan, Afghanistan, Bhutan, Bangladesh, the Maldives, Nepal, and Sri Lanka. Currently, Indians and Pakistanis make up the majority of South Asians living in the United States (Hoeffel et al. 2012). Most South Asian migrants that came to America in the early 1900s were Indians living under British colonial rule (Purkayastha 2005) and arrived between 1880 and the 1920s as unskilled laborers, including farm and industrial workers, who intended to go back to India (Prashad 2000; Bald 2015). The majority were Sikhs, but a small portion of these unskilled Indian laborers were Muslims who took up residence in port cities such as New York and New Orleans (Bald 2015). Both Arabs and South Asians have lived in the United States since the early twentieth century, but anti-Asian exclusionary immigration policies banned South Asians from entering the United States at various points in time. For example, as a result of rampant anti-Chinese sentiments, the Immigration Act of 1917 prevented anyone from Asia from migrating to the United States, including South Asian Indians. This policy created an "Asiatic Barred Zone" that prevented Asians, South Asians, and Southeast Asians from migrating to the United States. At the borders, South Asian migrants were denied entry based on undesirable characteristics, like being an "alcoholic" or having a mental or physical disability, or, for women, coming for "immoral" purposes (Bald 2013; Kibria, Bowman, and O'Leary 2014).

The Immigration Act of 1924 created quotas for migration into the United States, barring individuals who did not hail from Western and Northern Europe. According to Kibria et al., "The successful passage of the National Origins Act marked a great triumph for the forces of racist nativism" (2014: 30). This immigration policy limited the number of migrants from any country to 2 percent of people from a particular nationality living in the United States based on the 1890 census. Because there were so few South Asians in the United States at the time, only a small number were allowed entrance. Compared to Arabs, who were more likely to be treated like white ethnics such as Italians and Greeks, South Asians were residentially segregated due to their racialized status (Cainkar 2009). In cities like New York, many South Asian migrants, like Bengali peddlers, married Latinas and African American women in the late 1800s due to this residential racial segregation—they were in close proximity—as well as because South Asian women were denied entry into America due to the exclusionary immigration policies of the time (Prashad 2000; Bald 2015).

This early twentieth-century overview reveals how whiteness was constructed not only in opposition to blackness through legal regulations but also in relation to other immigrant groups like Asians, which often included South Asians. Excluding these groups and denying citizenship based on religious identity helped define what it meant to be white. But South Asians' exclusion was not that straightforward. Haney Lopez documents several legal cases where South Asian Indians were determined to be white by the courts. For example, in the early twentieth century, the courts used "common knowledge" and "scientific evidence" to argue about whether Asian Indians were white or not white (Lopez 2006). Common knowledge referred to popularly held notions about race, while scientific knowledge relied on naturalistic studies of humans. In the *United States v. Dolla* (1910) and *United States v. Balsara* (1910), the courts ruled Asian Indians were white based on scientific evidence. But in 1923's *United States v. Bhagat Singh Thind*, Bhagat Thind, an Indian immigrant, was denied citizenship because Hindus were seen as ineligible for naturalization—one that held even though Thind was actually Sikh. This ruling was based on common knowledge and set legal precedent for the cases that would follow by determining that Asian Indians who were Hindus could not become naturalized citizens because Hindus were not considered white. This case uncovered that a religious identity, being Hindu, distanced Asian Indians from whiteness.

The barriers to naturalization were lifted with the Luce-Celler Act of 1946, which allowed Indians and Filipinos to become American citizens (Dhingra 2012). However, it was not until the passage of the Immigration and Nationality Act of 1965 that America saw a significant increase in South Asian migration. This incoming population differed significantly from the previous Indian migrants. Due to preferences for highly skilled migrants, the post-1965 South Asian migration to America brought an influx of highly educated, middle-class, professional immigrants, from India in particular. Because the borders also opened to Arabs, a large number of Muslims migrated at this time. Muslim immigrants quickly planted roots by building mosques and religious cultural centers across the country, thus diversifying the American religious landscape. Between the 1950s and 1970s, South Asian Indians once again experienced confusion about their racial status during this time. Due to their complicated history around their racial identity, many South Asian Indians chose "white" or "other" on the U.S. Census. It was not until 1980 that they were racially categorized under the Asian classification by the U.S. Census Bureau at the request of Asian Indian migrants.[1] Some South Asians do not identify as "Asian" (Kibria 1998); their experiences are distinct from Chinese, Japanese, and other ethnic groups that have been lumped into this classification. For South Asians, their racial identification has been fluid from the moment they came to the United States, with a history of inclusion and exclusion in whiteness.

Arabs in the United States

In some ways, Arab migration to the United States was similar to South Asians', but there were notable differences. According to the U.S. census (2010), Arabs are defined as individuals who claim an Arabic-speaking ancestry.[2] There were three distinct waves of Arab resettlement in the United States. The first wave occurred from the 1880s to 1924, from what was once known as "Greater Syria," which included modern-day Syria, Lebanon, Palestine, and portions of

Jordan that were part of the Ottoman Empire (Cainkar 2009). Most of the migrants at this time were unskilled laborers seeking economic opportunities abroad, and the majority were Christians as opposed to Muslims (Suleiman 1999). Arab Christian migrants' patterns in terms of employment, intermarriage, and neighborhoods of residence were similar to those of other white ethnics, such as Italians, Slavs, and Greeks (Cainkar 2009). While there were certain geographic locations where Arabs experienced discrimination (including legal challenges to their rights to naturalization due to increased nativism of the early twentieth century), some were able to experience upward social mobility and participate more fully in American society.[3] Some Syrian Christians were able to access citizenship by proving their whiteness at a time when Japanese and Indians were denied citizenship and/or denaturalized (Lopez 2006; Gualtieri 2009). But the courts were not consistent in granting citizenship to Syrians. Arabs like South Asians had a unique history of being classified or denied naturalization because the courts were unable to agree on whether they were white. In *Ex parte Shahid* (1913), Faras Shahid, a Syrian immigrant, was denied citizenship because common knowledge was used by the courts to argue he was not white because of his darker skin tone and his inability to speak English. George Dow, also a Syrian immigrant, was denied citizenship by several lower courts, but in *United States v. Dow* (1915), the courts ruled based on scientific evidence that he was white. This was based on the intelligence he displayed to the courts but also because the courts decided Syria was geographically associated with Judaism and Christianity, and therefore those from Syria could become citizens (Lopez 2006).

In 1942, a Michigan court ruled against naturalizing Ahmed Hassan because Arabs were not white, while in Massachusetts, a Syrian man was able to access citizenship because the court ruled in 1944 that Arabs were eligible for citizenship (Lopez 2006; Love 2017). By 1943, Immigration and Naturalization Services (INS) determined that Arabs were white and eligible for citizenship due to having a shared culture and civilization with Western countries. INS relied on the case *United States v. Thind* (1923) to argue that Arabs were not like Asians, who were ineligible for naturalization. In other words, "the INS view was that Arabs were white and fully eligible for immigration and naturalization benefits (unlike most Asians at the time) and it issued an 'instruction' on the matter for INS offices across the nation" (Cainkar 2009: 77). At that point in time, Arabs were racially distinguished from Asians, with their perceived closeness to whiteness allowing them to access citizenship while distancing them from cultures and ethnicities marked as incapable of sharing white European cultural values. What this history reveals is that Muslims had difficulties becoming naturalized citizens because Islam was not associated with whiteness (Gualtieri 2009). For some Arabs, such as Syrians, their Christian identity and lighter skin tones afforded them certain key privileges that South Asians—who had darker complexions and were typically either Hindu or Muslim—were unable to access.[4]

The next major phase of Arab migration to the United States occurred during the post–World War II era. This period saw an increase in Muslim migrants. While the first wave brought sojourners who came in search of work opportunities and intended to eventually move back to the Greater Syria area, the second wave brought political refugees to the United States due to war and turmoil in their home countries. At that time, global interests and shifting international relations were causing America to move toward more inclusive immigration policies. For example, because China aided the United States in World War II, the Chinese Exclusion Act of 1882 was repealed in 1942 (Cainkar 2009).

The shifts between inclusion and exclusion of Arab migrants to the United States continued in the middle of the twentieth century. Due to political turmoil in Palestine in the early 1940s, there was an upswing in Palestinian migration to the United States. As a part of family reunification policies, women and children from the region began to migrate in large numbers. Congress passed two Palestinian refugee acts in 1953 and 1957, opening American borders to those who were being expelled after the creation of the state of Israel.[5] The 1950s also saw an increase in highly educated Arab professionals immigrating from Lebanon, Jordan, and Egypt to the United States. Unlike the previous generation of Arab migrants, this second wave was politically motivated and formed national organizations with the intent to influence American policies toward the Middle East (Suleiman 1999). The third wave of Arab immigrants arrived after the passage of the Immigration and Nationality Act of 1965, which came on the tail end of the Civil Rights Act of 1964 that provided the momentum to create more inclusive immigration policies. The 1965 act eliminated the quotas that had prevented migration from non-Western European countries, including those from Arab and South Asian countries. Consequently, professionals, unskilled laborers, and political refugees from Palestine, Iran, and Iraq were able to relocate to the United States in large numbers (Suleiman 1999). Between 1965 and 2000, more than six hundred thousand Arab migrants arrived in the United States. According to the Migration Policy Institute, by 2010, the immigrant population from Middle Eastern and North African countries living on American soil totaled more than eight hundred thousand individuals, who were largely Muslim (Batalova and Zong 2018).

As more Arabs migrated to the United States, negative stereotypes about them also began to flourish. The American media increasingly covered the Arab-Israeli conflict and the occupation of Palestine in the late 1960s, which led to racialized representations of Arabs in general. While the vilification of Arabs dates back to the eighteenth century, it is important to note that representations are fluid and fluctuate based on the sociohistorical context. In the late 1960s and 1970s, Arabs were portrayed as barbaric, greedy and dishonest—a characterization that was rooted in America's global interest in the Middle East and particularly Israel (Naber 2000; Cainkar 2009; Alsultany 2012; Shaheen 2014). For example, Jack Shaheen (2014) traces the media-based vilification of Arabs by examining their representations in nine hundred films over a twenty-year period. Through a content analysis of these films, Shaheen describes how the stereotype of Arab men as barbaric and greedy keepers of women in harems emerged, one that has morphed over time into the stereotype of the Muslim man as a terrorist, thus reflecting recent global concerns and changing political contexts.

While Arabs have had to contend with stereotypes, they are still faring well in some ways in the United States. According to the 2000 census, Arabs living in the United States had a median income similar to the national average and were more likely to have a bachelor's degree than the overall American population. But even with this success, they have always contended with a racialized identity that has been tied directly to America's foreign policy. The association of Arabs, and now Muslims, with terrorism, has justified U.S. military intervention in Arab countries. Once able to access some of the privileges of whiteness such as naturalization due to being seen as culturally similar to Western Europeans, the racialization of this group has grown exponentially over the past four decades. I show how Arabs who are Muslim are seen as incompatible culturally with Western values.

Arabs have experienced periods of both exclusion and inclusion since they first migrated to the United States. Although immigration laws were once more lenient toward Muslim migrants, the Trump era is likely to become hyperexclusionary toward this group.[6] In a political era that is marked by hypersurveillance and the costly War on Terror, Arabs who are also Muslim continue to move away from whiteness, regardless of their actual skin tone or pigmentation.

Shifting from an Ethnic Identity to "Muslim First" in America

Religion as a marker of identity started to grow as a result of the passage of the Immigration and Nationality Act of 1965. Immigrant Muslims began to carve out Muslim spaces in the American landscape by doing things like building mosques, motivated by the desire to teach their children Islamic values. These mosques have varied in size and architecture; furthermore, the racial and ethnic makeup of congregations has differed depending on geographic location (Smith 1999). Their establishment reflects the importance of a Muslim identity for South Asian and Arab migrants who feared losing it after migration.

In large metropolitan cities like Chicago, the Muslim community is less integrated with each other; South Asian Muslims and Arab Muslims tend instead to live in different, racially and economically segregated, neighborhoods. Cultural barriers, such as language and even religious practices, prevent these two populations from forming one larger Muslim community. One key example that demonstrates both differences in the practice of Islam as well as unique cultural practices based on ethnic identity is in how Muslim women cover their hair. Some women cover their hair fully, so that not even one strand is visible, while others cover their hair more loosely. In addition to cultural practices, Muslim communities are not completely integrated with one another due to their different reasons for migration to the United States. Palestinian, Lebanese, and Syrian immigrants who fled their countries as a result of war generally arrived without the resources of middle-class Pakistani and Indian professionals who migrated willingly to pursue economic opportunities. The latter group has tended to settle in white suburban communities in comparison to Arab refugees, who have relied on social services for jobs and housing. While divisions exist, there are certain instances in which these communities come together and attend the same mosque, particularly in places with fewer Muslims. In some cases, American mosques have become a unique space where South Asian, Arab, and African American Muslims join together with one another.

Second-generation South Asian and Arab Muslim Americans are exhibiting signs that a Muslim identity is becoming more prominent than ethnic identity. Naber argues that there are a few factors that influence young Arab Americans to claim they are "Muslim first." Some individuals feel their religious identity defines them more than their other identities, like ethnicity or even their national identity, and the increased media racialization of Islam after 9/11 has contributed to the stronger connection young Arabs feel to their religious identity. Furthermore, this group sometimes uses "Muslim first" as a tactic to convince their immigrant parents to support interracial marriages with other Muslims (Naber 2005). Due to an increase in religious classes and organizations that are available to them in America, second-generation Muslims are also learning more about their religion and making their own autonomous decisions about religious practices. As Peek (2012) found, many young Muslim women refused to take off their hijabs after 9/11, even when their parents asked them to do so out of fear for their safety. But it is not just Muslim youth who are turning toward this "Muslim first" identity. Muslim migration from nations that experienced political turmoil as a result of U.S. foreign policy, such as Palestine, brought a strengthened sense of religiosity. The Islamic revival that displaced Arab nationalism in response to American-sponsored imperialism in the 1980s also influenced Muslims in America (Naber 2005).

The American government has also played another role in producing the Muslim first identity by categorizing all Muslims indiscriminately through its policies. For example, state policies like the National Security Entry-Exit Registration System (NSEERS), which required Muslim men to register with the state, and Donald Trump's proposed travel ban have both targeted Muslims arbitrarily. South Asians and Arabs living in the United States who identify as Muslim are seen as potential threats to the state. While some may respond by downplaying their religious identity, many react by strengthening an identity that is under attack. As a result of these factors, second- and third-generation South Asian and Arab Muslims may find themselves associating first and foremost with their religious identity rather than one based on ethnicity.

Muslim Americans: Demographics and Attitudes

The anxiety that revolves around Muslims seems to be disproportionate because Muslims comprise a very small proportion of the total American population. Because the U.S. Census Bureau does not collect data on religious identity, there is no accurate count of the number of Muslims living in the United States, but the Pew Research Center has conducted surveys over the last decade to estimate the size of this population. In 2015, Pew projected that 3.3 million Muslims were living in America, comprising 1 percent of the total population (Mohamed 2016). Because Islam is one of the fastest growing religions in the world, Pew predicts that by 2040 Islam will be the second largest religion in the United States behind Christianity, with the number of Muslim Americans expected to grow to 8 million by 2050 (Mohamed 2016). These figures can be attributed to increased immigration to the United States and higher birth rates in the Muslim American community.[7] The majority of all American Muslims are foreign-born (58 percent); 25 percent are from Arab countries and 35 percent are from South Asian countries (see table 1).

Table 1
Foreign-born U.S. Muslims

Region	Percentage
South Asian countries	35%
Arab countries	25%
Other Asia/Pacific countries	11%
Sub-Saharan Africa	9%
European countries	4%
Countries in the Americas	4%

SOURCE: The Pew Research Center for the People and the Press, 2017

Fifty six percent of Muslim immigrants came to the United States after 2000, and 82 percent of Muslim Americans are citizens, with 40 percent being naturalized citizens. Roughly 60 percent are between the ages of eighteen and thirty-nine. Interestingly, there is a great deal of racial differentiation: 41 percent of Muslims identify as white (includes Arabs, Middle Easterners, and Iranians), 20 percent as black, 28 percent as Asian (includes South Asians), 8 percent as Latinx, and 3 percent as mixed race (Pew Research Center 2017).

Because of the exaggerated concern about Muslims as a threat to national security, state authorities and members of the general public are interested in attitudes held by Muslims living in America. Who are they, and are they anti-American? Will they bring sharia law—Islamic law—to the United States? Pew's (2011) study titled *Muslims in America: No Signs of Growth in Alienation or Support for Extremism* attempted to answer some of these questions by surveying Muslims in the United States. They found that the overwhelming majority of Muslims condemn Islamic extremism, but fewer than half of Muslims interviewed feel that the U.S. government's efforts to combat terrorism are sincere, and more than 80 percent felt satisfied with life in America. More than half feel that Muslims who come to America are eager to adopt an American way of life, while three-quarters of respondents believe that by working hard, one can get ahead in life. The survey revealed that Muslims are normal, ordinary Americans who mirror the general population in terms of educational level, income, and other aspects of American life.

Muslim political attitudes have shifted since 9/11, with many South Asian and Arab Muslim Americans changing their political identifications from Republican to Democrat. Interestingly, prior to 9/11, the majority of South Asian and Arab Muslim Americans leaned toward the Republican Party and voted for George W. Bush in the 2000 presidential election. Four years later, they overwhelmingly voted for John Kerry and then, in 2008, for Barack Obama. This shift can be attributed to the perceived anti-Muslim policies of the Republican Party (Pew Research Center 2011), such as the passing of the PATRIOT Act as well as the U.S. invasions of Iraq and Afghanistan by the Bush administration. While many Muslims have switched political parties, a report by the Institute on Social Policy and Understanding (ISPU) found that Muslims are the least likely of any faith group to vote (Mogahed and Chouhoud 2017). In the chapters that follow, I provide reasons there may be so little political engagement by the Muslim American population. I show that Muslim American men feel a sense of disempowerment because they are under hypersurveillance by the state, which can lead to lower political participation.

Another trend that survey data capture is the attitude Muslims have on same sex marriage. Homonationalism describes the process where Muslims are cast as inherently homophobic, which is used to align LGBTQ issues into a nationalistic agenda that perpetuates racist attitudes toward Muslims (Puar 2007). But Muslims' ideas on same sex are becoming more progressive over time. According to the Pew Research Center (2015), in 2007, 38 percent of Muslim respondents felt "homosexuality should be accepted" compared to 45 percent in 2014. While attitudes toward same sex relationships are not as positive as the rest of the U.S. population (33 percent did not think same sex relationships should be accepted), it does show a liberal trend occurring in the Muslim American population. This trend contradicts the stereotype that Muslim values are incompatible with Western values. This shift in attitudes may be the result of a Muslim American population recognizing their own marginalized status in the United States as a result of policies that have restricted their civil liberties. Research shows that more than half of Muslims surveyed believe that their lives have become more difficult since 9/11.

Arab and South Asian Muslims in Chicago and Dallas/Fort Worth

The interviews for this book took place in the two major metropolitan areas of Chicago and Dallas/Fort Worth, which are very different culturally, politically, and geographically. The Midwestern city of Chicago is the third largest city in the United States and is racially diverse. It is estimated that roughly four hundred thousand Muslims reside in Chicago (Logan 2003). Politically, Chicago is a Democratic city (U.S. Census Bureau n.d.). The Dallas/Fort Worth (DFW) area also has a large Muslim population. It is one of the fastest growing metropolitan areas in the country and also a racially diverse city, like Chicago. It has similar numbers of Asians and Latinx living in it, with smaller numbers of African Americans. Politically, Dallas is a centrist city consisting of conservative Republicans and Democrats, while Fort Worth is a Republican city.

Despite their differences, both Chicago and the DFW area have seen a significant growth in the South Asian and Arab Muslim populations, making them ideal locations for this study. Even though the two groups share a religious heritage, their cultural differences and migratory practices resulted in segregated communities in Chicago and the DFW area. The estimated Arab population in Illinois is more than two hundred sixty thousand, with Jordanians (including those with Palestinian passports), Iraqis, and Syrians comprising the majority of Arabs living in the state (Arab American Institute 2015). According to the 2010 U.S. census, the majority of Arabs in Illinois reside in Cook County (Arab American Institute 2014). Arab migration to Chicago, mirrored the general Arab migratory patterns to the United States described earlier in this chapter. The first wave brought Syrian peddlers and merchants while the second and third waves brought political refugees, Palestinian and Lebanese, as well as a large professional class seeking better economic opportunities.

Indians and Pakistanis also migrated in large numbers to both Chicago and the DFW area after the passage of the Immigration and Nationality Act of 1965. Professionals and migrants with specialized skills were prioritized, bringing affluent South Asians to the Chicago suburbs in the late 1960s and 1970s. Migration that followed in the 1980s and on brought South Asian immigrants who were refugees, both undocumented and documented, and unskilled laborers (Lal 2004; Mehrotra 2004). While the population is dispersed residentially in the city of Chicago and its surrounding suburbs, based on socioeconomic status, its visibility is prominent on Devon Avenue, a street that is populated with Indian and Pakistani restaurants and shops. A Pakistani and Indian presence can also be felt through the many organizations formed in Chicago, such as the Indo-American Center and the South Asian American Policy Institute. In Texas, the majority of Indians and Pakistanis work in fields such as medicine, technology, and engineering, reflecting their economic mobility in Texas. While the majority resides in Houston, there is a large South Asian presence in the Dallas/Fort Worth area that continues to grow.

Because there is a large, diverse Muslim population residing in both Chicago and the DFW area, mosques tend to serve a particular ethnic or racial congregation. According to Amaney Jamal, 90 percent of mosques in the United States are ethnically diverse, but one ethnic group tends to dominate. Arab mosques are tied to higher levels of civic and political engagement, while Asian mosques generally see a higher level of civic engagement but fewer connections with political participation (Jamal 2005). As of 2010, there were roughly ninety-one mosques in the Chicago area, and in 2011, the DFW area had thirty-nine mosques, representing a solid presence of Muslims in each city (Bagby 2012; Numrich and Wedam 2015). The mosques in Chicago and the DFW area reflect the racial and ethnic segregation of Muslims living there. Mosques may exhibit some racial and ethnic diversity—with Arabs, African, and African Americans attending the same mosque—but generally, these mosques are dominated by one ethnic group. Muslims are far from unified or homogenous but are culturally distinct and often live in various parts of the city.[8]

Both Chicago and the DFW area have seen an increase in anti-Muslim sentiments since 9/11, especially antimosque activity. Christopher Bail's (2015) study chronicles how the anti-Muslim rhetoric of certain fringe organizations has impacted these activities. For example, Pamela Geller's organization, Stop the Islamization of America (SIOA), campaigned to get public support to oppose the building of an Islamic center close to Ground Zero in New York City.[9] There have been multiple attempts across the country to stop Muslims from building mosques. In a suburb of Chicago known as Des Plaines, Bosnian Muslims found it difficult to build a mosque in their neighborhood due to a zoning dispute with the city (Blackburn 2014). In the same community, Muslims faced opposition from the city council to secure a permit to expand a parking lot for another mosque (Gaines 2014). In 2010, Muslims in Naperville, also a suburb of Chicago, were denied a permit by DuPage County to build a mosque in the neighborhood. The DuPage County board adjusted its zoning laws by unanimously voting that no new houses of worship could be built in the county. This law was passed after the board received five permit applications for the building of Islamic centers in the county (Goldsborough 2011).

In the Dallas/Fort Worth area, there have also been violent attacks on mosques. In 2010, someone burned playground equipment and painted a picture of Uncle Sam assaulting Allah at an Islamic center in Arlington, Texas (Tranchin 2010). In 2015, the Islamic Center of Irving had to increase its security upon receiving a series of violent threats after a man posted a video intending to highlight the traffic issues that the mosque brought to the neighborhood (Paul 2015). David Tyrer (2013) argues that this fear of mosques reflects an anxiety of the proximity of Muslim bodies to whites in the United States. It represents to many non-Muslim Americans an invasion of Islam in the West. According to the ACLU report on antimosque activity, "While mosque opponents frequently claim their objections are based on practical considerations such as traffic, parking, and noise levels, those asserted concerns are often pretexts masking anti-Muslim sentiment" (American Civil Liberties Union. n.d.[c]). The state of affairs for Muslim Americans in the United States has not improved in the decade after 9/11, but rather demonstrates how anti-Muslim sentiments have increased over time.

Another example of growing anti-Muslim sentiments, in the DFW area, can be seen in the case of Ahmed Mohamed. In 2015, Ahmed Mohamed, a fourteen-year-old high school student in Irving, Texas, built a clock and took it to school. His teachers accused him of building a bomb and subsequently called the police and had him arrested (Fantz et al. 2015). It is not surprising that the teachers in the Irving school responded to Ahmed as they did, given the political views of their mayor, Beth Van Duye—a staunch supporter of anti-sharia legislation in Texas. To provide a bit of context, in Texas, a sharia tribunal was set up to deal with family and business feuds in the Muslim community, similar to Jewish and Catholic tribunals that have existed without any interference from local politicians. While sharia tribunals are voluntary and Muslims can choose to use U.S. courts instead, Mayor Duye publicly stated she would never allow such tribunals and expressed her support for HB 562, an anti-sharia bill introduced to the Texas State Senate (Shehata 2015).[10]

The difficulties Muslims face in obtaining permits to build mosques and the introduction of anti-sharia bills in state legislatures reflect the growing hostility to the Muslim presence in the United States. One might assume that in a politically liberal city such as Chicago, anti-Muslim sentiments would be fewer. Yet the experiences of the Muslim Americans I interviewed suggest that these negative sentiments transcend political ideology. In other words, anti-Muslim feelings and Islamophobia are present regardless of the political leanings of the local population. An examination of Muslim American life in cities like Chicago and the Dallas/Fort Worth area sheds light on the increased racialization of Muslim Americans that has occurred in the years since 9/11.

Life Before and After September 11th

Although this book is not about the backlash that was brought about after 9/11 but rather about the long-term impact policies have had on South Asian and Arab Muslims, it is important to note how the men and women saw 9/11 as a turning point in their lives. All the South Asian and Arab men and women I talked to discussed its impact and how life changed in drastic ways. They each had some story to share. Many said they had some experiences related to race and ethnicity prior to 9/11, but after the terrorist attacks, they felt things were very different. They were treated with more hostility than before, and this treatment was tied more closely to their religious identity.

Aziz, a Pakistani American Muslim, recalled such a shift. He told me he grew up in a predominantly white neighborhood and that prior to 9/11, his family had a good relationship with their neighbors. I asked Aziz if he noticed any changes with his neighbors after 9/11. He remembered an incident that happened on a block in his neighborhood.

> AZIZ: I was driving one day with my mom back from work, and I think the whole time we were living in that neighborhood, like ten years previous, that no one had ever shouted anything offensive or anything like that. And I do remember probably within a week or two weeks after 9/11 driving back in our neighborhood but a few blocks down, still just maybe one or two blocks down. I'm not gonna forget. Some kid just shouted something, like it was either "Go back to where you came from" or something pretty offensive. And I was kinda surprised. We hadn't really gotten that in our neighborhood. We didn't think our neighborhood was like that.

Aziz, who does not pass for white, lived in a white neighborhood and attended white schools without a single negative encounter until that point. The heightened xenophobia that has plagued the United States since the attacks on September 11th was felt acutely by people who "look" like they are from another country. Due to his darker complexion, he told me he is often mistaken for

Latino. In the few weeks after 9/11, the American government and private citizens targeted people of color—including Asians, Indian Hindus, Sikhs, and Latinx—as potential threats to society.[11] There was little nuance in who was subjected to the hysteria that followed the attacks, but as time went on, there was a more targeted focus on Muslims. As I show in the chapters that follow, a Muslim name is what incited Muslim men's hypersurveillance, which was justified in the name of national security. Aziz's experience with racism shifted. Being yelled at in public was not the norm for Aziz before 9/11. But as the years passed, Aziz's encounters with the state and his fellow private citizens reflected his new shifting status as un-American because he is Muslim.

Omar's story also highlights how drastically things changed after 9/11. Omar, a sixty-eight-year-old Palestinian American, shared his story of migration with me, which shows how Arab experiences in America have changed over time. He first came to America in 1960 to study and remembered how life was like as an Arab in America at that time. He said, "At that time, it was wonderful. The people loved to speak to you and make a relationship [with you], as an Arab, in 1960." Omar was in a car accident and became homesick for Gaza, so he moved back to Palestine, a decision he later regretted. Shortly afterward he left Gaza and moved to Egypt to find work, he met and married his wife and found a job. But after the Six Day War, also known as the Arab-Israeli War of 1967, Omar was forced to leave Egypt because he was Palestinian. He and his wife and daughters moved to Libya, where he eventually found employment as an accountant, and lived there for more than twenty years. But when tension arose between Arafat and Qadafi, Palestinians were forcefully removed from Libya. Omar and his family moved back to the United States after they left Libya and settled down in Chicago. He was able to find work through family connections. Omar's wife and kids followed him to Chicago from Libya where they lived for about seven years prior to 9/11. His first wife died a few months after moving to the United States and Omar later remarried another Egyptian woman. He opened up a convenience store where he worked for several years. When I asked him how things had changed, he told me how he had been treated differently. Before 9/11 he had a very friendly relationship with his neighbor, who he identified as Irish American.

> OMAR: This lady used to be very nice with us. Sometimes she [would] call us [and] knock on the door and say, "Come, have some cake and Irish drink." Or she would say, "Hey, come on, help me. This needs to be taken out." We give her help, she give us. And she was nice, and we are nice together. [After] 9/11, she [told us], "You have to leave. You are terrorist."
> SAHER: Wow. Just like that?

OMAR: Just like that. "You are Afghani!" We left the house anyway. We left the house because of that. We used to be [there] for her better than her family, but suddenly, she wants us out.

Omar said at the store he owned, customers who were cordial to him before 9/11 suddenly treated him with hostility and verbally accosted him after the attacks. A regular customer came into the store and yelled at him, "Go back home!" and called him an "Afghani" and a "Pakistani." Omar felt sad that people who were once friendly to him suddenly turned on him and he blamed the media for their negative representations of Arabs and Muslims. He ended the interview with, "I came here for freedom. But I didn't find it."

Omar's story is heartbreaking in many ways. He has been unable to find a home due to his national and religious identities, forced to leave Palestine for a better life but also forced out of Egypt and Libya because he is Palestinian. While he thought he found a home in the United States, the events of 9/11 changed his feelings of belonging. The experiences he related demonstrate how quickly people changed their views of him and became hostile after the terrorist attacks. That he was misidentified by once friendly customers and neighbors as an "Afghani" or a "Pakistani" reveals how Arab and South Asian identities have become conflated with Islam.

Saima, a Palestinian American woman in her midtwenties, expressed the same sentiments both Aziz and Omar did about the impact of 9/11 on her Arab identity.

SAIMA: All I remember was that things were going really well for the community. It was one of those feelings where I was like, wow, like, we're actually—I mean we're not in the clear—but I just felt like there was a generally positive vibe between the Arabs and the non-Muslim community. And I feel like, even though there was still a lot of stereotypes, our name wasn't as jaded or wasn't as *black*. I just feel like our relations were clearing up. And then that all obviously changed, like, the day of. But yeah, afterwards it was—it was such a—I mean it was a different world, I guess. Everything changed in terms of, like, relations. You know, every time you meet a non-Muslim, for the most part, or a non-Arab—it's almost an apologetic relationship. Even to this day, 2010, I'm still, like, explaining or trying to convince people that we're not these barbaric people.

Although Saima acknowledges that Arabs were not treated as white before 9/11, she realizes they were distanced from blackness. Saima feels the events of 9/11 moved Arabs' location on the racial hierarchy further away from whiteness.

These stories highlight how 9/11 marked the beginning of a new racial-ized experience for Muslim Americans in the United States. While they may have never been seen as fully American, they were now treated as if they were unwanted. Being yelled at to "go back home" reveals a shift in how Muslims are now treated in their country of residence. Aziz's experience revealed the loss of his status as an honorary white, the racial location that Eduardo Bonilla-Silva (2002) argues is between white and collective black. Honorary whites, accord-ing to Bonilla-Silva (2002) are able to access some of the privileges of whites, like socioeconomic mobility, but do not experience all of the privileges that whiteness affords. He places Middle Easterners in this category, a placement that is tenuous, as Aziz's testimony highlights. Omar's and Saima's encounters show how the U.S. Census categorization of Arabs as white is no longer an accurate classification.

Losing Whiteness: Wearing the Hijab

Muslim women felt that their status as white depended on whether they wore the hijab. The Arab Muslim women I interviewed were cognizant of a stark shift, from being able to pass for white to being viewed as a racial other, incit-ing the gazes of their fellow citizens and surveillance of their bodies. In post-9/11 society, the hijab works in similar ways to skin tone to further distance Muslims from whiteness.

Samira, a young Palestinian woman, told me after she decided not to wear the hijab a few years after 9/11, she no longer felt like she had to apologize for all Muslims because she was not recognizable as one.

> SAMIRA: I feel that, when I was wearing the scarf and closer to 9/11, I was apolo-getic for 9/11. I was bearing the burden of 9/11, as if I had something to do with 9/11, and I felt that taking my scarf off not only empowered me to make decisions for me based on what I felt was right for me, but also empowered me to say to people in my country, "9/11 wasn't my fault. I don't know why you hate me. You can hate me if you want, but you know what? It wasn't my fault. I'm not related to any of these people. They don't even come from the country I originate from. I'm not gonna feel sorry for what happened, because it wasn't my fault."

Samira told me she had very difficult experiences when she wore the hijab after 9/11. She was in high school at the time and remembers a student blaming her for 9/11. She also recalled riding the bus to work and a passenger yelling at her, "Go back to your country, bitch!" She chose to remove the hijab because she no longer felt it was appropriate for her spiritually and noticed a stark difference in her experiences. In our conversations, she told me she passed for white after she stopped wearing the hijab, which empowered her in some ways. Samira enjoyed being able to feel like an individual rather than a representative of all Muslim Arabs, who were encountering a new form of racialization and the association of their bodies with barbarism or violence.

Aziza, a Syrian American, also felt that by wearing the hijab—which she began wearing in high school—she lost some of the privileges associated with whiteness. Prior to wearing it, she was treated as if she was white, and in fact, Aziza is legally classified as white according to the U.S. Census Bureau due to her Arab ethnicity. I asked her if she was recognized as Muslim or Arab before she started wearing the hijab.

> AZIZA: I guess, I mean I don't know because even though I'm Arab, I'm a little bit lighter skin. I mean, when I'm not wearing the scarf, I know people say that you can't really tell that necessarily I'm Arab or something. Even my friends seem to be like, "Oh, if you weren't wearing your scarf we would've just thought you were a white girl."

After she started wearing the hijab, Aziza began to frequently encounter the question, "Where are you *really* from?" when meeting people who wanted to know her ethnic identity. The terrorist attacks incited more hostile encounters for Aziza that related to the hijab, such as her high school bus driver chastising her religion.

> AZIZA: I was in high school, like the day after September 11, I can still remember my bus driver kinda like looked at me in the rearview mirror and he's like, "You know, it's a bad religion, it's promoting all of these things and it's all of the religion's fault."
>
> At that point, I was fifteen, and it's like I didn't know how to respond to him other than "No, no, that's not true." But he really made me upset because there were other students on the bus with me and I just got really upset. So right away when I got home, I told my mom and then my parents called the school. Because it's a small school, everybody kinda knows everybody, and then the next day, he wasn't driving our bus anymore. He got transferred to a different bus.

Encounters like these have persisted in the years since 9/11. As I describe in the following chapters, the belief that Muslims are innately violent and need to be watched and monitored is the new norm. With each new terrorist attack, the surveillance of Muslim Americans intensifies because of the association of Islam with terrorism.

Maryam, a Syrian American, told me she passed for white before she decided to wear the hijab. She grew up in a small Midwestern town where hers was one of only a few Muslim and Arab families. Growing up, she said her family was never overtly religious. They used to celebrate the major Muslim holidays, but other than that, culture played a more prominent role in her family's everyday life than religion. Maryam did not have Muslim friends in high school, but at college in Chicago, she began to meet other Muslims, and this strengthened her interest in Islam.[12] As a result, she started to wear the hijab, which is when she recognized her status as white beginning to change.

> MARYAM: I think that after 9/11, doing the job search with my internships and just even being in downtown Chicago, getting a sandwich or something, I was a little bit more aware of people staring at me maybe than other people who had been covering their hair longer, or maybe who had been identifying themselves as a minority for longer. But I really don't think that I identified myself as a minority until around that time.

Maryam went on to tell me that at a job interview prior to 9/11, the person interviewing her kept asking her questions about her hijab and why she was wearing it. After 9/11, these types of uncomfortable but more mundane interactions with people shifted toward racial slurs.

> MARYAM: I was walking around downtown Chicago, and it was like St. Patrick's Day. And people are just walking around downtown drunk, so they have no inhibition. So some guys yelled out, "Go home, you sand-nigger," or something like that.

As all these narratives demonstrate, a Muslim identity is a racializing agent in the current political climate of the United States. When white people convert to Islam, they experience reracialization and lose their privileges associated with whiteness (Galonnier 2015; Moosavi 2015). For Arabs who are racially classified as white, they lose this status when they wear the hijab. It is clear in the stories here that the women interviewed were not accustomed to these racial encounters before they wore the hijab. The men and women I interviewed were professionals who enjoyed a middle-to-upper-class lifestyle, giving them access to predominantly white spaces. While they may have never felt completely white due to the racialization of their ethnicity, their encounters in public spaces were not hostile in the ways they have been since September 11th. Since 9/11, a Muslim identity has triggered these racial experiences. Policies such as the USA PATRIOT Act have produced the current surveillance society that has made Muslim bodies susceptible to constant monitoring.

For Arab Muslim Americans who once passed for white, their religious identity has changed their racial identity in the public's eye.

In the chapters that follow, I further show how state policies, along with ideological constructions of Muslims as terrorists and a threat to Western values, result in the racialized surveillance of Muslim American men and women. Through conversations with Muslim men and women, I was able to uncover how their lives slowly transformed from being viewed as marginally American as a result of their ethnic identities to being seen as anti-American and unwanted because of their religious identity. The stories and testimonies of ordinary American citizens in this book reflect how cultural and political shifts can create newly racialized meanings in a society that is organized along racial lines.

2

Flying while Muslim

State Surveillance of Muslim
Americans in U.S. Airports

On Monday, November 20, 2006, six imams were removed from a U.S. Airways flight as they tried to head back home to Phoenix from the North American Imams Federation conference in Minneapolis. The *New York Times* reported that a fellow passenger passed a note to a crewmember claiming there were six suspicious Arabs on the plane who had said the word *Allah* several times and cursed the United States' "involvement with Saddam Hussein" (Sander 2006). In the note, the passenger also provided the seat numbers for the imams. As a result of this note, the imams were handcuffed, removed from the plane, and then interrogated for several hours by the FBI. The imams were released because they posed no threat to national security. Even though the men were refunded their money, U.S. Airways refused to book them on another flight to Phoenix.

On March 13, 2011, Irum Abbasi, an American Muslim of Pakistani descent, was pulled off of a plane because a Southwest Airlines crew member thought she heard Abbasi say "It's a go" on her cell phone. Abbasi actually said, "I have to go" because her flight was about to take off, but her hijab rendered her suspect in the eyes of the flight attendant, resulting in her removal from the plane and a search of her body. After she was cleared to return to the plane, the pilot refused to allow her back on because the crew was uncomfortable with her presence. She was issued a voucher and placed on the next flight (Quraishi 2011).

In March 2016, an Arab Muslim American family was removed from a United Airlines flight after they asked a flight attendant for help securing a booster seat for their young child. The mother wears the hijab. The couple were asked to show their tickets and then removed from the flight because of safety concerns (Ellis and Johnson 2016).

Incidents like these are captured by the phrase *flying while Muslim*. Muslims experience discrimination from fellow passengers, flight attendants, and pilots who read their bodies as signifying threat. They are often forced off of planes and reported to the authorities for questioning and searches. Though Muslims are not the only group who experience this type of treatment (Sikhs, Latinx, and South Asians have endured "random" stops and searches), this discrimination is rooted in a *fear* of Muslims. These instances warrant an examination of U.S. airports as a major site where Muslims become hypervisible and are placed under intense surveillance initiated by the state.

This chapter presents stories from Muslim travelers who were treated as potential threats to national security because of their religious identity. Profiling and surveillance of Muslim-appearing persons in airports are now widely accepted practices to promote national security. In these spaces, state-led screening initiatives take the form of a racialized surveillance that relies on religious cues to determine who is a threat. Bonilla-Silva argues that we live in a racialized social system that allocates "differential economic, political, social, and even psychological rewards to groups along racial lines, lines that are socially constructed" (2001: 44). Muslims are racialized via a differential allocation of rewards when their bodies are unfairly criminalized rather than protected by the state. In other words, their surveillance casts them as threats as opposed to citizens worthy of state protection.

Surveillance intersects with and depends on both religious signifiers and gender in this process of racialization. Muslim men's experiences differed from Muslim women's, and Muslim women who wore the hijab were treated differently in airports than those who did not. The interviews in this book show how surveillance of Muslim bodies has become institutionalized via the state's placement of innocent Muslim men on a Transportation Security Administration (TSA) list called the Secondary Security Screening Selection List. Muslim men on this list were informed that their names were similar to those of people on a government security list who posed a threat to national security and that they must go through additional security measures. Muslim women who wore the hijab were more likely to be routinely subjected to "random" stops and searches than Muslim women who did not wear the hijab; this public spectacle of being pulled out of the security line and having one's body and belongings searched because one wears the hijab is another way that a Muslim identity is racialized as a threat to national security. Not only was surveillance initiated by the state; non-Muslim travelers also participated in surveillance. Muslim Americans were aware they were being watched in airports and as a result carefully monitored their own actions and dress in these spaces, revealing how Muslims participate in self-surveillance.

Federalizing Security in U.S. Airports

Two months after 9/11, Congress enacted the Aviation and Transportation Security Act, which in turn created the Transportation Security Administration agency. Airport security—once a private industry—was transformed overnight into a federalized program (Carafano, Poole, and Roberts 2006). According to the TSA website, the primary objective of TSA is to prevent a terrorist attack in the United States.[1] As of 2014, TSA employed fifty thousand agents and had an operating budget of roughly $7.3 billion. TSA agents include transportation and security officers (TSOs), behavior detection officers (BDOs), and transportation security inspectors (TSIs) who are supposed to "deter and defeat terrorist activity."

Screening passengers and luggage for potential weapons is one of the many practices employed by TSA in order to prevent terrorism. New technologies, such as facial recognition tools and stereoscopic cameras to track physical traits like height, are continuously introduced in airports in an effort to improve security (Lipton 2006; Weissman 2015). Passengers' luggage and personal belongings are checked through scanners for suspicious devices or weapons, and metal detectors check passengers' bodies for weapons such as knives and guns. Full body scanners, also known as "advanced imaging technologies," allow TSA agents to detect nonmetal objects on passengers without needing them to remove their clothes at the security checkpoint. But there has been a lot of controversy surrounding the use of full body scanners by TSA. In 2015, a lawsuit was brought against TSA for their lack of regulations over the full body scanners in airports partially due to the impact this has on passengers' privacy (Jansen 2015).[2] Because body scanners were introduced in 2007 and were not widely used at the time of the majority of the interviews, the Muslim Americans I talked to discussed their experiences with metal detectors.

Another tactic employed by TSA agents are stops and searches of passengers, which they claim are random. During these stops and searches, passengers have their bodies and possessions searched at two locations: the security checkpoint and the airport terminal gate. At the security checkpoint, after showing identification and their airline tickets, some passengers may endure a pat down after they go through the metal detector or body scanner. Passengers who have already been subjected to intensive searches at the security checkpoint often go through the process again at the boarding gate, where their bodies may be inspected with a handheld magnetometer and they may undergo another physical pat down and have their belongings searched (Stoller 2005).

The Behavior Detection and Analysis Program trains behavior detection officers to conduct nonintrusive behavioral analyses to identify passengers who
display threatening or suspicious behaviors. BDOs are instructed in Screening Passengers through Observational Techniques (SPOT), a program where
agents are taught to notice behaviors that may signal terrorist activity, such as
recognizing passengers' facial expressions that indicate emotions such as the
fear of being exposed. If suspicious behavior is detected, BDOs approach
the individuals to interrogate them about their travel plans. If the answers
to these questions arouse more suspicion, the agents can detain the passengers and interrogate them further. TSA agents are supposed to document this
information and share it with various internal organizations, including the
Office of Intelligence and the Office of Law Enforcement Federal Air Marshal
Service (Department of Homeland Security 2008). Information on individuals may also be shared with local law enforcement, reflecting the influence of
Title II of the PATRIOT Act, which increased the scope of state surveillance
of both U.S. citizens and non-U.S. citizens by encouraging information sharing
across government agencies.

In addition to identifying suspicious behaviors, TSA agents rely on databases to know who to surveil. There is a history dating back long before 9/11
of airport security using databases containing the names of individuals who
may pose a threat to national security. In 1996, Northwest Airlines created
the Computer Assisted Passenger Prescreening System (CAPPS) to protect the travel industry from terrorism (Kleiner 2010). CAPPS consisted of a
computerized database of individuals identified as potential threats to airport
security. Though the Federal Aviation Administration (FAA) claimed that
racial, ethnic, and religious identities were not used to compile the list, the
FAA did not reveal what criteria were actually involved. Civil liberties organizations such as the ACLU responded to CAPPS with concern because of its
potential for discriminatory practices against passengers in airports. Yet even
with the complaints lodged against these lists, the state continued to justify
their use to protect the nation from a terrorist attack, and the government
continued to funnel resources into their maintenance. In 2003, the U.S. government provided Lockheed Martin with a multimillion-dollar contract to
produce a better version of CAPPS called CAPPS II, which was designed
to connect law enforcement to intelligence databases (Kleiner 2010). Civil lib-
erty organizations feared information unrelated to airline security would be
used against passengers. The ACLU was concerned that the state would secretly
collect data on passengers and produce lists based on racial, religious, and ethnic cues rather than criminal behavior, resulting in racial profiling (American
Civil Liberties Union n.d.[b]). CAPPS II was terminated in 2004 after the
U.S. Government Accountability Office found that it violated passengers' privacy (Kleiner 2010).

Although CAPPS II was terminated, lists are still used in airports for national security. TSA relies on multiple lists that are derived from the Terrorist Screening Database (TSDB) in order to determine who should not fly and who requires more surveillance in airports. Title I of the PATRIOT Act increased funding for the Terrorist Screening Center, which maintains lists of suspected terrorists, including the TSDB and the Terrorist Identities Datamart Environment (TIDE). TIDE comprises 1.1 million names, of which roughly 680,000 are shared with various local, state, and federal agencies (Handeyside 2014). According to the ACLU, the U.S. city with the most denizens on these watchlists is Dearborn, Michigan, which also happens to host the second-largest Arab American population in the United States (Scahill and Devereaux 2014). It is also the city that has the second-largest Muslim population in the United States. This strongly indicates the overrepresentation of Arabs and Muslims on these terrorist lists.

The two most widely used lists at airports are the No-Fly List and the Secondary Security Screening Selection List (or the Secondary Security Screening Selectee List). The No-Fly List contains names of individuals who are not allowed to travel by airplane within or outside of the United States because the state has determined that they pose a threat to national security. The ACLU has criticized the government for refusing to provide information on how someone gets on the No-Fly List or the number of names on it because it obscures state abuses. The Selectee List is also used at airports. Passengers who are on the Selectee List are prevented from checking in at airport kiosks and printing boarding passes at home (Pasquarella 2013). When they attempt to do so, these individuals are informed that they must see a ticket agent, who issues them their tickets after they are interrogated about their travel plans. These tickets are marked with four Ss (SSSS), flagging these passengers for extra surveillance in the security lines, such as having their bodies patted down and their belongings searched. Passengers on this list are usually allowed to board their flights only after they are cleared to fly through these additional security measures.

The No-Fly List and the Selectee List are both used by another TSA program, the Secure Flight Program. Under the Secure Flight Program, airlines are required to provide TSA with passenger information such as name, gender, date of birth, redress number, and travel number. TSA compares the Secure Flight List to the No-Fly List and the Selectee List (Transportation Security Administration n.d.). If the Secure Flight List matches a passenger on the No-Fly List, the passenger is unable to board the flight. If a name on the Secure Flight List matches a name on the Selectee List, the passenger will go through additional security measures at the gate. If a name comes up on one of these TSA lists, passengers may go through up to three layers of enhanced screening before being allowed on the flight.

TSA and its programs have endured several criticisms over the past few years because of their exorbitant budgets and reliance on profiling in airports. As stated previously, TSA has been repeatedly accused of relying on religious and ethnic cues to identify suspicious behaviors in airports. Critics argue that TSA lists have become a tool to profile travelers based on racial, ethnic, religious, and national identities. According to Kleiner, "Critics of airline passenger profiling have argued that computerized screening programs—such as CAPPS I, CAPPS II, Registered Traveler and the new Secure Flight program—are inherently 'biased against passengers with connections to areas of the world whose behavior or policies conflict with the interests of the United States—namely the Middle East. As such, critics believe that profiling promotes an unconstitutional categorization of travelers by ethnicity, race, religion or a combination of all three'" (2010: 115). Consequently, Americans who have a Muslim name are vulnerable to profiling because of the overrepresentation of Muslim names on these lists. Like the National Security Entry-Exit Registration System, these lists are overpopulated with names from Muslim-majority countries. It is possible the individuals I interviewed were actually on one of these lists, but based on the interviews, it is also likely that their Muslim names resulted in *false positives*, which happens when a name is similar enough to a name on one of these lists that it results in the person being targeted and stopped for additional surveillance (Nakashima and Klein 2007; FBI website n.d.).[3] The secrecy that clouds these lists makes it difficult to know how the government compiles them, but what is clear is that Muslim men find themselves unable to fly without hypersurveillance because of these lists. Inclusion on these lists perpetuates the notion that Muslims are a threat to national security regardless of their status as citizens. In other words, creating these inventories of Muslim bodies actively racializes Muslim populations.

Utilizing these lists does not curtail terrorism but rather justifies discriminatory practices by the state. Profiling in airports also creates a sense of distrust between communities of color and law enforcement (Ramirez, Hoopes, and Quinlan 2011). Lyon argues that in a post-9/11 society, the reliance on technology for surveillance has not made surveillance less biased but produced a system of social sorting: "[Passengers] . . . are coded to categorize personal data such that people thus classified may be treated differently. People from suspect countries of origin or with suspect ethnicities can expect different treatment from others" (2007: 162). In addition to being critiqued about racial profiling, TSA has also been criticized for its wasteful practices because of increased economic investment in security at airports. The mandate to search every piece of luggage that enters U.S. airports resulted in an increase in the number of airport security staff. Critics claim that the extra security does not reduce the chance of a terrorist attack but instead only increases travel times and costs

(Roots 2003). Complaints were also brought against TSA agents for misconduct, including theft of travelers' belongings (U.S. Government Accountability Office 2013). A *USA Today* story revealed that from 2010 to 2014, TSA paid three million dollars to roughly fifteen thousand passengers who filed complaints for damage to luggage or stolen property (Penzenstadler and Ptacek 2015). From 2007 to 2012, TSA also employed roughly three thousand BDOs and spent close to nine hundred million dollars on the SPOT program alone (U.S. Government Accountability Office 2013). A review of SPOT in 2010 by the Government Accountability Office concluded that despite this enormous budget, the program yielded little in terms of preventing a terrorist attack (U.S. Government Accountability Office 2013).

There has been an increase in passenger complaints against TSA by those who felt they were singled out because of their religious, racial, or ethnic identity for these supposedly random stops and searches (Bonikowski 2005). Behavioral detection officers have also come forward as whistleblowers of racial profiling in airports. According to the ACLU's website, former BDOs have come out and stated that these behavioral detection programs are "racial profiling programs" and give TSA agents the "license to harass" (Handeyside 2014). In 2015, the *Intercept* published an article about the "Spot Referral Report" that TSA agents use to determine suspicious behavior. Those listed on this document include exaggerated yawning, excessive complaining of the screening process, excessive throat clearing, widely open staring eyes, gazing down, and even a pale face from recently shaving a beard (Winter and Currier 2015). Anyone could be considered suspect based on these behaviors, yet my interviews revealed that not everyone is routinely stopped and searched in airports. Despite the critiques brought against airport security practices, TSA and its programs continue to operate under a multibillion-dollar budget.

The stories here unveil how airport surveillance is multifaceted and requires participation from several agents: the state and private citizens as well as Muslims. Airport surveillance unfairly targets Muslim passengers when TSA agents rely on visible cues such as Muslim religious signifiers like the hijab to determine which bodies should be stopped and searched and when Muslim men are subjected to hypersurveillance because their names either appear on a TSA list or are similar enough to one of those on it. This distrust of Muslims by the state sends a clear message to society that Muslims should be watched, monitored, and feared. As described earlier, private citizens also participate in this hypersurveillance of Muslim bodies by reporting them to flight attendants as suspicious because they wear hijabs or speak Arabic, because of the association of Arabic with the "enemy" (Naber 2006). I show that Muslims are aware that it is not just the state that surveils them in airports but also private citizens and that they consequently participate in self-surveillance as a result of their hypersurveillance.

Racially Profiling Muslims at U.S. Airports

The ACLU defines racial profiling as "the discriminatory practice by law enforcement officials of targeting individuals for suspicion of crime based on the individual's race, ethnicity, religion or national origin" (American Civil Liberties Union n.d.[d]). Based on this definition, racial profiling is not limited to discrimination based on skin tone but can include traits associated with religion or ethnicity. Religious signifiers, such as a Muslim name and clothing, inspire racial profiling in airports, which is captured in the phrase *flying while Muslim*, revealing the racial nature of this encounter, as it is a reference to *driving while Black*—abusive stops and searches of African American drivers that is triggered by skin tone.

The hypersurveillance of Muslims in U.S. airports is not the same as the inconvenience non-Muslim citizens encounter when they are forced to endure long lines because of additional security measures such as taking off one's shoes in the security line, making sure one's laptop is out of its case and in its own bin, going through a metal detector or body scanner, or having one's luggage scanned. Muslim Americans go through a more rigorous form of surveillance triggered by their religious identity. The Muslim American men I talked to who were on the Selectee List and the Muslim American women who wore the hijab were repeatedly stopped for "random" searches. Their surveillance at airports was a visible act that created a public spectacle, confirming in the minds of their fellow passengers that Muslims are a potential threat to national security. The stories here show how innocent, law-abiding Muslim American men and women are made to feel like potential criminals in front of their fellow passengers because of their religious identity. The act of surveilling Muslim American men and women, particularly when done in such a public format, racializes their bodies as potential terrorists.

Encountering the List at U.S. Airports:
The Surveillance of Muslim American Men

All the men interviewed for this study were at some point informed that they were on a TSA list or that their names were very similar to a name on a TSA list—a circumstance known as a false positive. The Muslim men were not told what list they were on or why, but after conducting the interviews, it became clear they were on the Selectee List, which subjected them to interrogation by TSA agents about their travel. Because they were on this list, several of the men interviewed were subjected to several layers of security checks after they stepped foot in the airport. These men were unable to use the self-check-in kiosk to retrieve their tickets. Instead, they had to get them at the ticket counter, where TSA agents interrogated them about their travel before issuing the tickets. Once they had their tickets, some noticed there were four *S*s printed on them. These *S*s marked them as those who should be stopped and searched at the security line, where they were often pulled out of the line to have their bodies and bags searched. Additionally, because of the Secure Flight Program, they were sometimes interrogated again and searched at the boarding gate because the flight passenger list had been compared to the Selectee List, marking them for yet another layer of surveillance. Muslim men who were on the list ranged in age and profession: some were college students, and others were professionals specializing in fields from advertising to law. The majority of these men were born in the United States and varied in their religiosity. Only a few of the participants were active in Muslim organizations. Nothing about their flying habits indicated suspicious behavior—they flew on round-trip tickets purchased with credit cards.

Hamza, a thirty-four-year-old Pakistani American man, was born in the northeastern United States and grew up in the Midwest. He went to college and law school in the Midwest and is a lawyer in the Chicago area, where he lives in an affluent, predominantly white neighborhood. He identifies as Muslim, but at the time of the interview did not belong to any religious organizations or go to a mosque, with the exception of on Muslim holidays or when visiting family. He was in Europe when 9/11 happened, attending a rock concert. He flew back to the United States on Air India and expected to have a hard time at customs because of his ethnic and religious identity. He was surprised to get through customs quickly that day, but described the next few years after 9/11 as a time when he felt unfairly targeted by airport security: "I would have to go through heightened security. Maybe two years after 9/11, I found out I was on put on the TSA list." I asked him if he knew why.

HAMZA: The reason I was given was because they had suspected someone with a name very similar to mine of being a terrorist, but they wouldn't give me any other information, they just told me to fill out a form. When you're on that, the effect of being on that TSA list is that you always have to go through heightened security at the airport, which sucks, especially if you travel the way I do, which is a lot for work.

Asked what this heightened security entailed, Hamza described requirements consistent with being on the Selectee List. He had to check in with a ticket agent, where he had to answer a series of questions about where he was traveling and why. At the security checkpoint after he showed his ticket to a TSA agent, he was always singled out, pulled out of the security line, and subjected to the handheld magnetometer and a pat down.[4]

Hamza remembered how humiliated and helpless he felt when he first realized he was on a TSA list. He had visited his family for Thanksgiving, a little more than a year after 9/11 and was flying back to Chicago.

> HAMZA: I remember getting in the airport and I couldn't do the electronic check-in on the kiosk. I had to go up to the ticket counter to get my boarding pass, and this was the first time I noticed that I was on the TSA list, because I went to the ticket counter because I was running late for my flight anyway. And I asked the person, "Why can't I get my boarding pass through the kiosk? I'm not checking any bags." They were like, "Sorry, sir, but you're on the TSA security list." And honestly, I remember I thought I was going to cry. I was so livid. Every emotion inside of me was just—it drove me nuts that they couldn't tell me any real reason why I was on this list. And that went on for two years. I could never go to the kiosk; I always had to go to the ticket counter.

Hamza is your average American young urban professional who happens to be Muslim. It was his name that triggered suspicion of him, resulting in his placement on a government watchlist. Regardless of his status as a citizen and lack of criminal record, Hamza was treated like a potential terrorist because of his religious identity and gender. Men like Hamza do not warrant state surveillance, yet they have become targets of it. Although Hamza was taken off the list after a few years, the experience left him bitter.

> HAMZA: I filed my report with the TSA and I don't know what happened, something must have happened 'cause I can do that now [referring to the self-check-in at the kiosk]. But it's not like I got a note in the mail saying, "Congratulations. You are no longer a terrorist."

The state racializes Muslim men's bodies as potential threats to national security when it places them on a security list simply because they are Muslim. Bilal, a thirty-year-old Bengali American man, was working at a Chicago advertising agency at the time of our interview. Bilal is also a local musician and artist. He stopped self-identifying as a Muslim shortly after 9/11, but when I asked if he was easily identifiable as a Muslim, he told me that while most people are unable to determine his racial or ethnic background based on appearance, after hearing his name, they could identify him as a Muslim. Like Hamza, Bilal was aware that he was put on a list immediately after 9/11.

> BILAL: I was put on some list where they won't let you check in right away. You have to see an attendant, and they'll ask you some questions. I don't know,

normally, you know I travel with people too. You notice the discrepancy, that they can just walk in and then I have to go through this. It wasn't too much of an inconvenience, which is why it didn't bother me, but it's some kind of profiling. It's to be expected, I guess.

What resonated with Bilal was the differential treatment he had in airports compared to his non-Muslim traveling companions. His traveling companions were able to use the self-check-in kiosks, while Bilal was unable to do so. Passengers who are allowed to enjoy the full privileges of citizenship may still experience the inconvenience of long lines at security checkpoints where they have to take their shoes off and pull out their laptops, but they are not isolated from the rest of the passengers on a regular basis and interrogated by TSA agents. Bilal's Muslim name triggers suspicion even though he no longer identifies as a Muslim, revealing how this interaction is best described as racial as opposed to religious discrimination. Bilal is not discriminated against because of his beliefs, but rather his body is essentialized as a threat because his Muslim name categorizes him as a potential terrorist.

There were a few cases where Muslim women mentioned facing this type of surveillance, but it was always when they were traveling with a Muslim man. I interviewed a married couple, Aziza and Mahmoud, together. Aziza was a stay at home mother in her early twenties, while her husband Mahmoud was finishing medical school. Both ethnically identify as Pakistani, and both were born in the United States. Aziza does not wear the hijab and was one of only a few women who told me that she was on a TSA list. I asked her why she was on a list.

> AZIZA: I think because my father was the president of [his local] Muslim Society and then I was the president of my MSA. That's my guess. Who knows? We were on the security list, a TSA security list, where you have—you're going through and you have three or four Ss on it. I guess you can write to TSA and request for your name to be taken off, which we haven't done, but we had a really difficult time flying.

Like the other participants, Aziza was not aware the Ss on her ticket meant she was put on the Selectee List. I asked Aziza if she'd noticed whether she was still on some list.

> AZIZA: It's gotten a lot less since I moved to Texas—I think I'm in the Denver International Airport system, but flying out of Dallas or Lubbock, I haven't had that problem. But immediately after 9/11, the next year, we flew to New Jersey for my mamu's wedding, my mom's cousin's wedding, and there were

five [of us, including] my father, my mom, and my two sisters. We were flying and they called out my father's name right before boarding the flight,
and they were like, "Can passenger Zaid please come up to the front?"

Aziza and her sisters watched as airline agents interrogated their father. They
noticed their father was getting agitated so they approached the counter to see
what was going on.

> AZIZA: So we all went up there and we're just like, "Okay, what is the problem?"
> They're like, "You guys are traveling together as a family?" They brought two
> guards that were standing there. It almost seemed like they were about to
> take him to the back and do some kind of extra questioning or whatever . . .
> and they were like, "This is random, sir." My dad's like, "I'm sorry, it's not
> random." And they're like, "Yes, it is." And my dad was getting upset, and
> we're like, "Dad, calm down. Don't make a scene," but we would have that a
> lot for the first two to three years after 9/11.

If Aziza and her sisters were also on a list, they would have also been called
up to the gate to undergo additional surveillance. It was Aziza's father who
was targeted because he was on the Selectee List and therefore had his name
come up again on the Secure Flight Program, where the passenger flight list
was compared to the Selectee List. Aziza may also have been one of the few
women on the Selectee List, or she may simply have encountered such experiences when she traveled with men on the list, explaining why her experience
varied at different airports.[5] Aziza's father was correct in noting his surveillance was not random, but inspired by a system where government lists, the
Selectee List, and the Secure Flight Program, are used to hypersurveil Muslim
men in airports.

Naveed, a thirty-one-year-old Palestinian American, accurately described
the feelings of the majority of the Muslim men who encountered racialized surveillance at airports. He is an American Airlines platinum flyer who
had a first class ticket when he was stopped and searched right before boarding
a flight because of the airline's use of the Secure Flight Program.

> NAVEED: The whole gate was watching . . . And I'm just thinking, Wait, I'm
> not boarding? I'm like, your best customer. I only fly American Airlines.
> You are my only carrier. All my money goes to you! So I was like, "Wait, so
> I'm not boarding?" "No, you have to go through extra screening." And I'm
> like, "Why? Why?" [And] then I was just like, Shut up. Just go through the
> screening, you know . . . And they went through my bag, and they frisked me
> again, and then I was just like, what, is this really random? Because it doesn't
> feel random to me.

Because Naveed was on the Selectee List, he had to go through additional security, being searched and interrogated at the terminal gate. Naveed thought his status as a platinum flyer should protect him from this surveillance. But privileges associated with class do not protect Muslim bodies from surveillance in a nation engaged in hypersurveillance. Muslim men are left feeling humiliated in front of their fellow passengers. Most of the men interviewed felt they have no choice but to comply with their surveillance rather than contest it.

Saleem, a thirty-year-old Arab American physician living in Chicago, was also profiled at the gate because of the Secure Flight Program. He told me he had several encounters at airports, but this one confirmed how Muslim men are specifically targeted.

> SALEEM: The worst time was when I flew American Airlines, and at Charles De Gaulle Airport, which is a Paris airport, they actually announced the names of the people, mainly of Middle Eastern descent, they actually announced maybe twenty-eight names. And they said, these people are going to undergo extra security, and I was searched three times. The last time was at the entrance of the aircraft in front of all the passengers—which freaked them out because they're like, "We don't want this guy sitting next to us!"

The agents who searched Saleem and the other twenty-seven Middle Eastern passengers were French, but Saleem remembered this as an American Airlines policy:

> SALEEM: These were American Airlines regulations. Which is interesting, because Air France also flies to the U.S., but they never do this. And it was humiliating because it was in front of everyone. Like I said, "Can't you do it in a private room?" And they were nicer to me, because I speak French, and I was speaking French with them, but they still said, "This is the policy, we have to search you here." So that was unpleasant.

Saleem was humiliated by this experience because of the public display of his surveillance. The search that occurred directly in front of the gate made Saleem appear to be a potential terrorist in front of his fellow passengers. He worried that passengers on the flight would think he was guilty of something.

While Saleem felt it was a shared Middle Eastern heritage that resulted in their profiling, other interviewees reveal that this is not limited to just Middle Easterners but also includes South Asians because it is the religious identity that is targeted. The calling out of Muslim names for additional security screening serves to further associate Muslim bodies with terror in front of their fellow passengers, creating an inequitable flying experience.

This public display of security segregates passengers into two groups: those who are a potential threat, and those who are worthy of protection from this threat. The fact that nearly all the names called out for additional security were Muslim names supports the claim that the Selectee and No-Fly lists target Muslims. In this instance, American Airlines performed security in front of some passengers by racially profiling its Muslim clientele. It is no surprise, then, that passengers feel justified in reporting Muslims as suspicious to flight attendants on airplanes; they take their cues from the state. When the state participates in racially profiling passengers based on a religious identity in a public fashion, citizens feel justified in reporting their fellow passengers as suspicious for doing things like speaking Arabic or wearing the hijab when flying.

Anwar, a twenty-year-old premed college student, also felt he was subjected to random stops and searches of his body and bags when he flew. He was finishing college when we met. He had just recently applied to medical schools. Anwar told me what it was like traveling home from college:

ANWAR: Oh yeah. Freshman year, I would take planes home every now and then, just because I'll get sick of the train because it would be like six hours if you get stalled, every single time. And then there [was] a string of three or four times in a row where, I was just by myself, just had a backpack, so I guess, I mean, I might've looked shady—just me, by myself, with a backpack—but yeah, every single time, just randomly selected, randomly selected, three or four times in a row.

I asked Anwar whether he could check in at the airport kiosk, and he responded that he always had to go to the ticket counter to receive his ticket. Because of these experiences, Anwar chose to ride the Megabus home rather than fly.

Like the other Muslim men interviewed, Anwar often went through the three layers of security, first at the ticket counter, next at the security line, and sometimes at the gate. These encounters were so embarrassing for Anwar that he avoided flying when he could. He told me he had to fly for his medical school interviews and that he was stopped and searched: "And recently at the airport someone checked my backpack, and he was this guy [who had a Muslim name] and I was looking at him like, 'No. Come on. What are you doing here?' He was just looking through my bag. He found biology books but that's all he found." The frustration Anwar felt when profiled by someone who appeared to be another Muslim comes through in this testimony. But Anwar was not aware that he was marked for surveillance the minute he stepped into the airport because he was placed on the Selectee List. He assumed it was his behavior, like carrying only a backpack, or his appearance that triggered TSA's suspicion of him. But many passengers fly with only carry-on luggage and are not subjected to intense interrogation by TSA agents. When I asked if there were markings on his ticket, he told me they were marked with four Ss, which, unknown to Anwar, ensured he would encounter more security as he navigated through the airport.

The secrecy that surrounds these lists is daunting for Muslim American men. They are told they are on some list, but it is never specified which one, creating a state of uncertainty. Some are told their names are similar to one on a "terrorist watchlist," making these men fear being associated with terrorism. This feeling of being watched but not knowing why or when, makes Muslim American men feel vulnerable. Although all the men interviewed are American citizens, they are still situated on the margins of society because their bodies are monitored and watched.

Twenty-three out of the twenty-four Muslim men interviewed were told they were on the Selectee List for a period of time after 9/11. The one man who was not on the list admitted he had not flown since 9/11. The ineffectiveness of these lists is best exemplified by the experience of Abdul. Abdul, a twenty-four-year-old Pakistani American Muslim who lives in Texas, recalled flying from Dallas to Chicago when he was twelve years old. He was flying with his father and brother, and when his father went to swipe his credit card into the ticket kiosk, he was unable to retrieve their tickets and instructed to see a ticket agent. Abdul and his father's names came up on a list. Abdul recalled that it took a while to clear up the issue, but he was finally given a boarding pass and allowed to board the flight. His older brother, Usman, added that both he and his father have had several issues using the check-in kiosk at airports since 9/11. When I asked them how this made them feel, Abdul responded:

ABDUL: I mean, it annoys me because I'm just like, Why would I be on a list? You know, I was born here. I was raised here. I've never been put in jail for anything. I haven't done anything. I come from a good family. What's your issue? Why would you think about putting me on a list?

Both Abdul and Usman grew up with American notions of justice, but they have become increasingly cognizant of their racialization after 9/11 because of their surveillance. Abdul is infuriated by his criminalization. Although he is a citizen, he is still unable to avoid profiling and he knows it is not based on criminal activity or behaviors but rather because of his religious identity. For Muslim Americans, their status as a citizen does not protect them from surveillance. The state defines Muslim men as a threat to security through these surveillance practices, revealing that all Americans do not enjoy the same privileges associated with citizenship, such as being viewed and treated as a loyal member of society. Even at the age of twelve, Abdul was racialized and marked as a threat due to his religious identity and gender.

The majority of the men I interviewed mentioned the lists they were on, but only one participant told me about how she and her husband were detained and interrogated by TSA agents. They were a married couple I interviewed separately. Saima, a twenty-seven-year-old Palestinian American school teacher who wears the hijab, told me she and her Indian Muslim American husband, Aziz, were detained for a few hours and interrogated after they deboarded a plane in Chicago. They were coming back from their honeymoon abroad in 2006, when TSA agents detained and interrogated them. Agents escorted them to another room where they proceeded to interview them about where they were from, what their favorite types of food were, and what they did on their vacation. After hours of questioning, the agent finally said to them, "I guess you're not terrorists." This comment shows that Muslim bodies are equated with their potentiality to commit terror until proven otherwise. The irrelevance of the questions the TSA agent asked Saima and Aziz reflects the misuse of resources on surveillance. Saima and her husband pose no real threat, but by detaining and interrogating them, the state upholds the illusion that they are protecting the nation from terror while confirming which bodies are threatening. In the interview, Saima mentioned she thought she and her husband were detained because Saima wears the hijab. But it is more likely that his Muslim name came up on a list subjecting them to this type of surveillance. Muslim men and women are sometimes swept into one another's surveillance, even though gender does predict what type of surveillance Muslim American men and women will routinely encounter in airports.

The Muslim men I interviewed all shared the same experience of U.S. airports. Their Muslim names mark them as violent and dangerous to the state, and their bodies were consequently treated with scrutiny. The government maintains secrecy regarding the procedures for these lists, making it difficult to know how names are selected or why one actually appears on the lists. None of the Muslim American men interviewed exhibited travel behaviors that might raise suspicion of involvement in terrorism. They are ordinary American citizens who are routinely humiliated in airports on the basis of their Muslim identity. Muslim men are subjected to the Orientalist stereotype that they are incapable of loyalty to the United States (even when it is their country of origin), which strips them of the basic privileges associated with citizenship. The utilization of the Selectee List is one of the ways airports have become a racial terrain where some bodies are criminalized and scrutinized through hypersurveillance.

Using federally funded lists in airports is one example of how the state institutionalizes and participates in the racialization of Muslim bodies through hypersurveillance because of the War on Terror. The profiling of Muslim men in airports is not random, but systemic. Even after TSA agents interrogated Muslim men and it was determined it was safe for them to board an airplane, they were still subjected to surveillance the next time they flew. The act of being stopped, searched and interrogated publicly because of one's religious identity confirms to the public your body is suspect and should be surveilled. The examples provided previously show that the state is not targeting specific nationalities or ethnicities, but Muslims in general. This is why a Pakistani Muslim American man had similar experiences in airports as a Lebanese Muslim American. State surveillance impacts Muslim men, not just Arab men. This was apparent in the way the U.S. government focused on twenty-four Muslim-majority countries through NSEERS and visa holds after 9/11: Arab countries (Syria, Lebanon, and Iraq) and African countries (Sudan and Somalia) as well as South Asian countries (Pakistan and Bangladesh).

All the participants in this study were connected to one of these twenty-four Muslim-majority countries. They were either second-generation Americans or naturalized citizens, whose families migrated from Pakistan, Syria, Lebanon, Egypt, and India. It is likely the FBI terrorist lists are inundated with names of individuals from the same twenty-four Muslim-majority countries that have been placed under suspicion since 9/11, explaining why the people I interviewed either were on the list or triggered a false positive. As a result, these Muslim men were surveilled because of their religious identity—because Muslim-majority countries are prioritized for surveillance. This hypersurveillance of Muslim American men in airports unveils the process of how the state actively participates in racializing Muslim men as terrorists and threats to national security.

Performing Security: Wearing the Hijab while Flying

Talking to Muslim men and women who traveled after 9/11, it became clear they were surveilled differently. Muslim American women's experiences varied based on whether or not they wore religious signifiers, such as the hijab and jilbaab (a loose garment many Muslim women wear over their clothes to hide their figures). The hijab, the headscarf many Muslim women wear, is one of the most recognizable religious symbols of Islam (Williams and Vashi 2007). Muslim women I interviewed who wore religious signifiers were repeatedly pulled out of security checkpoint lines and subjected to searches of their bodies and their belongings. These Muslim women were not on the Selectee List; rather, TSA agents relied on racial cues to identify potential threats to security and profiled them as a result of these discretionary decisions. All the Muslim women who wore the hijab were consistently pulled out of security checkpoint lines, stopped, and searched. Most were forced to endure a pat down, were swiped with the handheld magnetometer, and had their personal belongings searched. The women who wore the hijab experienced this treatment the majority of the times they flew.

Sarah, a thirty-two-year-old Pakistani American Muslim, travels frequently. She recalled her experiences flying as a Muslim woman who wears the hijab: "I've noticed that I do get pulled over in lines a lot. When I travel, I am always patted down." I asked if she made the metal detector go off, giving the TSA agents reason to pat her down and search her belongings.

> SARAH: That's interesting that you say that. Now that I think about it, I
> don't think I make the alarm go off all the time. Now that you say that,
> I don't think I always make the alarm go off. Maybe once in a while, I will
> wear a safety pin and forget about it. I remember last time—my husband
> and I, we went to Albuquerque about a month ago. And I'm very particular
> when I travel. I mean, I understand that there are rules and regulations,
> and I'm going to follow them. So I don't wear tons of jewelry, I just don't
> do it. I wear shoes that are easy to slip off 'cause I know I am going to have
> to take them off in the line. And a woman pulled me aside and said, "I just
> have to pat down your scarf." And they are very respectful because they have
> all learned how to do it now, so they have a very particular way of doing it.
> And my husband says to me, he goes "Why did she pull you aside?" But you
> know, honestly I just didn't care. I'm like, "Fine I'll just do it." But it's inter-
> esting, because I have noticed that. I have noticed that.

As a frequent traveler, Sarah knew what would trigger the metal detector and therefore avoided wearing anything that would cause it to go off. She was also careful to abide by the security norms in airports, therefore Sarah wears slip-off shoes and makes sure her carry-on luggage has TSA-approved items in it, so as to pass through security smoothly. In spite of her precautions, her Muslim identity still triggers additional inspection by security agents.

Ayesha, a twenty-nine-year-old Pakistani American Muslim woman and self-employed entrepreneur, also wears the hijab and has been subjected to "random" stops and searches in airports. She told me she was always searched at the security checkpoint line and she suspected that airport security agents intentionally made the metal detector signal an alert when her husband walked through. She and her husband took great care to remove any items that might cause the metal detector to go off, yet it still went off every time he passed through it. I did not interview Ayesha's husband, but there is a possibility that he was on the Selectee List and was thus subjected to more surveillance at the security line because his ticket had four Ss on it. She told me her husband was routinely stopped and searched by TSA agents and how they both felt they were unfairly profiled. After 9/11, she said she did not want to fly United Airlines because it was one of the airlines that was hijacked and she feared facing extra scrutiny because she is easily identified as a Muslim. She recalled that the last time she flew, a TSA agent asked her to take off the hijab.

> AYESHA: I was quiet because I couldn't believe he just asked me that. Then I was like, "Well, I wear it for religious reasons. I'm not going to take it off." And then he was like, "Oh." And then he called the female person over and then I was so confused. So then she was like, "Okay. You can do it yourself. Just reach under your scarf and move it around or something, make sure there's nothing there." I was like, "I fly quite a bit and this is the first time I'm experiencing this." And she was like, "I personally don't think it's right." And she said herself, "I think it's discrimination and profiling."

The act of stopping Ayesha and searching her hijab is a spectacle of security. I refer to this as *performing security*. If the TSA agent truly felt Ayesha was hiding a dangerous weapon underneath her scarf, she would not allow her to pat herself down.[6] This act shows how stopping and searching Muslim women who wear the hijab is a symbolic gesture of security that makes some bodies feel more secure while vilifying others. Even the TSA agent recognized the racial aspect of this practice in her comment that it was discriminatory. This performance of security creates the illusion that the state is protecting its citizens, justifying the new security structures, such as utilizing databases and stopping and searching passengers at the security line. Neither Ayesha nor Sarah are real threats to the state, but surveilling them in public creates the illusion that the state is protecting the nation while simultaneously producing a narrative that Muslims are to be watched and monitored.

Fatima was born in Palestine and moved to the United States in 1998 with her ex-husband. She wore both the hijab and the jilbaab. At the time of the interview, she had flown four times since 9/11 with her young children and described her experiences as humiliating because of the scrutiny she endured as a Muslim traveler.

> FATIMA: When I go to any place that has security, most of the time I am asked to take the jilbaab off. They say take your coat off and I tell them, "It's not a coat, I can't take it off." So they make you stand aside [at airports] and they search you while people are watching you to make sure you aren't hiding anything.

I asked Fatima how this made her feel. She said, "Really uncomfortable. Totally embarrassed, like I am a target for everybody's eyes, that I did something wrong and people are watching me thinking, 'Why are they doing this to her? Maybe she did something wrong. Maybe they'll catch something with her.'" Fatima dreaded her public surveillance. She worried about how her fellow passengers would interpret it, fearing they would think she had done something illegal. She told me her children would get upset when she went through these stops and searches. This enactment of publicly profiling Muslim women who wear religious signifiers accomplishes what Fatima fears. It associates Muslim bodies with terror, racializing them as bodies to distrust, watch, and closely monitor.

There were a few instances where Muslim men told me they were stopped and searched based on appearance alone. Bilal recalled that shortly after 9/11, he was "randomly" stopped and searched in customs upon returning to the United States from Canada because of his Muslim identity. Bilal was on the Selectee List, but this encounter was the result of a TSA agent profiling him upon reentry into the United States after he had already been through airport security in Canada because of his ethnic identity and then his religious one.

> BILAL: I've been searched very thoroughly at *lots* of airports. Actually, when I came back to Chicago about six months after 9/11, I was coming in from Canada after doing this hip-hop project. I was stopped at the border and this was the most ridiculous invasion of privacy I've experienced as a result of being a Muslim. The guy asked me my name and asked me if I was Muslim and then proceeded to read my journals, and was just flipping through my journals and just sitting there for twenty minutes reading my journals that I had on my carry-on bags. It was really a bit much.

Bilal's darker skin may have incited the security agent to ask if he was Muslim. When he confirmed the officer's suspicion that he was a Muslim, the TSA agent proceeded to search his personal belongings. Bilal's American passport should have granted him reentry into America with ease, yet because he was a Muslim, the borders tightened when he attempted to come back in. His status as an American citizen did not protect him from being profiled because his Muslim identity negates his status as an American.

The supposed randomness of the act of surveillance perpetuates the false notion that security is colorblind. The experiences of Muslim women in this sample contradict the notion that these searches are random, confirming that it is a form of profiling guided by a racialized understanding of religious identity. Its appearance of ambiguity supports the myth that in a democratic society, no one is treated unfairly due to the color of one's skin or one's religious identity. Yet Muslim women who wear the hijab are routinely subjected to stops and searches, revealing the bias toward Muslims in this practice. The notion of the randomness of these stops and searches works to dismiss claims of racial injustice by Muslim Americans. Consequently, most of the participants admitted they did not complain to a TSA agent but instead endured the humiliation of being singled out.

Flying without the Hijab: Passing through Security

Comparing the experiences of Muslim women who wear the hijab to those who do not wear it demonstrates how clothing can become a racial marker for Muslim women because it triggers surveillance. Women who did not wear the hijab had very different experiences while flying. Samira, a twenty-five-year-old Palestinian American who worked as a domestic violence advocate, told me she was stopped and searched at the security checkpoint when she wore the hijab but has no longer been "randomly" searched at airports since she stopped wearing it. Experiences like this suggest that the hijab is what motivates TSA agents to stop and search Muslim women.

Sommer, a thirty-four-year-old Syrian American Muslim woman, is very light skinned with green eyes. Her experiences at U.S. airports were drastically different than those of Muslim American women who wear the hijab. I asked her if she was stopped and searched at the security line.

> SOMMER: You know, you take off your shoes. My kids are used to it because we travel to New York quite often. They take off their shoes, they are cute, they take off their little jackets and stuff. [But] because I'm not veiled, they assume I'm French before anything else. So no, I don't.

I asked her if her Muslim husband experienced issues in the airport. She said, "My husband's name doesn't sound Muslim. It's not Muhammad or anything like that. So they don't know what he is, so no, he doesn't either." Sommer told me her husband Anglicized his name, changing it from an Arabic-sounding one. Sommer is able to pass as a white American because she does not wear the hijab and has a lighter skin tone. She admitted in the interview that people do not identify her as someone from a racialized ethnic group. As her testimony reveals, when she is mistaken for anything, it is a white European ethnic. Because her husband Anglicized his name and is also light skinned, he was not on the Selectee List or subjected to random stops and searches. Sommer and her husband are not racialized as a threat to national security in front of their fellow passengers through searches. Likewise, many other Muslim women who did not wear religious signifiers were able to go through airport security without facing routine stops and searches.

Arab and South Asian Muslim women who did not wear the hijab were able to avoid the hypersurveillance in security lines that Muslim women who wear the hijab could not. While some women, like Sommer, were able to pass as white, even women with darker skin tones were not routinely stopped and searched at the airport like Muslim women who wear the hijab were. This is not to say that skin tone does not racialize individuals as suspect—skin tone may trigger surveillance in times of hyper insecurity, like when there is a terrorist attack—but the hijab triggers stops and searches routinely. Leila, a forty-one-year-old stay-at-home mom who does not wear the hijab, is a Palestinian American Muslim woman. Leila does not pass for white because of her skin tone, but because her name does not sound Muslim to most people, she is often mistaken for being Mediterranean. She told me that her experience flying was very different from that of her mother-in-law, who wears the hijab.

> LEILA: My mother-in-law was stopped when we went to California, just her and
> I. She wears the hijab and all they wanted her to do was take off her jacket,
> but she had worn a sleeveless shirt underneath, she told them "No I can't."
> They said, "Well, we have to search you then." Well, she got really upset
> about it. . . . She felt it was not random and that it was on purpose. And I
> just told her to take it easy and don't let them get the better of you. And
> it really took her a few days to get over it, because she was very, very upset
> about it. Nobody feels that it is random. And I think that is the hardest part.

Leila's and her mother-in-law's starkly different experiences highlight what it means to be marked as Muslim in airports and how religious signifiers, such as the hijab, serve as a racializing agent. Leila and Sommer were both cognizant that they were privileged to avoid surveillance at airports because they were not identified as Muslim. This juxtaposition of Muslim women who wear the hijab versus those who do not is evidence that it is bodies that are identifiable as Muslim that are subjected to consistent and repetitive profiling. The comparison also reveals how racial privileges associated with skin tone—that is, passing for white—become muted if someone chooses to wear the hijab. The hijab marks women as foreigners who need discipline, demonstrating that clothing can work in the same way that skin tone marks someone as dangerous or a criminal. In a post-9/11 society, the hypersurveillance of Muslim women who wear the hijab in U.S. airports clearly shows how religious signifiers associated with Islam have come to acquire racialized meaning, resulting in differential treatment of American citizens.

Self-Surveillance in Airports

The impact of hypersurveillance is that those who are under a watchful eye begin to participate in their own self-discipline. Nadine Naber (2006) coined the term *internment of the psyche* to describe how Arab Muslims she interviewed in San Francisco responded to the fear and anxiety of state surveillance immediately after 9/11. Some of her participants expressed deep paranoia, while others altered their actions and behaviors, like avoiding too much time in public spaces, in order to prevent their surveillance. I also found that Muslim Americans responded to their surveillance by monitoring their own actions and behaviors in order to prevent hypersurveillance, particularly in airports. For example, Ayesha changed the way she dressed when she flew to avoid being stopped and searched by TSA agents.

> AYESHA: Well, my husband and I have traveled a lot. We don't do it anymore, but we know what we are comfortable wearing when we go to the airport. We have a certain way we like to do things. We are just those people who like to travel comfortably. I just realized that now I'm getting older and because people judge me, you know a lot of people judge others solely based on appearance. You know? It would probably be better if I was more put together when I went to the airport. . . . I'm not so concerned about security at the airport. They know seasoned travelers, but [its] more for the passengers. The people watching.

Ayesha attempts to avoid the public performance of security by wearing nicer clothes when she travels. Rather than traveling in comfortable clothes, she surveils her body before she enters the airport. Ayesha told me her husband, who has a beard, also monitors his actions in airports. He goes out of his way to help passengers lift their bags into the overhead compartment on the airplane.

These actions may seem insignificant, but they reveal that for Muslim Americans, airports have become what Foucault (1995) called a *panopticon*, a space where discipline is unpredictable and ever present. In this panopticon under the watchful eye of the state and private citizens, Muslim Americans are not free to be themselves but must constantly demonstrate they are loyal and trustworthy citizens to escape discipline. Sarah told me that when she and her husband fly, they avoid reciting any Islamic prayers because they fear it will frighten their fellow passengers. Flying can be an anxiety-inducing experience for many Americans, and for some, praying is one way to alleviate this stress. However, for Muslim Americans, getting caught speaking Arabic or reciting anything from the Quran could be interpreted as a threat to national security. Hamza, who was on the Selectee List for a few years, told me he avoided playing a video game on his phone that involved airplanes. He told me he turned it off because he feared it could be interpreted as suspicious behavior because of his religious identity. Faisal, an Indian American man in his midfifties, was very careful about the language he used in public, particularly when flying.

> FAISAL: I mean, you know, it's like you heard so many stories about in the plane . . . somebody heard somebody say "bomb," [or] "Oh, they are speaking in some Arabic, Middle Eastern language." . . . I think it's more precautionary and avoiding unnecessary hassle. Or, you can take the other route. "I have my freedom. I can say whatever I want to say," and all that. You can take

that route also, but you know some people don't think it's worth it. Some people think, you know, "I don't care really." So maybe I am a little more on the side of "it's not worth it to me."

The reality is that Muslim men and women do not have the ability to act or speak freely in airports. They are afraid to speak Arabic, let alone words like "bomb." Their bodies and actions are closely monitored by both the state and their fellow passengers. As a result, they are stripped of the ability to occupy airports without concern for how their actions and behavior are interpreted. Because airports are spaces where national security is heightened, Muslims are not able to exist freely in these spaces and instead participate in their own self-surveillance.

Muslim Americans experience what DuBois referred to as "double consciousness" in *The Souls of Black Folk* (1903)—where they are incapable of being one self but instead are made up of multiple selves because they have to shift their identities in public—because of their hypersurveillance in spaces like airports. This inability to be one's true self, to even speak one's native language out of fear of surveillance, reflects the psychological wage Muslim Americans experience because of their racialization. Thus flying while Muslim creates undue anxiety for Muslim Americans. They must navigate airports carefully in order to avoid discipline from the state or their fellow passengers.

While the majority of Muslim Americans I spoke to felt they had to tolerate their profiling and therefore participated in their own surveillance, there were few occasions where Muslims openly expressed their anger. Saima was one of only a few participants who argued with TSA agents.

> SAIMA: I also just get angry a lot at what—you know, the crap we go through. So the last time they did that—that was when [the TSA] agent finished patting down my head—I was like, "Why don't you just go ahead and pat the rest of me down?" And I actually got really upset, and it was an African American woman, and she was like I understand blah, blah. And I was like, "No, pat the rest of me down. Do the whole thing. If you're going to humiliate me just go through the whole process." And she was like, "I'm really sorry."

This expression of anger was unusual, but the sentiment was not. Muslim Americans do not want to irritate TSA agents because they fear the consequences of contesting this behavior, like being detained or prevented from flying. Hamza was the only interviewee who told me he filed a complaint with TSA about being on a list. Perhaps because Hamza is a lawyer, he knew his rights and felt more confident filing a complaint, but in general, the response by the majority of the Muslim Americans interviewed was to minimize surveillance through self-discipline instead of resisting or challenging it. The reasons for opting to self-surveil as opposed to reporting discriminatory practices in airports can be best understood by looking at Fatima's experience flying. She was traveling with her two small children overseas when a passenger refused to sit next to her in his assigned seat.

FATIMA: The first time I flew after September 11th was a little hard. It was a year or two after September 11th. I was flying to Palestine and we went to Israel first. I remember a guy refused to sit next to me because I was wearing the scarf [*laughs*]. It was Continental Airlines. I was flying from New York to Israel.

When I asked how the airline responded to his request she told me, "The manager of the plane told him this is your assigned seat or you have two empty seats in the back of the plane. And he chose to sit in the back." Although the flight attendant told the passenger it was not the airline's policy to allow customers to choose their seatmates, the attendant accommodated his request by allowing him to sit in the back of the plane. The compliance of the airline to the request of the passenger is telling. By accommodating racist attitudes toward Muslims, the message is that Muslims are not worthy of protection from humiliation and racism because the state has confirmed they are dangerous through its security policies. Passengers are able to report their fellow passengers as suspicious to flight attendants just for being Muslim and consequently have them removed them from flights. This practice normalizes fears of Muslims and thus racializes them as a threats. The humiliation of Muslims in airports is justified in the name of national security and their racialization is ignored.

State Surveillance: Racializing Muslim Bodies

Since 9/11, U.S. airports have become highly policed spaces where surveillance is heightened. Whereas other citizens are protected by the state, Muslim Americans must work to avoid being marked an enemy of the state. Foucault wrote, "Disciplines are techniques for assuming ordering of human multiplicities" (1995: 202). For Muslim Americans, power is exerted on their bodies through formal and informal surveillance by the state and private citizens. Through federal policies such as the creation and use of the Selectee List and stops and searches, and TSA programs like SPOT, Muslim bodies are racialized as a threat to national security. The public display of this surveillance signals to the rest of the population that Muslims are potential terrorists. They are not treated like Americans who are protected by the state, which thus strips them of the privileges citizenship should entail and racializes them as violent and dangerous.

In racialized social systems, rewards are allocated along racial lines (Bonilla-Silva 2001). U.S. airports constitute a racialized social system where bodies are organized into those worthy of protection and those who are a potential threat. Being able to fly without suspicion is a privilege. The ability to print out a boarding pass and get through security without being stopped and searched is also a privilege. Travelers who are identified as Muslim are often denied these simple rights regardless of their statuses as citizens. Power is exerted on a Muslim population when they have to take extra precautions to avoid profiling and surveillance from TSA agents. They must avoid wearing items that could set off the metal detector and overtly display signs of helpfulness and cooperation. As a result of being observed in public spaces, Muslims monitor their own behaviors and actions. They internalize the surveillance as a form of discipline.

The interviews confirm that state-initiated surveillance is racially motivated and gendered. Profiling based on religious, ethnic, or racial identity contradicts the basic provisions of the Fourth Amendment, which states that stops and searches are illegal without probable cause. Relying on physical cues rather than behaviors as a basis to determine criminality results in a judicial system that is inherently flawed. It also does not make America any safer from a potential violent attack.

In a post-9/11 society, U.S. airports are spaces where we can pinpoint the rearticulation of racialized meanings. The experiences of Muslim Americans in these spaces provide evidence that the racial state is constantly evolving based on shifting political and social contexts. In the years after September 11th, Muslims have witnessed the erosion of their cultural status as Americans and the privileges of their citizenship. Although anti-Muslim racism and Islamophobia existed well before 9/11, it has become institutionalized through surveillance policies in an effort to prevent another terrorist attack in the years since 9/11. The state does not treat them as citizens worthy of protection but instead criminalizes them because of their religious identity.

3

Citizen Surveillance

In 2010, the building of a thirteen-story Islamic community center in Manhattan, known as Park 51, was met with public anger and hostility. Public figures, like anti-Muslim political activist Pamela Geller, brought national attention to the building of this center. Geller ignited anger around its construction due to its location, two blocks away from the World Trade Center site. Although there had always been mosques close to the site where one of the terrorist attacks occurred, the media frenzy that followed the building of this center resulted in mass protests. *Time* magazine reported that people came out holding signs with slogans such as "Sharia," "Go Home!" and "We Will Never Forget!" (Chua-Eoan 2010). Even though Geller's organization, Stop Islamization of America, has been labeled a hate group by the Southern Poverty Law Center her message that Islam is a threat to the United States is a view that many Americans share. In 2012, she bought ad space on New York subways and put up pictures of the Twin Towers in flames along with a quote like "Soon Shall We Cast Terror into the Hearts of the Unbelievers," citing the Quran as the source. The Metropolitan Transit Authority (MTA) initially banned the ads for their defamatory nature. One ad in particular stated that anyone who opposed Israel was a savage. After the MTA refused to display these ads, Geller sued and a judge ruled in her favor stating it violated her First Amendment rights.[1] But the MTA changed their policy to prohibit controversial political ads, preventing Geller's incendiary ads from being placed in subway stations and on buses in New York City.

The American media also perpetuates the rhetoric that Muslims are terrorists, antimodern, anti-American, and misogynists. Bail's (2015) study reveals that anti-Muslim fringe organizations control the discourse about Muslims in the media. The social construction of Muslims as violent and threatening is not new. Jack Shaheen's studies *Reel Bad Arabs* (2014) and *Guilty: Hollywood's Verdict on Arabs after 9/11* (2008) chronicles hundreds of films, dating back to silent films in the early twentieth century, and how they perpetuate the myth that Muslims and Arabs are violent and dangerous to American society. Alsultany (2012) argues that after 9/11, representations of Arabs and Muslims in the media as terrorists were coupled with a positive image of an Arab or Muslim that contributed to the false notion of a postracial era.

These narratives of Muslims as terrorist, backward, misogynistic, and anti-democratic impact Muslim Americans in their everyday lives. Since the terrorist attacks, the American population has been encouraged to participate in surveillance in order to ensure national security. The messages the media perpetuates about Muslims, coupled with Islamophobic rhetoric by groups like Pamela Geller's, reinforce the idea that Muslims are the bodies that require surveilling.

Racialization of Muslims is not just a state-led process but one that also occurs through interactions in daily life. Racialized meanings attached to Muslim bodies by the state are politically motivated, such as to get public support for maintaining and investing in a surveillance state or foreign policy like the invasions of Iraq and Afghanistan. Private citizens internalize the messages given to them by both the state and the media and then interact with Muslims in ways that reflect their misperceptions of Islam. The state encourages citizen participation in the War on Terror through the Department of Homeland Security's publicly placed slogans and ads like "If You See Something, Say Something." This state-run program emboldens private citizens to report any suspicious activity they see. As a result, private citizens are invited to participate in the surveillance of Muslim bodies. By observing, monitoring, and policing Muslims, private citizens also participate in the racialized surveillance of Muslim Americans.

Just like state surveillance, Muslim surveillance by private citizens is gendered. Muslim women and Muslim men are subjected to surveillance for different reasons. Muslim American women who wear the hijab have their nationalities contested in very public ways, while Muslim American men are questioned through interactions with private citizens at work, school, or social gatherings when their identity as Muslim is made known. Women who wear the hijab are targets for public contestation because of the visibility of their religious identity. They have their cultural values questioned because of their choice to cover their hair. Their fellow citizens consider actions like wearing the hijab a foreign cultural threat to Western values. Muslim men are pigeonholed as potential terrorists once their religious identity is known.

When they identified them as Muslim, private citizens began to question and interrogate the Muslim Americans in this study about their nationalities, cultural values, and their loyalty to the United States. Muslim Americans are stripped of their status as an American through these interactions. They do not enjoy the privileges citizenship should entail, including feeling like a valued and loyal member of society. Instead, since 9/11, Muslim Americans are told they should "go back home," situating them as foreigners in their own country. They are repeatedly questioned about their connection to terrorism. Their identity as American is continuously called into question through their foreignization and constant surveillance since 9/11. In this unique time in history, Muslim Americans experience fragility around their national identity as a result of their racialized religious identity. As this chapter shows, private citizens participate in the racialized surveillance of Muslim Americans, which is guided by gender.

Surveilling Nationality

One of the ways private citizens surveil Muslims is by questioning their nationalities. Interactions with private citizens reveal that Muslim Americans are often treated as if they are enemies who have trespassed American borders. Private citizens participate in the racialization of Muslim Americans when they watch, monitor, and interrogate them in public and private spaces. The encounters the Muslim Americans interviewed had with their fellow citizens show how ethnicity and race become less prominent in their interactions when religious signifiers are present. Muslim American women who did not wear the hijab were not subjected to the same verbal harassment or the same watchful eye as those who did, regardless of skin tone. The hijab is clearly equated with foreignness, and as a result, Muslim women's bodies are under the gaze of their fellow citizens. They are racialized through this surveillance as forever foreign and never American.

"Go Back Home!": Never American, Forever Suspect

Muslim women told me they were often yelled at in public spaces to "go back home." It was only Muslim women who wear the hijab who were the recipients of this verbal abuse, reflecting the gendered nature of this interaction. These encounters frightened not just the Muslim women who experienced them but also their family members and friends. Verbally accosting Muslim women is one of the ways private citizens exert their authority regarding who belongs in society. By targeting women who wear the hijab for trespassing, the message sent is that Islam is not welcome in America.

Irum, a Pakistani American woman who wears the hijab, related an experience she had after 9/11 that she characterizes as "a defining experience." A young white man yelled at her to "go back home" in the parking lot of the grocery store she frequented in Chicago.

> IRUM: I was in the parking lot, and this young guy [in his] twenties, a white guy . . . saw me get out of my car, and he was walking towards me, and he stopped and he started yelling at me. He was saying to me, "Go back to your country" . . . and that's all I heard, and I actually got back into my car, and I drove out of the parking lot 'cause I've never experienced anything like that before. And I'd been going to this [grocery store] forever, and you know for the past year I never had that before, but I waited for him to leave and I came back to my car. I figured, "I'm not gonna be afraid; I'm just gonna go," and that shook me up just a little bit . . . and my roommate insisted that I not go shopping anywhere in [the neighborhood] without her for the next couple weeks.

Irum was not used to this treatment, but after 9/11, she realized things had changed. Her Muslim identity marked her as a foreigner who was not welcome in the United States. Because the War on Terror does not engage with a specific nation but instead with a region defined as Islamic, Muslim women who wear the hijab are also marked as being from a part of the world that is associated with terror instead of a specific nation. As a result, they are subjected to being watched, yelled at, and in some cases, even aggressively approached. Even though Irum was not told to go back to a specific country, she was told she does not belong in her own country. This statement highlights the "us" and "them" that is constructed in order to signal who is to be watched and who belongs. A Muslim identity situates someone as the "them" that does not belong here, even though it's not specified where the Muslim belongs. This interaction caused Irum to fear for her safety, so she got into her car quickly and drove away. Muslim women who wear the hijab have become targets for verbal and, in some cases, potential physical abuse by their fellow private citizens.

Reema, a forty-five-year-old Pakistani Muslim woman, discussed how it angered her that Muslim women who wear the hijab are verbally accosted in public when they are doing their normal activities, like going for a walk: "[My friend] said one time she was walking 'cause she just takes her walks, and this car like slowed down and they were telling her to 'Go back!'" Maham, a thirty-eight-year-old Indian American woman, told me, "I was filling gas the other day and [a man] driving by yelled out of their window, 'Go back to your country, you camel jockey!'" *Camel jockey* is a racist slur used against Arabs and Middle Easterners. Irum, Reema, and Maham's encounters confirm that Islam is racialized and equated with foreignness. Because private citizens are unable to distinguish between Muslim countries, they equate Islam with an ambiguous region of the world. They are unable to distinguish the various nationalities and ethnicities that Muslims comprise. Scholars have shown how Islam is most commonly conflated with the Middle East (Volpp 2003; Naber 2007; Cainkar 2009; Love 2017). Thus South Asians who are identified as Muslim can also be marked as Arab when they wear the hijab, but it is important to note this was not always the case. Sometimes the general "Go back home!" comment reflects that private citizen's inability to identify where he or she thinks a Muslim is from.

Muslim men were not targeted publicly like Muslim women who wear the hijab unless they were in their company.[2] Farooq, a thirty-nine-year-old computer scientist and Jordanian American, immigrated to the United States when he was seventeen years old. His accent and darker skin tone incite questions about his ethnicity. He told me some people mistake him for Mediterranean. But when he is out in public with his wife, a white American convert to Islam who wears the hijab, he has been yelled at to "go back home." Her visible religious signifier results in the assumption they are both presumably Arab regardless of the fact that she is a white American convert. Farooq said that once, they were yelled at to "go back to Arabia." Like Farooq, Faisal is also married to a white convert who wears the hijab. Faisal is an Indian American, and he told me that when he is out with his wife and daughters who wear the hijab, they have been yelled at to "go back home." But when he is by himself in public, this never happens to him. Faisal has dark skin and cannot pass for white. Furthermore, like Farooq he is a naturalized citizen and speaks with an accent. Yet it is when these Muslim American men are with their white wives who wear the hijab that they are yelled at to leave America and go back to wherever they came from. The hijab thus signals to non-Muslim Americans a foreign unwanted presence in the United States.

These experiences also clearly demonstrate how the hijab mitigates the privileges that whiteness affords. White women lose their privilege of whiteness when they wear the hijab. The white women's experiences are no different from the Pakistani and Indian women who also wear the hijab. They too are marked as potentially Arab. The hijab becomes a racializing agent, and those who wear it are told to "go back home" by their fellow private citizens, which denies them the ability to claim their national identity. American women are made to feel unwelcome and marginalized in their own country because they are Muslim. Furthermore, they are made to feel uncomfortable in public doing their normal everyday activities. Not only are they stripped of a sense of belonging in the United States, a privilege citizenship should afford; they are unable to freely occupy public spaces.

This verbal abuse reflects the prevalent ideology that there is a conflict between Islam and the West or, more specifically, that there is a war between Islam and America (Grewal 2014). Private citizens participate in policing the boundaries of America through these interactions. Surveilling nationality is a way private citizens become gatekeepers of citizenship. A particular form of white masculinity is performed through this nationalistic surveillance of Muslim women's bodies. This act of racializing Muslim women by verbally accosting them and telling them to "go back home" is closely tied to performances of masculinity and nationality: "The project of establishing national identity and cultural boundaries tends to foster national ethnocentrism. As a result nationalism and chauvinism seem to go hand in hand" (Nagel 1998: 248). The policing and surveillance of Muslim women's bodies reflects this "nationalistic chauvinism," constructing the ideals of who is and who is not able to claim an American identity.

The Gaze: Observing and Monitoring Muslim Women in Public Spaces

Another way that Muslim Americans are surveilled is through the gaze. Foucault writes that the gaze is a powerful tool of control and discipline (Foucault 1995). The *gaze* is the intent watching of people. It is a form of surveillance utilized by those in society who wield power. An examination of the gaze provides insight into power dynamics in society. The gaze is also dangerous, because it has been used to intimidate and show racial domination over African American women (hooks 1992). Muslim American women who wear the hijab told me they encountered hostile stares by white citizens. The gaze on their bodies is a tool of intimidation and control. Not only did the gaze make them feel unsafe; they also were cognizant their bodies were being surveilled for any illegal activity. Private citizens are able to enforce discipline on Muslim American men's and women's bodies through their surveillance.

Maham, an Indian American who wears the hijab, told me she remembers September 11th vividly because it was the same day she took her one-year-old daughter to the emergency room.

> MAHAM: So we're sitting in Edwards Hospital Emergency Room in the evening waiting for her to be seen, and all that's coming on the little screens is all the Twin Towers, the bombing—and here I am sitting here with my hijab. And I felt really uncomfortable that day just because it had just happened. It was so fresh, and here I am sitting in a public place. And that's when they were all hypothesizing, "This happened. That happened."
>
> It was all just coming out at that time, and I was just dying. I remember sitting there for a good part of an hour and [that was] all that they were showing on TV, and I felt like, "How can I escape? because I see people looking at me. I see eyes."

The gaze on Maham's body felt to her like she was being implicated in the attack. The hijab is the object of the gaze because it signifies Islam, and Islam is equated with terror. The gaze took away from Maham the right to feel the shock and anger of the terrorist attacks with her fellow citizens. She was no longer a member of a national community but was singled out through the gaze as someone who did not belong and was the object of suspicion and anger. This is one of the ways that Muslim women who wear the hijab are racialized. Maham became the target of surveillance because her religious identity equates her to a foreign threat to the United States.

Afia, a fifty-year-old Pakistani Muslim woman who wears the hijab, told me she started wearing it before 9/11, but the "stares" were a regular occurrence after the terrorist attacks. Initially, the gaze limited Afia's mobility in her life. Afia told me she felt uncomfortable attending her son's middle school basketball games in the years after 9/11. Her two sons attended a Catholic school in Texas, and she recalled telling her husband he would have to go to their eldest son's basketball games because of how uncomfortable she felt: "I always felt that I was the outsider. I always felt it." At her son's sporting events, she said she felt the gaze on her from other parents. As a result, when her son had a track meet, she would wait in the car for hours for him to avoid the awkward interactions with the other parents: "I [would] take [my eldest son] for track and I would sit in the car for four hours and had my youngest son [with me]. I would help him with his homework while we waited for my eldest son." Afia felt avoiding these encounters would benefit her sons.

> AFIA: I didn't want even a tiny bit of [a] self-esteem or confidence issue to come in my sons. I wanted them to be very self-confident, very proud of their heritage and their roots and their religion at all times. So I didn't want even once for a kid to make fun or say something—that, "Oh, your mother wears this, your mother wears that."

Afia felt she was protecting them from having to witness other parents treat their mother differently because of her religious identity. She did not want them to feel embarrassed or ashamed of their religious identity. At the same time, the gaze limited her ability to participate in her children's school activities.

The gaze is not harmless but a powerful tool that limits the abilities of Muslim Americans to participate in society as Americans. It strips Muslim Americans of the right to respond to terrorist attacks like every other American citizen: with shock, sadness, fear, and anger. It also limits the mobility of Muslim Americans in their everyday lives by making them feel unwanted or unwelcome in public spaces. The gaze works to prevent Muslims from feeling a sense of belonging in their own country, a privilege associated with social citizenship (Glenn 2002).

Surveilling Culture

In the public's mind, Muslims are thought to be opposed to democracy and Western liberal values. Scholars note that the stereotype is that Muslim men are misogynistic and violent, while Muslim women are oppressed and anti-feminist (Ahmed 1992; Razack 2008). Ayaan Hirsi Ali, a writer and public speaker who promotes Islamophobic rhetoric, argues for the complete reform of Islam because she claims it is an oppressive and violent religion that is inherently antimodern.[3] The prevalence of this kind of ideology can be seen in the interactions of private citizens with Muslim Americans. Islamic practices, like that of wearing the hijab or praying in public spaces, are viewed as backward and are treated with disdain and even suspicion. Private citizens justify monitoring Muslim bodies for participating in religious practices and rituals they view as threats to American society.

Surveillance of culture is racialized when cultural practices are essentialized as innate to Muslims, subjecting them to intense scrutiny. For example, any abuse that Muslim women experience at the hands of Muslim men is reduced to religious cultural values perpetuated by Islam. The Taliban's treatment of women in Afghanistan is an example of this culturally fueled racism. Muslim women were constructed as in need of saving from Muslim men, which in turn justified the invasion of Afghanistan (Razack 2008 Abu-Lughod 2013). Another example of this is the misconception that Muslim women are forced to wear the hijab. Private citizens chastise Muslim American women who wear the hijab because for them it represents subservience to patriarchy, rather than being understood as a choice. Wearing the hijab is treated as a cultural aberration to American societal values and individuals who wear it are understood as antimodern and antifeminist. Interviewees spoke of being verbally abused and accosted by strangers who told them they were oppressed and looked "ugly" in the hijab, leaving Muslim American women feeling unwelcomed in public spaces.

Oppressed and "Bad" for Society

Muslim women who wear the hijab have to contend with various assumptions that are made about them. One of the most prominent stereotypes about the hijab is that women are forced to wear it and are therefore oppressed. Reema, a Pakistani Muslim American and mother, started wearing the hijab after she traveled to Saudi Arabia to perform a religious pilgrimage called "Umrah." Reema lives in an affluent suburb of Chicago and works in the financial industry. She told me that after the pilgrimage, something clicked with her. She just felt the desire to start covering her hair. I asked her if she noticed any changes in her experiences when she returned to the United States. She told me that because of her skin tone, prior to 9/11 people thought she was either Latina or Indian. She never passed for white and was rarely identified as Pakistani.[4] But after she started wearing the hijab, her experiences did change. She told me she was in a currency exchange with her sister-in-law, waiting in a line, and they overheard people in line behind them making derogatory comments about them. She also relayed a story of what it was like to go back to work after she started wearing the hijab. She was very fond of her boss and had a good relationship with her coworkers before wearing the hijab, but her supervisor's response to her wearing it was very telling of how she was now perceived in the United States.

> REEMA: So my coworkers were like, "Are you OK?" and asked me, "You're still covering your head? How long do you have to do that after coming back?" And I said, "I don't have to, this is what I want to do." A couple people thought that somebody died in the family. And then a week or so into it, my boss at that time, he came into the room and he said, "I need to talk to you," and he sat down, and his concern was not so much the actual covering, [but that] he thought that I [was] doing it under some sort of pressure. So he wanted to understand the reasoning. And after I told him, he said, "As long as you are OK, it's a choice that you make, then it's all right, but I just want to make sure that mentally and all that, you're OK." He was also concerned if I'm going kooky or something, you know.

This interaction reveals that private citizens make negative assumptions about the choice to wear the hijab. The first response is that Reema may be abused or oppressed by her husband. After she confirms it was her choice to wear the hijab, she then has to prove to her employer that she is not suffering from any mental health issues. It is not just strangers who interrogate and monitor Muslim women who wear the hijab but also their coworkers and friends.

Irum, a Pakistani American optometrist who wears the hijab, was confronted by a patient of hers about her choice to wear the hijab. The patient assumed she was a nurse who could not speak English.

> IRUM: [The patient] had seen me in the hallway with the hijab and . . . said, "Well, when she comes in here, I don't know if I'll be able to understand her language," and he assumed that I didn't speak English fluently. So [the medical assistant] came out and [said], "I don't know if you wanna go in there or not, just 'cause he kind of has a perception of you." And I was like, "I have nothing to hide; I'm gonna go in." So I went in and just was myself, and I guess he was a little taken aback—he wasn't really expecting an American—and then he says to me . . . "You know, you got to lose that. This is America." He goes, "It's sad that you people are still oppressed," and you know, I just totally excused it. And then he kept on it. I thought it was

interesting because it was very busy that day, and I was a little frustrated
because he kept holding me back because I just wanted to do his exam . . .
but he wanted to chitchat with me and insist that I not wear this and insist
that, you know, this is backward . . . Then his whole attitude was "You're in
America, you need to act like an American," you know.

The patient made several unfounded assumptions about Irum. First, he assumed
she was a nurse and also not American. He was surprised when she spoke
English without an accent. He also associated the hijab with the oppression of
women. He viewed wearing the hijab as an un-American act. Irum was being
surveilled for her cultural practices associated with Islam and made to feel that
by wearing the hijab, she was not behaving as an American. It is in these social
interactions that private citizens behave as gatekeepers to citizenship. By surveilling Muslim bodies and situating their religious values as unequivocally un-
American, Muslim Americans feel their national identity is vulnerable. While
Irum chose to ignore the comments, other Muslim women felt they had to
prove that their religious values were not in conflict with American ones.

Nazia, a thirty-seven-year-old Indian Muslim woman who is a naturalized citizen, did not wear the hijab at the time of the interview but wore it
for several years. Her experiences while wearing the hijab were similar to the
other Muslim participants I interviewed. She was in the mall one day when a
stranger interrogated her about wearing the hijab.

NAZIA: I used to wear a hijab, and there was this lady who came and asked me
why I did this. She told me, "Why do you have to do this? You don't have to
do this here in America." So I said, "You know what, I just started doing
this after coming to America. I didn't do it before when I was in India. I did
[it] after coming to America because I learned more about Islam." And so
she just kinda gave me a look . . . So she was thinking since Muslim women
are seen as being oppressed, she probably thought that she would let me
know that it's not the case here in America.

Being approached in a public setting like the mall by a stranger shows how
Muslim women's bodies are subjected to constant surveillance. Not only are
they watched, but they are also interrogated. Nazia is questioned about reject-
ing American values by wearing the hijab because the assumption is that she
was forced to wear it. Nazia contests the belief that Muslim women have
no agency regarding their bodies by explaining how she chose to wear the
hijab after she migrated to the United States and never wore it in India. Nazia
attempts to demonstrate that wearing the hijab is not an affront to Western
values of freedom but rather reflects her free will as an American citizen. These
interactions emotionally taxed Muslim women who wear the hijab with the

responsibility of demonstrating that Islamic and American values are not in conflict with one another.

Maryam, a twenty-nine-year-old Syrian American who was born in the Midwest, decided to wear the hijab after her second year of college. She grew up in a predominantly white small town in the Midwest. Maryam said she passed for white before she decided to wear the hijab. She said she felt like a minority for the first time in her life when she started wearing the hijab. She described an experience she had in a café a few months after 9/11.

MARYAM: One time I was at [a chain restaurant], and there was this woman who was reading a newspaper. She kept staring at me, and like reading her paper, and then giving me this evil eye. And so, I was just like, "Oh, can I help you?" And she was like, "You and your people all ought to just go home. You're no good to this society." And I got real upset, and I was like, "Well, you know, you should really read some of your statistics, 'cause I think an overwhelming majority of us have done more good for this society than anything else."

Maryam, like many Muslim women who wear the hijab, are often stared at in public spaces. In this instance, Maryam decided to disrupt the gaze by confronting the woman. Maryam encountered cultural racism, where her religious values are racialized as "bad" for American society, situating her as someone who is incapable of positively contributing to the nation. Unfortunately, this was not the only negative experience Maryam has had regarding her values because of her religious identity. She told me a white man approached her in the grocery store and yelled at her for "ruining America." She was frightened by the man and feared the verbal abuse would become physical. She was grateful to the other customers who intervened on her behalf, but the experience made her realize how vulnerable she had become in public spaces because of her religious identity.

These confrontations about values are paradoxical. On the one hand, Muslim women who wear the hijab are viewed as oppressed and in need of saving. The need to "save" Muslim women from abusive Muslim men is an ideological tool to justify imperial projects, such as the U.S. invasion of Afghanistan in 2001 (Abu-Lughod 2013). This misconception of Muslim women as victims of abuse and in need of saving is not a new phenomenon that developed after 9/11, but has been perpetuated in the West in order to justify colonial projects in Muslim countries (Ahmed 1992; Razack 2008; Al-Saji 2010). On the other hand, in the United States, religious signifiers attached to Muslim women's bodies racialize them as un-American, oppressed and culturally backward. These encounters with strangers make Muslim women who wear the hijab feel as if they are transgressing Western cultural norms and are an unwelcome presence in society. Private citizens fail to recognize the right to choose what one wears is how Muslim women express their democratic values. While Muslim women abroad are seen as in need of saving, Muslim women in America are unwanted and treated as if they are polluting American society.

Muslim men rarely told me they were surveilled for their cultural values the way Muslim women who wear the hijab were. However, there was one interview where Saleem, a Lebanese American doctor, told me of an encounter he had with a nurse and a patient that highlighted this dichotomy of the "good" and "bad" Muslim. Although he was born in Lebanon, Saleem is an American-born citizen because his father was naturalized. He moved to Chicago to complete his medical residency. He told me people think he is a European immigrant when they encounter him because he has a lighter skin tone. He said that when they realize he has a Muslim name, their interactions became more hostile. He recalled an incident where his patient demanded a new doctor after he realized that Saleem was a Muslim by reading his name tag.

> SALEEM: When the patient saw my badge, he really got scared. So one of the nurses wanted to make him feel better, and he said, "You're a Muslim?" and she said, "But he's a good one." Kind of like the default is I'd be bad . . . I had a patient call me a fascist. I don't think he knows what that word means, because—I don't think anyone knows what the word means.

When the patient identified Saleem as a Muslim, he no longer wanted him to be his doctor. The patient's distrust of Saleem is triggered because of his Muslim identity. The nurse attempts to defend Saleem by categorizing him as a "good" Muslim as opposed to a "bad" one. This dichotomy of the "good" versus the "bad" Muslim is meant to ease the patient's anxiety about Saleem, but it also confirms the limitations of Muslim existence in the United States.

On one end of the spectrum, there are the Muslims who assimilate and downplay their religious identity, the "good" ones (Mamdani 2004; Shryock 2010). These Muslims do not transgress what are perceived to be American cultural norms, by doing things such as wearing the hijab. They do not display their religiosity in public. On the other end of the spectrum, there are the "bad" Muslims. These Muslims display their religious identity through behavior and dress. These Muslims are viewed as having the potential to be radicalized because their adherence to religious codes is seen as a rejection of American values (Mamdani 2004; Shryock 2010; Kundnani 2012; Kundnani 2014). In a neoliberal society, this notion of "good" and "bad" Muslims segregates citizens into deserving and undeserving. Being labeled a "good" Muslim does not protect Saleem from potential job discrimination. He is still vulnerable to the anti-Muslim prejudices of his fellow private citizens and as a result could lose patients. Social interactions with private citizens reveal how Muslims are reduced to religious subjects and understood only in relation to terror

(Tyrer 2013). Thus the "good" Muslim is someone who is secular and perhaps not practicing and therefore less prone to terror, while the "bad" Muslim is more susceptible to terrorism because he or she is religious and practices Islam.

Surveillance of Beauty

The surveillance of beauty is another way that Muslim American women who wear the hijab are surveilled for their cultural practices. Whiteness has become a marker of beauty and privilege both in the United States as well as in countries that make up the southern hemisphere, such as India (Hunter 2011). This is evidenced by the increased interest and use of skin lightening creams both in the United States and internationally. Hunter (2011) refers to "racial capital" as a material benefit people possess based on their skin tone. In a racialized society, the lighter one's skin tone, the more access one has to economic resources such as jobs or social networks (Glenn 2009; Hunter 2011). Muslim women who wear the hijab were told wearing it made them ugly; they are also racialized for their beauty.

Nasreen, a forty-two-year-old Palestinian American and mother of five, said that before she started wearing the hijab, she sometimes passed for white or a white ethnic, like an Italian or Greek. Once she started wearing it, she had some interesting experiences with her neighbors, who she considered to be her friends. After 9/11, the father of her son's neighborhood friend would come over and engage her in conversation about religion. She felt he was trying to persuade her to give up her religious beliefs. He would try to convince her to take off the hijab. He said, "But you're so good, Nasreen. You're so good. And why do you have to put that on? It's not making you better. It's ugly." She told me that his wife did not like her because she wore the hijab. She said her son's friend would tell her stories of what his mother said about her. He told her his mother said, "She's white. She's an American. Why the hell does she have this on?" Another neighbor, an older white woman, said she would be more beautiful without the hijab.

> NASREEN: I had a neighbor—to this day she'll call me [and say], "You have that stupid"—what does she call it? "Tablecloth" or something—"You still have it on?" I sa[y], "Yes, I do. I'm not taking it [off]," [and she responds,] "But why? You're so beautiful. You don't have to put it on. And you know, you're an American. You shouldn't put it on."

The comments reflect an association among beauty standards, whiteness, and nationality. Nasreen was told that she is "good," but the hijab does not make her "better"—it must make her worse. Nasreen was made to feel she could become more beautiful and consequently more American without it. These neighbors implied that Nasreen was a race traitor because choosing to wear the hijab is giving up one's whiteness, something scholars note that white converts to Islam often encounter (Galonnier 2015; Moosavi 2015). Nasreen's neighbors acted as gatekeepers of what it is to be an American by trying to police physical beauty. By wearing the hijab, Nasreen was not losing her beauty but her standing and status as a citizen.

In some cases, it was strangers, not friends, who approached Muslim women about their clothes and beauty standards. Maham, who is Indian American and lives in a suburb of Chicago, told me about an experience she had one day when she was out with her daughter.

> MAHAM: I was in the library, and my daughter was looking around somewhere. She wasn't with me when the woman said something to me. [The woman] was a librarian who worked at the library, and she turned to me, and she said, "Must you wear black from head to toe? You know, it's really morbid." I turned to her and I said, "I'm sorry. I didn't mean to offend you with the way I dress." And then she suddenly got all flustered and realized that what she had said was probably inappropriate and started to make small talk . . . "No, no. Is it part of your requirement in your culture?" she said. And I said, first of all, "No." I said, "The color of my clothing has nothing to do with culture. It just so happens [that] today I happened to be wearing these trousers and I thought the scarf matched."

Maham dresses like many other American women who live in an urban area like Chicago—she wears black or darker colors. She feels her black hijab matches the colors of her clothes. Black is not an unusual aesthetic for individuals who live in large cities. (In fact, in a 1994 *New York Times* article on fashion, John Tierney theorizes about the affinity New Yorkers have for black clothing.[5]) But Maham is not seen or treated like any ordinary American citizen who prefers to wear black. The hijab marks her as someone who is morbid. The librarian tried to explain that she was assuming this was a cultural practice of Maham's, regardless of the fact that she was wearing jeans and a black sweater that day. Cultural practices like wearing the hijab are viewed as unattractive and as an eyesore in American society. Muslim women are repeatedly told that beauty is equated with showing more of one's body and the practice of wearing the hijab is beneath American standards of beauty. It creates assumptions of what constitutes American beauty and situates Muslim women outside of this norm. Thus through a rejection of American cultural norms such as beauty, the hijab works as a racializing agent on Muslim women's bodies.

One of the privileges of whiteness is the uncontested association of it with citizenship and its unquestioned rights to resources (Garner 2006): you are viewed and treated like a valued member of society, something that has been denied to racialized groups in the United States. Racialization of culture is not a new phenomenon. Eduardo Bonilla-Silva argues white Americans participate in *cultural racism* toward African Americans, where cultural differences replace biological differences. For example, the stereotype of African Americans as lazy or not hard working is attributed to deficiencies in black culture, so they are blamed for any inequities in education and wealth (Bonilla-Silva 2002). The pitting of Muslim values against American values is another example of cultural racism. Cultural racism does not replace the reality that skin tone still matters in a racialized society but highlights the importance of racialized cultural attributes.

Muslim American women who wear the hijab are made to feel like they are oppressed, bad for society, un-American, and even unattractive. The mentioned interactions reveal that Muslim women are told that the removal of the hijab would be an act of citizenship. Their interactions with private citizens show who wields power in defining who is an American. Private citizens participate in the rearticulation of what it means to be an American. At a time when the nation is engaged in a War on Terror, a Muslim is excluded from this definition. Not only are Muslims criminalized through state surveillance, but private citizens also engage in their surveillance when they observe, monitor, and challenge Muslim American women for participating in their cultural practices because these practices are racialized as anti-Western and un-American. Arab women who could once pass for white, are no longer able to do so when they put on the hijab. For South Asian and Arab American women who wear the hijab, their experiences begin to mirror one another because of it.

Disloyal and Dangerous: Muslim Americans Policed by Fellow Citizens

The state actively recruits private citizens to participate in surveillance by encouraging them to be on the lookout for suspicious activity in order to prevent terrorism. The "If You See Something, Say Something" campaign by the Department of Homeland Security gives citizens permission to profile Muslim Americans. The Department of Homeland Security's website states, "Become a partner and join the 'If You See Something, Say Something™' campaign's efforts to protect our nation by raising awareness of the indicators of terrorist activity and the importance of reporting it to local law enforcement. By disseminating the campaign message, you'll play an integral role in keeping our communities safe" (U.S. Department of Homeland Security 2017).

Advertisements and announcements on buses, subways, and airports that encourage private citizens to pay attention to their surroundings is one of the ways citizens are told to participate in surveillance. The state does not provide a description of what entails "suspicious behaviors," leaving the public to rely on their own assumptions and stereotypes of what constitutes terrorist activity. The social construction of a Muslim terrorist occurs through the interactions of Muslims with private citizens. Private citizens made comments, sometimes in the form of an innocuous joke, to their Muslim friends and acquaintances about their association with terrorism.

Nasreen, a forty-two-year-old Palestinian American woman and mother who lives in an affluent suburb of Chicago, told me that immediately after 9/11, she felt tensions with her neighbors. She said one of her neighbors joked about whether or not she and her family were making bombs in the basement.

> NASREEN: When 9/11 hit, we all—you know, of course everybody stood inside. The neighbors that knew [me] knocked on my door and said, "What are you doing in your basement? Are you making any bombs? Are you creating anything?" They claimed it was a joke, but I was really offended. I go, "I'm not finding this very funny." "Oh, but we're just joking." But I know they're not joking. They're worried. They're looking at you. So the people that used to always come over as neighbors started roaming around my house. And I'm not dumb. They would go downstairs and look. One of them was the wife of a cop.

This interaction with Nasreen and her neighbors demonstrates how quickly her interactions and relationships with them changed after 9/11. She told me she was particularly concerned that the one neighbor who was married to a police officer could cause a lot of trouble for her and her family if she suspected Nasreen's family of being connected to terrorism. As a result, instead of expressing anger at their insensitive jokes at such a tense time, she felt she had to remain silent because of the power they wielded over her and her family. Nasreen feared her neighbors because they had the ability to report her family as a potential terrorist, which could result in the detention of her family.

Private citizen surveillance is justified in the name of national security, so Muslim bodies and property become fair game. Their privacy is sacrificed for security, and they have no recourse to protect themselves from this injustice because it is performed under the guise of making America safe. The state grants permission to its citizenry to racially profile Muslims. By using coded language about terror, there is ambiguity regarding who requires vigilant monitoring. The close association of terrorism with Muslim bodies provides cues as to who should be watched and who should be protected.

Several of the Muslim men and women I interviewed told me they were associated with terrorism when they were in school. Aziza, who is Indian American, was a high school student on September 11, 2001. She vividly recalls how a student blamed her for the attacks.

AZIZA: I remember sitting down in my chair, and there was this kid. He was this white, blond-hair, blue-eyed, really cute guy, [a] baseball player, and he patted me on the back and he's like, "Thanks for what your people did." And I was just literally in shock, and you don't even know what to say at that moment, 'cause you're just like—I mean, what does even "my people" mean? What does that refer to—anyone who's brown? The entir[ety of] India, Pakistan, Afghanistan, [the] Middle East?

This was not the first time this happened to her. When she was in the seventh grade, a parent approached her about the Oklahoma City bombing. The interaction happened at a Halloween party, and Aziza recalled fondly how she was dressed up like an Indian princess for the party. It was not the outfit she wore that made this party memorable, though; she remembers it vividly because she was accused of being responsible for a horrific terrorist attack.

AZIZA: When I was in seventh grade, I had gone to this party. It was a Halloween costume party, and I dressed up as an Indian princess. We dressed up as Indian princesses every year, and so I'd gone to my friend's house, and there were a whole bunch of seventh graders and our parents there. [My friend's] father was like, "So where're you from?" and I said, "My parents are from India and I'm from Oklahoma, and I'm Muslim," and he's like, "That's great." He's like, "I'm sure you were involved in the Oklahoma City bombing." And he wasn't being funny. It wasn't a joke, and, I mean, I was in seventh grade. I didn't even know what to say to that, but the reason I was bringing that up is I feel like there is hatred that existed before 9/11.

It is important to note that not even children are exempt from this association with terror by private citizens, nor did the association with Muslims and terrorism arise out of nowhere on 9/11. But after September 11th, anti-Muslim bigotry increased and surveillance of Muslim bodies became institutionalized.

"Are You a Terrorist?": Surveillance of Muslim Men for Terror

Muslim men recalled friends and acquaintances joking around with them about being a terrorist. Because the state surveilled Muslim men, these accusations made them very uncomfortable. Some of these interactions happened at school as well as at work. In these spaces, Muslim men avoided talking too much about religion or politics in an attempt to deflect negative associations of Islam off of their bodies. Nabeel, a twenty-two-year-old Pakistani American college student living in Texas, described the types of jokes he encountered about being a terrorist.

NABEEL: I went to high school starting in ninth grade at a Catholic school, private, all boys' school. And that was a little different. Kids weren't . . . I wouldn't say "racist," but like, you know, high school boys joke around a lot. They would make jokes, you know, like, "Oh, don't blow me up," and stuff like that. You know? But they wouldn't mean it in a racist way. It would be joking around.

Nabeel's response to this incident reflects the prevalent notion that these jokes are not racist. It highlights the invisibility of the racialized aspect of these anti-Muslim attitudes. These jokes are far from harmless and remind Muslims their bodies are associated with terror. They also let Muslim Americans know they are not trusted in their own country.

Jamil, a twenty-year-old Indian American college student in the Chicago area, told me that when he was in high school, he was teased several times about being a terrorist.

JAMIL: There have been times my friends will joke around and call me a terrorist.
SAHER: Does that bother you?
JAMIL: When I was in high school, I used to laugh it off, but in college, I've found more Muslim friends, which is how I avoid these types of jokes.

Jamil told me he grew up in a predominantly white community in the Midwest where there was a very small Muslim community. Like Nabeel, he was one of only a few Muslims in the school, and most of his friends were white and non-Muslim. Even though Jamil claimed these jokes did not bother him, when he found more Muslim friends in college, he chose to avoid spending time with people who made these types of jokes to him, indicating they did make him uncomfortable. Having Muslim friends did not completely protect Jamil from these unwarranted accusations. He was in an elevator of a dormitory with an Indian American friend when a college student, a white male, asked them, "You two aren't terrorists, are you?" Jamil and his friend were shocked at this question, and Jamil responded "No," accompanied by an awkward laugh. In this case, Jamil felt it was their skin tone that incited this interaction. The student did not know Jamil was a Muslim, but his ethnicity triggered the assumption that he might be a terrorist. Jamil's experience was somewhat unusual. The majority of the Muslim men I talked to told me they were usually targeted as a terrorist after they revealed their Muslim names.

Aziz, a thirty-year-old Indian American management consultant, recalled an experience he had with a professor when he was getting his MBA at an elite institution in the Northeast.

AZIZ: I did *hear* things and comments in classes, though. There was a professor I remember in one of our classes. I had told him before that I was Muslim. I was a practicing Muslim and prayed five times a day. We would talk about Muslim countries [the course had nothing to do with the Middle East], which was for some reason a favorite topic of his, [and] I would always say, "Actually, oh, I've been there or had the opportunity to travel [there]." But I remember in the middle of one class or [the] beginning of one class, he's like, "Oh, we're talking about Afghanistan today." But he's like, "Aziz, have you been to any camps there?" And that really was like crossing the line to me.

The professor was referencing a terrorist training camp. By asking Aziz if he was there, this professor created the association of him with Islamic extremism and terrorism. This stigmatized Aziz in front of his fellow classmates by suggesting he was capable of being disloyal and dangerous to his own country because he was a Muslim. The power dynamic in this relationship prevented Aziz from registering a complaint against his professor because he feared it would impact his grade and status in the program, as well as potential job opportunities.

This was not the last time Aziz experienced such insinuations. Aziz works in the corporate world and told me of an encounter he had with a partner of the firm. It was a Monday morning, and the weekend before, there had been a terrorist attack in India. Aziz ran into the partner, who questioned Aziz about where he was over the weekend.

> AZIZ: I remember this partner I was working with who, after there was a terrorist attack in India, . . . asked me on Monday morning jokingly, "Ah-ha, where were you this weekend?"

Aziz, like the majority of the Muslim men I interviewed, was on TSA list and had been interrogated by TSA agents. Therefore these comments were not received as harmless jokes but reflected the power that private citizens hold over Muslim Americans.

Private citizens wield an incredible amount of authority over Muslims. Muslims are susceptible in schools and in their places of employment because of the negative views their fellow citizens have of Muslims. They fear being labeled as terrorists and reported to the state. These interactions are a constant reminder that Muslims are being watched. Their association with terrorism can have detrimental consequences for Muslims, such as being arrested or detained without due process.[6] Hamza, a Pakistani American lawyer in his midthirties, stated that for a period after 9/11, he avoided talking about politics or religion at work. He feared being labeled a terrorist sympathizer for expressing certain political views, such as those on the Palestinian-Israeli conflict.

Abdul, a Pakistani Muslim American, was a premed student volunteering in an emergency room in a hospital in Texas at the time of the interview. He recalled an uncomfortable interaction he had with a patient.

ABDUL: I work in the ER, and so I was seeing this patient. Usually patients don't talk to us; they talk to the doctors. But he asked me, "What's your name?" And I said, "My name's Abdul." He said, "Is that an Arabic name?" and I said yeah. And he was like, "So are you gonna blow something up?" And I was kinda shocked, and I was like, "No, I'm not." I mean, I was in the room with my doctor, and my doctor didn't say anything. I kind of chuckled, and I said, "No, I'm not," and kinda chuckling at the guy's ignorance.

Abdul told me the doctor he was working with was not a Muslim. The doctor's silence speaks volumes. It shows that Abdul's racialization is not seen as a valid form of prejudice worthy of speaking out against. Muslim Americans feel powerless to speak out against racial hostility they encounter when there is little support for them. Abdul told me he did not want to jeopardize his position at the hospital, so he chose to remain silent.

This was not the only experience Abdul had with being accused of terrorism. When he was in junior high, his classmate asked him if he was related to Osama bin Laden. His older brother, Usman, who attended the same high school, told me a teacher would make derogatory remarks about Muslims in the classroom. When I asked Usman and Abdul (I interviewed them together) if they complained about these comments, they both said they felt nothing positive would have come from making a complaint. Usman's words sum up perfectly how Muslim men feel about making a complaint.

USMAN: Even if I made a complaint, it's all political in that school. I didn't have the money or the political power to actually get this guy into trouble. If anything, I was just gonna get myself into trouble by doing it. I mean, one of the people that went after me was a really popular person in the school—he was a history teacher, so we were talking about world history, but he focused mainly on European and Christian history, and he would go after the Muslims and stuff like that, and he tried to embarrass me in class. And all the students would side with him. The whole school sided with him. I mean, I knew I couldn't go after him for anything, so, I mean, there wasn't much I could do in high school.

The responses by Abdul and Usman were echoed by several of the other Muslim men I interviewed. None of them felt they had the power to contest these encounters because the belief that Muslims are terrorists or violent has been so thoroughly ingrained into the American psyche that to argue against it seemed futile.

Syed, who is an American-born Pakistani Muslim, was in his midtwenties and worked at a bank in Texas at the time of the interview. He wore a nametag at work and interacted with customers regularly. He told me that one day at the bank, he noticed an agitated customer speaking to his coworker and gesturing at him. The coworker told Syed the customer was unhappy and concerned that a Muslim was working in the bank. The bank did not appease the customer by firing Syed, but they also did not discipline the customer for his racist attitude toward Syed. The incident reflects the vulnerability of Muslims to anti-Muslim prejudice in the workplace. Sommer, a light-skinned Palestinian American Muslim, told me her husband Anglicized his name at work to avoid losing business. Her husband works in the corporate world and interacts with executives. She told me his boss supported him changing his name because his Muslim identity could result in them losing lucrative business deals. The complaints lodged against Muslim Americans have the potential to make them less desirable employees, particularly if hiring them results in loss of business. Their Muslim identity makes them suspect and untrustworthy, and as a result, they are surveilled and discriminated against at work and school.

The interviews reflect the rising trend in employment discrimination for Muslims in the United States (Acquisti and Fong 2015).[7] While highly educated professionals who are Pakistani and Indian were once characterized as a model minority, in today's era, Muslim American men are losing racial privileges they once were afforded because of how their religious identity racializes them. Stereotypes of Muslims are pervasive and far-reaching in the lives of Muslim Americans. While South Asian and Arab Americans I interviewed have higher levels of education and of the American population, the narratives presented suggest a Muslim identity may continue to complicate their achievements and successes.

Calling the FBI on Muslims

After 9/11, there was a surge of FBI interviews of Muslims. According to Cainkar (2009) upward of hundreds of thousands of Muslims were interviewed by the FBI in the years after 9/11. A few of the Muslim men and women I talked to shared stories of the FBI visiting them at their homes. The majority of the interviewees admitted they knew someone, mostly Muslim men, who had met with the FBI. They told me how their neighbors or strangers they encountered reported them for suspicious behavior. Hina, a Pakistani Muslim American woman, told me that after 9/11, her husband had the FBI visit him several times: "He had neighbors who would call the FBI and say that 'we have a terrorist-looking guy living next to us.' They said, 'He comes and goes at weird hours, you need to check him out.'" Hina said the FBI visited her husband several times over the course of three weeks because of phone calls made by private citizens.

Maham also told me about a time the FBI visited her at home late one evening. One afternoon, shortly after 9/11, she went to the post office to mail some clothes to Pakistan to her relatives. Her husband waited in the car while she went into the post office to mail the package. Later that evening, Maham, who wears the hijab, was putting her young kids to bed when there was a knock on the door.

> MAHAM: I asked my husband, "Who's knocking at our door at this time of night?" And I was upstairs trying to get the kids to bed, but I peeked from the loft to look down . . . it was a man in uniform with a badge, and I'm pretty sure he identified himself as the FBI, and he wanted to follow up on a civilian call that had come in in regards to something that had been mailed at the post office. And my husband's like, "Sure. Come on in." I was standing at the top of the stairs, and he's like, "Please come on in." [The FBI agent] was like, "No, no, sir. That won't be necessary." [My husband said] "Do you want me to get my wife?" [The agent]'s like, "Well, no. We're just following up [about] what was mailed, and where was it mailed, and the details of it." And so [my husband] said, "Yeah. Someone had sent her some clothes, and she was shipping them back to her because they were for sale. We have all the paperwork."
>
> And [the agent]'s like, "No, sir. That won't be—" He was very apologetic, and he kept saying, "Sir, that won't be necessary. That won't be necessary." Of course we were just like [an] open book, whatever you want to know. And my husband said, "I'm just curious. What is this about?" And [the agent] said, "Someone jotted down your license plate, sir, as you left [the post office]."
>
> So someone went out of their way to not only watch me at the post office, but basically got our license plate number, turned it in to the police as someone suspicious mailing something, and then the police [were] able to track license and registration and find us. And after, [the agent], he just said, "That's fine, sir. Thank you so much. We're very sorry to disturb you." And he said, "I must explain. This is our job. We have to follow up." And he's saying to my husband, "You can imagine how many of these calls we get daily these days."

This experience captures what most Muslim Americans fear. They are afraid their fellow neighbors and citizens will report them to the FBI. This particular interaction highlights how racial privilege operates in society. Even though the FBI agents behaved in a way that indicated they understood there was no real terrorist threat, they stated they had to respond to a private citizen's call. If Maham was a real threat, the FBI agents would have gone to the post office and seen what was in the package that Maham mailed earlier that day. If they were able to track her down from the license plate, surely they would have been able to find her package and see what was in it, especially if national security was at stake. Perhaps they would have even searched her home. The ever-present threat of terror has created an environment where a citizen can have the state come and surveil a Muslim citizen simply for mailing a package.

I should note that Maham's experience with the FBI was unusual. Men were more likely to be visited by the FBI than women; several of my participants told me of times their fathers were surveilled by the FBI. Tariq, a young Palestinian American doctor, said his father was visited before and after 9/11, as was the father of Maryam, a Syrian American woman. Neither Tariq nor Maryam knew if these visits were inspired by private citizen surveillance or if it was because the FBI had been surveilling their fathers for their political views: Tariq suspected his dad was under surveillance because he had been vocal about his pro-Palestinian views, and Maryam thought hers was visited because of his political views on the Middle East. I also had several Muslim men tell me they knew other Muslim men who were interrogated by the FBI.

What these encounters reveal is that private citizens have the power to report Muslims to the FBI just because they are Muslim. Muslim men are more likely to be suspected and targeted because the state has constructed the image of the terrorist as Muslim and male, but on occasion, women who wear the hijab can also be caught up in this type of surveillance.[8]

Private Citizens and Racialized Surveillance

The interactions between Muslim Americans and their fellow private citizens reveal a power dynamic where one has the authority to watch and monitor the other. In a post-9/11 society, a slight majority of Americans support curtailing the civil liberties of Muslims in the name of increasing national security (Sullivan and Hendriks 2009). In a society hyperconcerned with protecting the nation's borders from another terrorist attack, surveillance of Muslim bodies has become an acceptable practice, supported by the state through policies such as the PATRIOT Act. The state encourages private citizens' participation in this surveillance in an attempt to curtail terrorism. The Department of Homeland Security's Nationwide Suspicious Activity Reporting Initiative (NSI) is a collaborative project where federal, state, local, and tribal agencies gather information on suspicious behaviors that could be related to terrorism. In the case of post-9/11 America, this distrust is rooted in xenophobic attitudes toward Islam and Muslims. Muslim Americans are treated differently than the rest of the population because they are categorized as potential terrorists and threats to Western values due to their religious identity. This justification of their surveillance is a part of their racialization.

When private citizens participate in the hypersurveillance of Muslim Americans, they create an environment of exclusion. Public spaces are not welcoming ones for Muslim Americans. This private surveillance of Muslim Americans is guided by gender. Muslim women who wear the hijab are open targets for the public. They are subjected to verbal abuse and threats of violence. Muslim American women are treated as though they are a danger to American cultural values in a myriad of ways, like having their beauty contested or being told they are no good for society. Private citizens surveil their fellow Muslim citizen when they continuously question them about their nationality. When Muslim Americans, particularly Muslim women who wear the hijab, are yelled at to "go back home," they are stripped of their status as American citizens. They are also made to feel vulnerable when they are called terrorists, even if it is done in a flippant way. Muslim American men were more likely to be treated as violent threats to national security. The public has internalized the construction of Muslim men as potential terrorists and consequently refers to them as such through offhanded comments and jokes. The laws and policy shifts in this country in the name of national security have made labeling someone a terrorist a serious offense, and Muslim Americans are cognizant the state has the ability to take punitive action against them without due process because America is engaged in a War on Terror. Private citizens hold enormous power over Muslim Americans because of their ability to report them to the state.

These experiences reveal that the United States is a racialized social system that now allocates different rewards and privileges based on a Muslim identity. It is important to note that a racialized society creates unique experiences based on gender. Muslim American men and women encounter differential experiences in this racialized social system that mark Muslim women as a threat to American values and Muslim men as a threat to national security. The War on Terror has created an era of hypersurveillance and the institutionalization of a racialized Muslim identity, one where the state and private citizens watch and monitor mosques and Muslim bodies. As a result, South Asian and Arab Muslim men's and women's location on the racial hierarchy is shifting based on their racialized religious identity. Although immigrant Muslims and their American-born offspring may have always been viewed as foreigners, now they are suspect and dangerous to society. The current racialization of Muslim Americas has to be understood within the context of American policies, both foreign and domestic, in the War on Terror, but it is also an ideological tool espoused by the state to justify surveillance of Muslims. Thus racializing Muslims as a threat to both cultural values and national security is a necessity in maintaining a surveillance state, and private citizens play an important role in this racialized, gendered surveillance.

4

Self-Discipline
or Resistance?

Muslim American Men and
Women's Responses to Their
Hypersurveillance

There is an argument to be made that surveillance can have positive outcomes. Surveillance technologies, such as carefully placed security cameras, have been useful in identifying criminals. These cameras aided in identifying and capturing the Boston Marathon bombers, Dzokhar and Tamerlan Tsarnaev.[1] While surveillance has been used by the state to identify criminals, citizens are also able to use it to capture abuses by the state. Personal cameras on smartphones have been utilized to document instances of police brutality and the deaths of innocent black Americans. But there are also several critiques about surveillance that warrant attention—one concern is that surveillance is an invasion of privacy.

A surveillance society thrives when individual privacy is sacrificed for national security. In a surveillance society, it is not just the state and private citizens who surveil. It is only complete when those surveilled begin to self-surveil. To clarify, not everyone has an equal chance of being surveilled. The state designates which bodies require vigilant monitoring, and a surveillance society becomes oppressive when it unfairly monitors and watches particular groups of people based on their race, ethnicity, religion, and gender, resulting in a loss of privacy and consequently one's civil liberties. In the context of the War on Terror, Muslim Americans are cognizant they are being watched and monitored. They are uncertain of when the surveillance will occur and whether or not it will be followed by punishment. In some instances, surveillance is visible, and in others, it is not, rendering it unpredictable. Foucault states, "The major effect of the Panopticon: to induce in the inmate a state of conscious and permanent visibility that assures the automatic functioning of power. So to arrange things that the surveillance is permanent in its effects, even if it is discontinuous in its action; that the perfection of power should tend to render its actual exercise unnecessary" (1995: 201).

Living in an environment where surveillance is a possibility but not always exercised creates a state of unpredictability for Muslim Americans. Because of the fear of surveillance and in order to avoid it, Muslim American men and women participate in their own surveillance. This act highlights power dynamics in society. Some citizens are empowered to surveil in order to protect the state, while others are cast as suspicious and targets for surveillance, resulting in their disempowerment.

Gender was central to understanding whether or not Muslims resisted or participated in their surveillance. While some found unique ways to resist their hypersurveillance, revealing that agency is always exerted in the face of oppression, others felt disempowered. For example, the Muslim men I interviewed told me they feared being classified as a terrorist by someone misinterpreting their beliefs about religion and politics. They were less likely to participate in political and religious discussions at work and in public spaces because they feared it could cast them as anti-American or suspicious. Men were aware the consequences of being cast as anti-American could be dire for them because most Muslim men were on government lists at the airport or knew someone who had been visited by the FBI. They were cognizant this classification could result in punitive repercussions. Because of this fear, Muslim men were more likely to silence themselves and avoided standing out or bringing attention to their bodies.

Muslim women's responses were complicated. Because women were not on government lists and their religious attire triggered their surveillance by private citizens, they tried to both mitigate their surveillance and resist their racialization in various ways. Muslim women described the various ways they altered their behavior and dress in public spaces because of their constant surveillance. They told me stories of how they were careful to wear colorful hijabs and smiled more often in public to avoid appearing morose or oppressed. They attempted to reclaim their American identity while wearing the hijab because they knew they were being surveilled. In some ways, Muslim women felt they had more agency and power to contest their surveillance. Their responses lie somewhere between self-surveillance and resistance.

Muslim American Women: Self-Discipline or Resistance?

In an attempt to escape the gaze and control the narrative about Islam, Muslim American women were purposeful in how they navigated public spaces. Muslim American women altered their dress, made attempts to smile more and appear assertive, and tried to perform what they saw as American values to the public. Many women told me they felt it was their duty as Muslims to represent Islam in a positive light and in order to counter the stereotypes that have racialized them. Monitoring one's behavior and actions like this is a form of self-discipline enacted by the threat of surveillance.

House Arrest: Avoiding Public Spaces

In this new racial terrain, Muslims fear for their safety. Muslim American women who wore the hijab told me they were frightened to leave the house out of fear for their safety. Lori Peek (2012) shows that Muslim women who wear the hijab were afraid for their safety immediately after 9/11. In the years since 9/11, any time a terrorist attack has occurred in Europe or in the United States, the Muslim community has had to brace itself for anti-Muslim backlash, since hate crimes against Muslims spike afterward. Immediately after the Boston Marathon bombing, a Muslim woman who wears the hijab was physically attacked by a man in Boston.[2]

Several of the Muslim women I interviewed told me they avoided going out in public when not necessary out of fear for their safety. Aziza told me she and her family avoided going to the mosque immediately after September 11th because they were afraid it might be attacked.[3] While the fear eventually subsided, the weeks after 9/11 were a period where Aziza felt she could not leave the house because she wears the hijab.

> AZIZA: I mean me and my mom and my sister and my brother's wife, we all wear the hijab, so even going out to eat in a big group—we would try to avoid [going out].

For many Muslim women who wear the hijab, the act of avoiding public spaces when an event occurs, such as a terrorist attack, results in self-imposed house arrest. The fear for their physical welfare limits their mobility in public spaces. Private citizens are able to place boundaries on public spaces through social interactions with Muslim Americans. They accomplish this by creating a hostile and unwelcoming environment.

The anxiety surrounding racial violence may have seemed like an overreaction right after 9/11, but violence against Muslims has increasingly become a reality. On February 10, 2015, three Muslim American students were shot and killed by their neighbor. Deah Shaddy Barakat, Yusor Mohammad Abu-Salha, and Razan Mohammad Abu-Salha were all Arab Americans and in their early twenties. They were preparing to eat dinner at home one evening when Craig Hicks, a forty-six-year-old white male, knocked on the door and proceeded to shoot them all in the head. Deah was in dental school at the University of North Carolina, Chapel Hill, and had recently married Yusor, who was planning to attend dental school with her husband in the fall. Razan, Yusor's sister, was an undergraduate majoring in architecture and environmental design and was living with them. Senseless murders like these produce fear in the Muslim American community.

After 9/11, there was a 1600 percent spike in anti-Muslim hate crimes (Southern Poverty Law Center 2017). This statistic shows that hate crimes against Muslims were minimal prior to 9/11. According to the Southern Poverty Law Center, the backlash against Muslims died down immediately after 9/11 but has slowly been on the rise since then. In 2010, there was a 50 percent increase in anti-Muslim hate crimes, which coincided with anti-Muslim rhetoric perpetuated by politicians opposed to the building of a mosque in New York City close to where the World Trade Center was located.[4] FBI statistics revealed that 2015 saw a 67 percent increase in anti-Muslim hate crimes compared to the previous year (Federal Bureau of Investigation 2015). Anytime there is a terrorist attack committed by a Muslim, either in Europe and the United States, Muslim Americans brace themselves for the repercussions that will follow. Many Muslim women avoid public spaces for a while out of fear for their safety.

Being Visible: Reclaiming an American Identity while Wearing the Hijab

Muslim women who wear the hijab varied in how they responded to the anti-Muslim sentiments that grew after 9/11. While some women felt limited in their mobility in public spaces, others responded by reclaiming their right to participate in the public sphere. Some felt it was important to be seen in the public, participating in their everyday activities, to show that they were as American as any other citizen. By doing so, these women were actively pushing back against their racialization and their hypersurveillance. Rather than taking off the hijab or avoiding public spaces, some Muslim women made a conscientious effort to occupy these spaces to show they belonged. Zara, an Indian American mother of three kids, wears the hijab and lives in a suburb of Chicago. She told me that a week after 9/11, she decided to go to a garage sale with her kids.

ZARA: [After 9/11,] I realized that I wanted to take a more proactive role. 'Cause, you know, I can't just sit back and hide in the house or look outside the house from the inside. I love going to garage sales, and I think there is just such a social element, and I love taking my kids there and finding books. It's a fun social thing to do with the kids, and they meet other people and negotiate, keep charge of their money and things like that. And I thought to myself, "I used to go to garage sales on the weekends, why wouldn't I do that now?" And so I did go, and it was really interesting talking to these people because we would end up getting into a conversation, and I would stay and talk to these people for like fifteen to twenty minutes. And we talked about Palestine and foreign policy and why people react the way they do. And a lot of the people were just wanting to talk.

The act of going to a garage sale was a conscientious attempt to reclaim her right to space. Through this act, she was affirming that she was a part of the fabric of American society. Rather than stay home and hide from society, Zara wanted to show she had every right to be a part of the public sphere because she and her children were American citizens. She also accepted the responsibility of dispelling myths about Islam to her fellow citizens by staying and talking to strangers about it. Zara's actions were not necessarily the norm in the immediate days and weeks after 9/11. While the immediate response Muslim women had to 9/11 was to lay low out of fear for their safety, in the years since the attacks, many Muslim women have willingly acquired this new responsibility to dismantle the stereotypes of Muslims in public spaces.

Because women who wear the hijab are incapable of hiding their religious identity in public, they are forced to deal with the public hostility, as I chronicled in chapter 3. Many Muslim women who wear the hijab have become more vigilant since 9/11 and subsequent terrorist attacks in Europe and the United States because the anger toward Muslims, with hate crimes and anti-Muslim violence, continues to rise. For Muslim women to avoid public spaces out of fear of physical and verbal abuse is understandable. However, as emphasized in Zara's testimony, there has been an alternative response to a self-imposed house arrest: the conscientious decision to try claim a place in American society by showing the compatibility of a Muslim and American identity. For women like Zara, a Muslim identity did not impede one's mobility in public, even if it inspired hate and potentially violence. By going to the garage sale immediately after 9/11, Zara tried to connect with the larger American public and show that she too was one of them, even if she was also a Muslim. This can be seen as an act of resistance to one's hypersurveillance.

Controlling Dress

Because the hijab incited so much hostility and anger toward Muslim American women, they often felt pressured to remove it. In a few instances, Muslim women told me that Muslim men pressured them to take off the hijab because they knew it could trigger hostility or discomfort in public spaces. Zara, an Indian American schoolteacher, and I talked about how she decided to start wearing the hijab.

It was the summer before seventh grade, and she attended a Muslim youth camp. At the time, she said she didn't know anyone who wore the hijab; her mother did not cover her hair back then. She told me at the camp, she watched and observed two groups of girls. She said one group would get up early in the morning and put on makeup, dressing up for the boys at the camp. The second group of girls would wake up and put on their hijabs and pray. She found herself drawn to them because they were not concerned about the things teenage girls are typically focused on, such as boys. She decided then that she wanted to start wearing the hijab, and so she did. She told me this decision to wear the hijab was not supported by all of her family members.

> ZARA: My uncle came and picked me up [from camp], and he's like, "You know, you don't have to wear that." In the middle of camp, he wanted to pick me up to go get junk food, so we went into the store, and he's like "You don't have to wear that," and I'm like, "No, I'm comfortable; I could wear it. It's not a problem." So we got our junk food, and I went back.

Zara's parents did not try to force her to take it off, but she told me they thought it was a phase, and a few of her cousins teased her for wearing it. But the decision to wear the hijab was entirely hers, similar to all of the Muslim women I interviewed for this book. Yet she too was aware that after she decided to wear the hijab, her experiences changed. Zara told me that after 9/11, the mosque she regularly attended put up a barb wire fence in front of the windows because bricks and rocks had been thrown at these windows. Like mosques, Muslim women who wear the hijab symbolize the threat of Islam in America, and so their bodies are also subjected to violence and harassment.

Reema, an Indian American woman who wears the hijab, told me her husband asked her to take it off. She was at work on 9/11, and her husband at the time (they have since divorced) wanted her to pick him up from the train station. He pleaded with her to take off the hijab because he feared for their safety. Zainab, a Palestinian women in her forties, told me that after 9/11 her mother begged her to remove the hijab because she was afraid she would get attacked in public spaces. In addition to her mother pleading with her to remove it, Zainab told me that when she was in college, a few professors also encouraged her to take off the hijab for her own safety. She said, "A couple of professors said, 'You are attracting more attention.' They said, 'We understand Islam is for modesty and respect, but you're attracting more attention and not the positive attention.'" Muslim women who wear the hijab are under a lot of pressure to change or control their dress because of fear of violence from strangers and pressure from family members and loved ones who want to protect them. The interviews I conducted confirm Lori Peek's (2012) findings that refusing to take off the hijab can create stress for Muslim women with their family members.

Muslim women responded to this by controlling their dress. They exerted their agency by trying to change the narrative that Muslim women are oppressed and abused. Several of the Muslim women I interviewed admitted they tried to dismantle the myth that they were oppressed by wearing colorful hijabs. They felt darker colors made them appear oppressed and morbid to their fellow citizens. Ayesha was annoyed that a black scarf brought negative attention to her body.

AYESHA: One thing that would make me really upset is if I wore a black scarf, you get so much more attention walking to work. Even if I'm going shopping or something and wearing a black scarf, people look at me more. And it's not like a positive vibe . . . it's so annoying. Everyone wears black. Everyone wears black pants or black shirts. Most people love the color black and love wearing black. I had to stop wearing a black scarf because people would look at me negatively because of it. That really annoyed me.

By changing the color of her hijab, Ayesha was responding to her surveillance. She altered her dress because the gaze made her so uncomfortable that she wanted to avoid it, exemplifying how powerful discipline can be. In this case, external surveillance became internalized and self-imposed. Ayesha did not feel she had the freedom to dress as she would like but instead had to think carefully about what she would wear in order to avoid the gaze on her body.

Maryam also told me she was conscientious of the color of the hijab she wore. She preferred lighter colors to darker ones, but realized some people did stop wearing black hijabs because they felt they would be treated differently if they wore a lighter color.

MARYAM: I never wear black hijabs, really, just because I like wearing bright colors. But one of my best friends, who lives in Boston, used to wear black hijabs all the time. Like, she just felt like that was her personality and that matches her clothes, and she just always wore it. And then after 9/11, she kind of slowly stopped wearing black hijabs. And it was like the biggest joke, because we used to fight with her to just put on something other than black. And now she never wears black hijabs. And she says she feels like people respond to her better when she's wearing a brighter color.

Muslim women such as Maryam's friend and Ayesha refused to take off the hijab but instead tried to influence its representation in order to prevent it from racializing their bodies. While some women told me they chose colorful hijabs in order to match the clothes they were wearing, many women admitted they were afraid they appeared grim and oppressed in black hijabs. Sharmeem, a young Indian America physician, told me that although she liked to match her hijab to her outfit, she was aware that wearing darker-colored hijabs attracted negative attention.

> SHARMEEM: I guess me and my sisters are kind of big about matching [our hijabs]. We don't really wear dark colors, and people actually notice that. I didn't think they really would, but I've gotten those comments from people: "I noticed that you're pretty trendy and fashionable with your hijabs," and so I feel like [I] am more approachable when [I] wear something with a little more color.

These acts are complicated. On the one hand, Muslim women expressed their agency by controlling the way their bodies were imagined in public spaces. In this sense, it was an attempt to rearticulate the common narrative of Muslim women as oppressed and abused. Muslim women wanted to demonstrate that the hijab is not threatening. Wearing brighter colors was an attempt to take away from the hijab the misconception that wearing it exemplifies their oppression.

It can also be understood as a reflection of power relationships and dynamics in society. Private citizens, through their surveillance of Muslim women's bodies, create an environment where Muslim women feel pressure to alter and change their dress because of these antagonistic stares. The act of changing one's attire to disrupt the gaze reveals that although there is a power dynamic in these social interactions, Muslim American women still exert some agency in response to their surveillance. By altering their appearances, Muslim women are trying to limit their racial experiences in public spaces. The uncomfortable gaze and the scowling looks create a hostile environment they have to navigate. Ironically, Muslim women feel they lack choice or free will in how they dress not because Muslim men oppress them, but because they are under the watchful eye of their fellow citizens. Controlling for dress is one of the ways Muslim women participate in the discipline of their own bodies while they rearticulate what it means to wear the hijab.

Not Timid and Not Oppressed

Because of the prevalent stereotype of Muslim women in constant peril (Razack 2008), Muslim women who wore the hijab worked to counter this negative image of them as timid and oppressed in public through their actions. Irum, a Pakistani American optometrist, told me about her love of outdoor activities. She recalled a time when she went rock climbing with another friend.

> IRUM: I remember very clearly when we went rock climbing at a big facility out in [a small Midwestern town]. And it's a great facility, and my friend and I were both wearing the hijab. We just kinda showed up, and the guy was just like, "I don't think I've ever seen Muslim women here before . . . are you sure you want to do this?" And then he was like "Cool, yeah—let's do it!" He was just all excited that we were there, but I think—I mean he was just kinda perplexed when we first got there.

The man working at the rock climbing facility was initially shocked to see two Muslim women who wear the hijab. After he got over the shock of seeing them, he expressed excitement that they were rock climbing. It should not be surprising that Muslim women who wear the hijab like to participate in athletic activities as well, but the prevalent image of these women is they are submissive and fragile and therefore they could not possibly participate in physically engaging activities. Irum also enjoys white-water rafting and received the same initial response when she and her husband went to rent a raft. She said, "I think it's people don't expect that Muslim women, especially when you wear a hijab, could be, you know, cool or outdoorsy or open. They think you're just kinda sheltered, and they're just worried that you'll fall and hurt yourself." In a sense, Irum is simply living her life and doing the things she loves to do, regardless of the hijab. But she is also aware that by participating in these activities, she is actively showing that the hijab does not restrict her from enjoying them and that it challenges the idea that Muslim women are passive and submissive. By white-water rafting and rock climbing while wearing the hijab, Irum feels she is directly challenging the idea that she is oppressed.

Ayesha, who is Pakistani American, also described how she purposefully avoids coming across as submissive because she wears the hijab.

> AYESHA: The thing about wearing [the] hijab is you have to counteract it a little because people think you're timid. They think that maybe you're forced to wear it and stuff. But by just being a confident and strong person, [it] takes those misconceptions away. I know a lot of Muslim women think that they've been discriminated against in an interview setting.

Ayesha felt it was imperative for Muslim women who wear the hijab to behave in ways that counter the stereotype of Muslim women as timid. She told me she speaks in a confident manner and looks people in the eye when she talks to them. Ayesha makes sure her behavior in public spaces does not in any way reinforce existing stereotypes of Muslim women. And while Ayesha tries to control her representation, her statement reveals how confined Muslim women are by their hypersurveillance. They are not free to just be themselves but have to constantly think about their behavior and the way they present their bodies in their daily interactions.

Sharmeem echoed Ayesha's sentiments. She told me it was important to smile more and be assertive to demonstrate that Muslim women are not oppressed because of the misrepresentation of them as women who do not speak up or express their thoughts. At the time of the interview, Sharmeem was completing her residency in Texas. She told me her fellow residents had a lot of perceptions of Muslim women that were not true.

> SHARMEEM: I've noticed when you're more quiet and don't say anything, people have this perception that you are oppressed or you're not really able to speak your own mind. But then once you smile or you're open with them or you're talking comfortably, they see that you're just kinda like them. And I've gotten that from other residents too. This last month, I was with some of the other residents from my program, and there are a lot of Iraqi refugees and just a lotta refugees that come in, and [one] of the residents was like, "It was always kinda my perception that Muslim women were maybe a little more conservative or they didn't really speak their mind," and then he had a personal experience with an Iraqi Muslim woman and he was really kinda taken aback, because she was really persistent with looking up some diagnosis. She was like, "Well, I really want you to work this up," and kinda concerned about this. I guess he was just like, "I didn't realize they could be so open and so vocal."

Being labeled as oppressed is in itself a form of oppression that Muslim women who wear the hijab encounter frequently. They are under pressure to demonstrate that they are not voiceless but have agency. This stereotype of them as antifeminist and weak is humiliating for them. By countering this impression, they are doing two things simultaneously. First, they are regaining their dignity by making their agency visible. Second, they are also contesting the prevalent notion that Muslim men are abusive. In this way, not only are Muslim women rearticulating what it means to be a Muslim woman; they are also redefining and challenging common sense understandings of who a Muslim man is—that is, someone who oppresses them or subjugates them.

Along with asserting oneself in public spaces, Muslim women also made a huge effort to smile more. Nazia, a naturalized citizen who is Indian American, no longer wears the hijab, but when she did, she tried to positively represent Islam while wearing it. In order to dismantle the association of Islam with violence and terror, Nazia felt she had to create a new association with

Islam. She said, "Because to wear a scarf and go out and be nice, just be a normal human being and still show people that you are a Muslim, I found that to be very encouraging. So I still wore my hijab just to show that I am Muslim." Nazia's comment highlights that Muslim women are under constant pressure to demonstrate that they are ordinary Americans; they have to do a lot of work to demonstrate that they are just like everyone else. They are aware of their power to confirm or dismiss racialized understandings of their bodies through their actions and dress. They take cues from their interactions with private citizens and shift their behavior accordingly. Muslim women carry with them the responsibility of dismantling myths about Muslims, which often places limitations on their behaviors. To further this point, Nazia compared her experiences with and without the hijab. She still felt that as a Muslim, she had a duty to educate society about Islam, but since she took off the hijab, she said she no longer felt the pressure to carefully think about her actions in public like she did when she wore it.

Some Muslim women who wore the hijab recognized how restricted their actions were because of the way private citizens interacted with them in public spaces. Maham told me that when she was wearing the hijab, she was constrained by how she could behave in public because she felt pressure to represent all Muslims.

MAHAM: I am very particular about my actions because I am identified as a Muslim. I think very carefully before I make any action, because I know that I'm not just representing me [because] the majority of the world doesn't see me as me. They see me as, "This is this Muslim woman. She obviously is. She's got that scarf on, and she just did this. Can you believe it?" Or, "Oh, wow. She did that. Isn't that wonderful?" I am the poster child for my religion, as far as I'm concerned, so you have to be that much more careful. If you're out there, and you've got a bad attitude, and you happen to be wearing a scarf too, well, guess what? You're not doing anybody any justice. Because you're not, you know, walking the walk that you're supposed to. That's how I feel. I mean, scarf or no scarf, but more so with the scarf—I think you have a bigger obligation because you're identifiable, you know? You don't want to leave that bad impression.

Responses like Maham's are understandable given the types of interactions Muslim women have had with their fellow private citizens. This collective responsibility they feel places a lot of stress on Muslim women to represent an entire religion. Women who wear the hijab are subjected to verbal abuse and threats of physical abuse, as mentioned in chapter 3, and are under constant pressure to perform under this surveillance. They want to convert the impression of Muslims from a negative one to a positive one by doing good deeds while wearing the hijab. They hope that by controlling their own behavior and performing American values while wearing the hijab, this will lift some of the surveillance off of their bodies. If Muslim bodies are seen as friendly and peaceful as opposed to violent and anti-American, there will be less need for surveillance. Muslim women who wear the hijab are thus stuck in between a rock and a hard place. They self-surveil because they are under scrutiny, yet they also see this as an opportunity to exert their agency and redefine the meanings associated with Islam. They try desperately to contest the stereotype of a Muslim through their behavior and actions while under surveillance.

Not only do Muslims self-surveil; they also surveil one another. Reema, a single mother, told me how she monitors her kids' behavior as well.

> REEMA: I tell my kids that when you go out—when you stand in the grocery line, you know, anything, anything we do, [when] we're out watching a movie, eating out, all of these things—it makes a difference how we are seen. If we put somebody down or if we cut them off on the road . . . you know, that's what we're [saying] about ourselves. And I said, "If you're in a grocery line and you see somebody like with two things, let them go before you, and they might not remember, but they might remember that [and think,] 'I think they were Muslims, you know.'"

The accountability for all Muslims felt by Muslim women who wear the hijab is so powerful that it can have an impact on Muslim children as well. In a post-9/11 society, Muslim children are growing up with the awareness that their religious identity is under constant scrutiny. Reema's statement reveals the pressure Muslim kids are placed under because of this public surveillance. They are raised feeling a responsibility to demonstrate they are good people, because it will counter the negative associations that the public has with Islam. Racialized surveillance can become deeply internalized when Muslim American children are taught to self-discipline and self-surveil. At a young age, Muslim American youth are learning they are not like other American children but are held to different standards. One of the consequences of this racialization is the denial of individuality. Muslim Americans are denied their individuality in public spaces and are forced to navigate society within the confines of an externally imposed collective identity. Because individualism is a key characteristic of American citizenship, when people are denied their individuality but instead are treated as a collective, they do not enjoy the privileges that citizenship should afford.

These experiences shed light on the complex situation Muslim American women are in. They censor their actions and behaviors in public spaces because of the discipline placed on their bodies. While Muslim women are imposing discipline onto their own bodies, they are not completely without agency.

Some women viewed these limitations as oppressive, while others felt it was an opportunity to educate and transform negative stereotypes.

Ambassadors of Islam: Muslim Women's Participation in Civic Engagement

Another tactic employed by Muslim women to alter negative stereotypes of Muslims was to volunteer. Volunteering in American society is highly valued and viewed as a democratic value. It is a quintessentially American attribute or characteristic (Bellah et al. 2007). Maira (2009) argues that civic engagement and community service have come to define the neoliberal citizen who must demonstrate his or her "worthiness" as a citizen. Many of the Muslim women I interviewed told me they volunteered at a variety of places in order to counter the notion that Muslims were no good for American society. Irum began volunteering two years after 9/11. Even though she was incredibly busy, she wanted to educate people about Islam because she felt it was both her religious and civic duty. She found an organization that connects Muslims with speaking engagements.

> IRUM: I was kinda looking for something to do; like I wanted to volunteer, and I wasn't quite sure [doing] what, but one day I came across [the organization] at a convention or something. I saw a presentation, a slideshow about what they were about and what they did. Basically, they do a lot of public speaking to any kind of place—like civic centers, public schools, and things—that have questions about Islam.

Irum spoke at a high school and gave lectures. She said she gained some gratification from this experience because she was able to counter the harmful narrative surrounding Muslim bodies. Students asked her, "Why are there suicide bombings?," "Why are there terrorists?," "Why do people believe Muslims hate America?," reflecting prominent cultural views of Muslims as both inherently violent and anti-American. The act of volunteering provided some Muslim women with a sense of empowerment at a time when many felt silenced. Not surprisingly, Irum told me that most of the volunteers for this organization were women as opposed to men, reflecting the gendered nature of this type of work.

Ayesha also sought out opportunities to volunteer. After 9/11, in addition to volunteering for several Islamic organizations in the Chicago area, she also contacted her former high school history teacher and asked if she could come to the class to talk about Islam. She grew up in a small town in the Midwest where she felt its inhabitants tended to harbor racist views.

> AYESHA: I went back to my high school and talked to one of my old teachers, [who taught] AP history courses, about Islam and what it really meant. I

contacted her. I grew up in such a secluded town. They were racist. I grew
up with confederates, people who thought the confederacy should still exist.
I did it voluntarily. I felt like it was my one thing I could at least do to just
inform other people and kind of stand up for what I believed in.

Just like Irum, Ayesha had very little spare time in her busy schedule, yet she
recognized the importance of volunteering to educate society about how
Islam is a religion that is compatible with American values. These acts were
not unusual for the women interviewed. Muslim women shared stories of
how they hosted lunches for their neighbors or would send treats to their kids'
classrooms in celebration of Eid (a Muslim religious holiday). These are conscientious efforts to demonstrate that Islam is not a cultural threat but a peaceful and misunderstood religion. Muslim women work carefully to subvert the
negative images of them.

Afia told me she wanted to volunteer at her son's private school in Texas
in the years after 9/11. Afia encountered some resistance to her repetitive
requests to volunteer in the main office of the school. She attributed this to the
fact that the school did not want a woman wearing the hijab in the main office.
Prior to 9/11, her requests to volunteer were welcomed by the school; however
after the attacks, she felt a change in the administration's attitude toward her.
This discouragement has not stopped Afia from offering her time to educate
people about Islam. She has participated in interfaith groups and given talks
about Islam in her community at churches and in college classrooms. I asked
her what motivated her to do this type of work.

> AFIA: First of all, I like to make a difference . . . whether by helping a person
> who is poor or helping to answer anybody's question as far as not only my
> religion, [but] as a woman also—that women have a very, very lasting and
> strong effect on a family, especially on the kids. [A mother's] effect on a kid
> is I think double the amount [that] a dad has.

Afia's desire to dispel the myths of Muslims was clearly gendered. It was her
identity as a mother that drove her to become a sort of ambassador of Islam.
In her studies on gender and work, Hochschild (2001; 2003) reveals that even
when women are employed in the labor sector along with their husbands,
they come home to do the unseen and unpaid labor of childcare, housework,
and community service.[5] As mothers, Muslim women were driven to make
these spaces more inclusive for their families. They know the impact anti-
Muslim sentiments can have on their children's lives growing up in America.
They wanted to protect their children from this racialization.

Volunteering by Muslim women is a gendered form of resistance to racialization. Because they are more likely to encounter racism through their

interactions with their fellow private citizens, they seek to feel some sense of control over this interaction. Muslim American women hope that through their personal interactions with their fellow private citizens and by informing people about Islam, they will be able to shift the public's attitude toward Muslims in an era of rising Islamophobia. Like most individuals, they are unable to recognize the systemic nature of anti-Muslim racism. It does not operate on the microlevel alone but is also institutionalized through federal programs that rely on the narrative of Muslims as terrorists to garner sustained support for security and surveillance. Because Muslim women were not surveilled by the state like Muslim men, they felt more agency in resisting their racialization. Muslim women work to rearticulate the narrative that surrounds Muslims in America through their actions in public spaces. These efforts did not come without a price. Muslim women often felt exhausted and stressed because of this responsibility that has been placed on their bodies.

The Psychological Toll of Being a Muslim in a Surveillance Society

Another common sentiment expressed by Muslim women was how surveillance induced stress in their lives. Arab Muslims report high rates of depression and anxiety since 9/11 (Abu-Raiya et al. 2011). Some of the Muslim women I talked to admitted they felt stress because of their surveillance and the need to respond to it. The pressure to represent an entire collective in a positive way eroded Muslim women's individuality, causing them emotional stress, tension, and strain. Muslim women who wear the hijab were unable to exist in public spaces freely, but rather had to navigate their racialized identity based on the way others viewed them. Saima, a Palestinian American, reflected on how it feels to exist in a space where strangers have preconceived notions of her because of her religious identity.

> SAIMA: I feel like whenever I see non-Muslims that the first thing that comes to their mind when they see someone like me—[may] not necessarily [be] *terrorist*, but it's a totally negative image. Like I really just want to walk into a situation where it's just a blank slate. Yeah, let me create my own image. Let me create my own identity. If you want to hate me or disrespect me at the end, let it be because of who I am and not because of your simplemindedness or your naiveness or your ignorance [or] from what you've been told.

The denial of an individual identity and the imposition of a collective stereotype on one's body creates an incredible responsibility for Muslim Americans. These women who wear the hijab are continuously reduced to religious subjects in public spaces. The inability to be seen as human beings without preconceived notions attached to their bodies was exhausting.

Maryam, a young Syrian dentist, also talked about the increased level of stress she experienced after 9/11. She felt anxiety over being detained and deported.

> MARYAM: I mean, like, especially after 9/11, I was like, "What if they wanted to round us up or deport us?" I couldn't live in Syria. I'm just totally American. And so that has made me realize that I am in this country no matter what, and I'm gonna contribute to this country and try to make things better. Because I think you can look at it kind of like, "Why are we dealing with this? Let's just move." I don't know anyone with that opinion who is a friend of mine. Or you can be like, "We need to make this a better place to raise our kids."

Maryam's fear reflects the impact surveillance has on American citizens. Muslim Americans did not feel the protection that citizenship should entail but rather worried the state could detain them and deny them due process because of their association with terror. The fear of being deported and detained comes with a psychological cost.

The USA PATRIOT Act brought back some of the language surrounding patriotism that was used to justify the internment of Japanese and Japanese Americans during World War II (Cole 2003). Specifically, the language used in the Enemy Alien Act, enacted in 1798, gives the president the authority to deport, detain, or expel any citizen of a country at war with the United States (Cole 2003). This act was a precursor to the internment of Japanese noncitizens and citizens alike. Muslims recognize that if another terrorist attack on the scale of the 9/11 occurs on American soil again, they could be detained and deported without due process or even interned. These anxieties are not unfounded. Republican presidential candidate Donald Trump has called for a ban on Muslims entering the United States and for Muslims to wear ID cards. After a terrorist attack in Nice, France, in 2016 former house leader Newt Gingrich said all Muslims in America should have to take a test to see if they believed in sharia law and that all who fail this test should be deported out of the United States (Etehad 2016). On June 5, 2017, Fox News contributor Nigel Farage suggested there may be a need for internment camps for Muslims after a terrorist attack in London, England.[6]

This fear is one of the motivating factors that drove Maryam to actively work to counter the racialization of Muslims. Maryam volunteered for a few Muslim organizations in the Chicago area that did work to dismantle the stereotypes of Muslims, such as by hosting community events and lectures on Islam. As a mother of young children, she was compelled to do this work to ensure her children would grow up in a society that accepted their religious identity. But this work did not come without a cost: "It's been a big source of stress for me. I think it's been a big source of stress for a lot of people." Volunteering is time-consuming. In addition to working and taking care of their children, women like Maryam took time out of their busy schedules to inform the public that Muslims are law abiding American citizens.

Muslim men and women have to worry about their children in a society that is filled with anti-Muslim sentiments. Nasreen told me how her children were repeatedly called terrorists shortly after 9/11.

> NASREEN: They were going to the just regular public schools. They got bashed on the bus. They were called terrorists. They were told to go home. They were told—they were being attacked by other kids. And the saddest part is that the principals or the deans had prejudice in them.

When Nasreen's kids told her how they were harassed on the school bus, she went to speak to the principal of the school about it. She was disappointed that there was no recourse or action taken to protect her kids from this abuse. The lack of response to anti-Muslim sentiments made both Nasreen and her children feel disempowered and devalued.

This incident was not an isolated one. Her children were with her at a restaurant when another customer yelled at them to "go back home." Nasreen told me how her children internalized these collective experiences.

> NASREEN: And that's when my kids felt like, where do we belong? And they would tell me, "Mom, where do we belong? What are we? What are we? Are we Arab? Are we American? Because we're"—and I'll never forget this—one of my daughters says, "We're terrorists."

Nasreen's ten-year-old daughter internalized her racialization. Nasreen was understandably upset by her daughter's response and told her daughter this was not true and that she did not understand what "terrorist" meant. Her daughter responded, "But Mom, that's what we're called. We're terrorists . . . every day they tell us we're terrorists." Muslim children who grow up in a surveillance society where their religious identity has been racialized are made to feel they do not belong.

A number of studies on discrimination and mental health found that discrimination experienced by Arab Americans who are Muslim since 9/11 is correlated with an increase in psychological stress (Moradi and Hasan 2004; El-Sayed and Galea 2009). Surveillance that is triggered by racialized understandings of bodies creates a hostile environment, which can lead to an increase in hypertension, stress, and depression. There is a psychological cost that young people endure because of their racialization. The term *racial battle fatigue*, psychological stress responses that people endure from exposure to constant racial microaggressions, could accurately reflect what Muslim Americans go through because of their racialization (Smith, Allen, and Danley 2007).[7] These responses include coping mechanisms, physical avoidance, exhaustion, and psychological withdrawal. Symptoms associated with racial battle fatigue can include stomachaches, migraines, and other physical responses to the stress of encountering racism in one's daily life. Racialization through surveillance creates an environment where Muslim American women are constantly under the watchful eye of their fellow citizens and must respond accordingly.[8] Limiting their behavior or actions in public spaces, performing American values through smiling, laughing or altering the clothes they wear or taking time to educate the public about Islam creates stress and takes a toll on the lives of ordinary Muslim Americans.

Political Disempowerment of Muslim American Men

Muslim American men told me one of the biggest changes they experienced after 9/11 was feeling they had to censor themselves in public spaces. Because Muslim men were more likely to be targeted by the state via TSA lists at airports and were not under the same kind of surveillance by strangers as Muslim women who wear the hijab, their responses to racialized surveillance differed. They told me they avoided discussing particular topics, such as religion or foreign policy, out of fear of being identified as a Muslim and associated or seen as sympathizing with terrorism. Some of the participants admitted to feeling nervous or afraid to speak freely about their religion or their political beliefs, such as their disapproval of American foreign policy toward Afghanistan, Iraq, or Palestine. This silencing angered many of the Muslim American men.

Aziz, a thirty-year-old Indian American who lives and works in Chicago, described how he has self-censored himself at work since 9/11.

> AZIZ: When [political discussion] comes up [at work], I definitely feel like if it's anything that has to do with foreign policy–type issues or things that are happening in other countries, especially if they're related to the Muslim world, I just don't feel like my opinion is going to be as taken as that of another American. You just don't have that feeling... and so when people ask me about Islam and stuff, I get super uncomfortable at work. It's super uncomfortable.

Aziz is unable to talk about his political beliefs or his views on U.S. foreign policy because he worries he will be misunderstood or misrepresented. He is cognizant that although he is an American citizen, he has been marked as a foreign other and a potential threat. His allegiance can be questioned easily because of his religious identity. For Muslim men, an increase in their religiosity can also incite suspicion about Muslim men. Aziz gets uncomfortable when he is asked questions about his religion at work because he worries that he is being "bucketed" as a type of Muslim, the "bad" kind. Aziz self-surveils through silencing himself because of the anxiety of surveillance. The inability to contribute to public discourse is a form of political disempowerment. When citizens are made to feel they cannot participate in political debate or dialog in society, they are excluded from the democratic process. A true democratic society thrives on its citizens' political participation and civic engagement. Like other Muslim American men in this sample, Aziz is cognizant that an association with terrorism could have severe consequences. In addition to being on a TSA list at U.S. airports, most Muslims know someone who has been visited by the FBI or state officials. Aziz told me he avoided fraternizing for too long with his fellow coworkers who were more visibly Muslim. He worked with a few Muslim men who wore beards, and even though he had friends who had beards and his father wore one, he admitted he avoided talking to those men for too long at work because he worried he might be associated with Islamic fundamentalism.

> AZIZ: As a guy, I spend a lot of time at the office and [notice] the psychology of the way I'm thinking people are viewing me and who I should maybe talk to or who not to spend too much time with—like the guy with the really long beard that you always find in every IT department. You're like, "Oh, OK. I'll talk to that guy for a couple of minutes, but not too long."

Aziz censors who he spends time with because he wants to downplay his religious identity when possible. Aziz openly acknowledges he spends time and energy calculating his behaviors and actions in front of his fellow colleagues. This is something that Americans whose bodies are not cast as suspect do not have to deal with on a day-to-day basis. Muslim men and women, on the other hand, expend a lot of energy and time thinking about how their bodies are perceived by their fellow citizens.

Hamza, a Pakistani American lawyer, also censored himself for a few years after 9/11. Prior to the date, Hamza was comfortable talking about his political views and openly disagreeing with coworkers and acquaintances regarding American foreign policy toward the Middle East. Although at the time of the interview he claimed he no longer felt silenced, for several years after 9/11, Hamza explained how he had lost his voice.

HAMZA: The other distinct post-9/11 thing that I felt—probably the two or three years after 9/11—I felt that as a Muslim and as a minority that I kind of lost my voice a little bit. I lost the ability to really speak my mind and have discussions with people on sensitive topics, just because you felt like you couldn't do that for a long time.

SAHER: Was this with friends or coworkers?

HAMZA: It was more coworkers. I never felt like that with my friends. For example, with coworkers or acquaintances, I never had a problem talking about politics and policies. But immediately after 9/11, you couldn't really question policies towards Palestine or Israel. I felt like I couldn't anyway. You felt muzzled. The discourse was very nationalistic and, yeah, you felt like you lost your voice a little bit.

For Hamza and Aziz imposing these actions of self-surveillance was one of the ways they tried to protect themselves from further surveillance, which they feared could lead to punitive measures by the state. Surveillance creates an environment where Muslim men feel vulnerable. Adil, a twenty-year-old Indian American who was a college student at the time of the interview, also described his fear of expressing his views on foreign policy or religion because it could create an unnecessary association with terrorism. He also admitted he silenced himself.

ADIL: I just feel that . . . if you express any sort of view, political view or religious view, the connotation jumps to 9/11 and extremists, like all Muslims are lumped together. And I definitely don't feel at ease just walking into a grocery store and talking about the situation with Israel and Palestine, because I know that a lot of people wouldn't be welcoming to that and that naturally people just jump to that conclusion, where maybe I'm not a terrorist, but I harbor [the same] views.

In a society where citizenship has a history of being associated with whiteness and Christianity and where a heightened sense of nationalism reflects the overall political tone, many Muslim American men are afraid to speak openly against the government because they did not want to be seen as terrorist sympathizers, as Adil's testimony highlights. This fear of being associated with terrorism is not mere paranoia but steeped in the political and cultural context in the United States after 9/11. In addition to increasing the surveillance capacity of the state, the USA PATRIOT Act criminalizes individuals who inadvertently fund terrorism through donations to charitable organizations. It is not just individuals who commit terrorist acts who are punished, but anyone associated with terrorism. Ahmed, a Palestinian Muslim American physician, recalled how the FBI visited his father.

AHMED: Yeah. I mean, [my dad has] actually been visited by the FBI before. He's very politically outspoken even though he's a pacifist. So it's not anything new. It's not surprising. I wasn't surprised. I was angry.

According to Ahmed's testimony, his father's political views were enough to warrant state surveillance and even a visit by the FBI. Even though Ahmed said his dad never espoused anti-American views, the FBI surveilled him because he is a Palestinian immigrant and is vocal about Palestinian rights. Visits by the FBI are one tactic used by the state to exert power over Muslim men. They instill fear in Muslim men and send the message that they are not allowed to express any political views that may be misinterpreted as anti-American. It is no surprise that Muslim men silence themselves when their political views can be used against them, to cast them as disloyal or un-American.

Because the Muslim men I interviewed did not wear religious signifiers, like the hijab, they did not feel the pressure to alter their dress, but they felt the gaze on their bodies when they accompanied Muslim women who wore the hijab. In one instance, a Muslim man attempted to control his wife's dress. Reema recalled an exchange she had before she went to pick up her ex-husband from the train station on 9/11.

REEMA: I was talking to [my husband] and he was like, "Okay, are you on your way?" And then he's the one who really asked me something I was completely caught off guard [by], because he was like, "Are you coming? Are you wearing your scarf?" And I said "What?" and he's like, "Are you still wearing your scarf?" and I said, "Yeah," and he's like, "No, I was thinking you should take it off when you come to pick me up." And I was like, "No, I am not, I am going to come like I am."

This experience highlights the contradiction in the dominant notion that Muslim men force their wives or kids to wear the hijab. In this example, Reema's husband desperately wanted to avoid any surveillance or negative interactions, so he tried to persuade his wife to remove her hijab. The fear that Muslim men felt from the state was real, and the attempt to control Reema's dress reflected the stark difference in how men responded to their surveillance compared to women. Muslim men did not express the desire to transform the narrative of Muslims through their actions. Instead, they wanted to make invisible their religious identity. Their participation in self-surveillance reveals how citizenship is racialized in America.

Self-surveillance via silencing their voices is a form of censorship that strips Muslim American men of a fundamental right that citizenship entails, the ability to participate in a public forum and debate. By refraining from speaking out about injustices that Muslims in the United States and abroad face, Muslim men are unable to influence the discourse that directly impacts their daily experiences. Their voices are muted, while those who espouse anti-Muslim or Islamophobic sentiments are becoming more acceptable. When Muslim men are unable to exercise the rights associated with citizenship, like freedom of speech, we need to question the state of our democracy. In a true democracy, all citizens are able to enjoy the privileges that citizenship affords. Yet in a state defined by hypersurveillance, some citizens are criminalized, while others are protected. The United States is a racialized social system that shifts and fluctuates over time. The institutionalization of hypersurveillance has created a new racial terrain that Muslim Americans must navigate.

Feeling Un-American

One of the speakers at the 2016 Democratic National Convention was Khizr Khan, father to an American Muslim soldier who died in a suicide attack in Iraq. Khan spoke of his son's limitless patriotism, exemplified in the sacrifice of his life for his country. Appealing to an American public that harbors extreme Islamophobic sentiments that have been fueled by political rhetoric like Donald Trump's call to ban all Muslims from coming to the United States, Khan wanted to show that Muslims are Americans and Americans are Muslims. The speech highlighted something important. For Muslims to be seen as American, they have to do extraordinary things to demonstrate their patriotism and loyalty to the United States. Former president Bill Clinton's speech at the convention also drew attention to this sentiment that Muslims have to prove they are loyal and patriotic citizens. He said, "If you're a Muslim and you love America and freedom and you hate terror, stay here and help us win and make a future together, we want you" (Beinart 2016). Muslim Americans must pass a litmus test on their patriotism before they are able to claim their American identity. The men and women I talked to commented on this feeling of having to prove their American identities.

Saleem moved to America after 9/11 to do his residency in medicine. He was born in Lebanon and has always been an American citizen because his father is a citizen. He told me he always identified as an American citizen, even though he grew up in Lebanon and how excited he was to finally be living in the United States. Saleem felt that his experiences in the United States have changed his perceptions of what he thought America would be like.

> SALEEM: I feel I was a bit naive, in the sense that I thought that Americans were more open-minded, more accepting of people from other cultures. And I don't know whether it's my experience in the Midwest—whether it's different on the coasts. But I feel like I was naive in the sense that I was expecting people to be more open, more curious, more liberal, and they're not.

Saleem has been stopped and searched several times at airports. He was called a fascist by a patient in the hospital. He told me that when he applied for a job he received an email saying the position was for American citizens only. When he told them he was an American citizen, the person refused to believe him. He felt this treatment was because he has a Muslim name. As a result, Saleem feels rejected from his American identity: "There are certain times where I feel extremely alienated from mainstream America, and I know that a lot of minorities do . . . [Even] despite the fact that I'm a professional—you know, middle-upper class."

Like Sameer, Aziz has had a host of negative interactions with his coworkers and in airports, chronicled in the earlier chapters. Aziz told me how this has left him feeling distant from his American identity.

> AZIZ: Generally, there's just a feeling of people judging what I say, especially if it comes to foreign policy, especially if it comes to things about American identity, especially if it comes to things of Americanness. You just feel like everyone is now judging what you say and think that's not in the best interests of the country. That's the feeling that you get, and people look at me as someone who's outside first and then American second . . . even if you were born and raised in the country.

The alienation Muslim Americans experience from their national identity is not surprising given it is within the context of national security that Muslim men and women are hypersurveilled. They recognize everything they say is scrutinized because of their religious identity.

Because Aziz felt he was constantly judged, he told me he has changed some of his actions. For example, after a terrorist attack in India, he made sure to contact his friend who grew up in India to inquire about his family's safety in order to show him he condemned the terrorist attack. He knew his friend was not from the region where the attack occurred, but he also worried his friend would have negative feelings toward him because he was Muslim. September 11th brought an intense questioning of citizenship for South Asian and Arab Muslims. Aziz's interview revealed that his citizenship was contested because his religious identity marked him as a foreigner.

Nabeel expressed that his Muslim identity situated him as different than someone who was Christian or Jewish. Nabeel said he was often bombarded with questions about whether or not he practiced Islam. Because they equated Islam with terror, people asked these questions to gauge whether Nabeel was a fanatic as well.

> NABEEL: People ask, "Oh, so do you pray five times a day?" You know, stuff like that. "Have you been on the pilgrimage?" It's like, "No, I'm twenty-two years

old. I haven't been on the pilgrimage." Like, I mean, "Have you visited the Vatican?" You know? It's just like, "I'm just a kid, just like you. It's just I was brought up in a different culture and religion."

This line of questioning is one of the ways Nabeel is marginalized from being seen as a normal college student and a typical American. He recognizes the discrepancy in how Christian or Jewish students his age are not grilled about their religious practices because they are seen as the norm in America. Because a Muslim identity and an American identity are treated as if they are contentious, the more religious a Muslim seems to be, the less American they appear in the public's eyes. American citizenship is guarded by borders of race, ethnicity, and religion. South Asians and Arabs felt they existed within these borders, if not close to the edge, yet after 9/11, they started to realize they had been ejected from their identities as American citizens.

Nowhere to Go: Lack of Protection from Hypersurveillance

In *Structural Transformation of the Public Sphere* (1961), Jurgen Habermas argues that in order for a democracy to thrive, there must be a space for political participation for all its citizens. According to Habermas, the public sphere is a space located in between individual private areas, such as one's home and government-run spaces. It is in these public spaces where members of society meet and have rational debates about politics and matters pertaining to public life. These discussions provide citizens with a political voice and a sense of empowerment. The ability of citizens to participate in these discussions within the public sphere is one characteristic of a healthy democracy and a privilege afforded by citizenship. The inability to participate in debate and a public forum reflects an ailing democracy.

The notion that we have always been a society where anyone could participate in public discourse is a false one. Race has always determined who could and could not be a part of the democratic process in the United States. The exclusion of anyone who was not a free white man from accessing citizenship reflects this truth about public discourse and democracy. While the War on Drugs maintained a system of oppression and surveillance of African Americans, the War on Terror places Muslim bodies under the watchful eye of the state and citizens, resulting in their exclusion from participation in democratic processes.

In light of increased anti-Muslim sentiments and surveillance, there has been a rise in civil rights organizations to protect Muslim civil liberties. Organizations such as the Council on American Islamic Relations (CAIR) and the ACLU have taken on the legal battles for Muslims who have had their civil liberties challenged in the United States. Although the purpose of these Muslim organizations is to work hard to protect the civil liberties of Muslims in the United States, their status is also tenuous. The state has questioned Muslim organizations, such as CAIR and the Islamic Society of North America (ISNA), about their associations with terrorism in an attempt to discredit their efforts (Shane 2011). The Snowden leak also revealed that Nihad Awad, the executive director for CAIR, was under intense surveillance by the U.S. government. If the civil rights organizations that are supposed to provide Muslims with civil liberties protections are being surveilled, it is no wonder that Muslim American men feel they are unable to speak out about the injustices they experience. Because they work to avoid any associations with terrorism, they may be deterred from participating in efforts to stop their surveillance if there is a threat the organization or group could be targeted for even more surveillance or marked as a terrorist organization.

According to Brayne, *system avoidance* is when individuals who are subjected to hypersurveillance avoid surveilling institutions like medical and financial organizations (Brayne 2014). There are signs in this chapter that Muslim Americans are beginning to exhibit this behavior. When Muslim men go to great lengths to silence themselves because they want to downplay or make invisible their religious identity in order to avoid surveillance, it may very well be a sign that they will also avoid institutions that they fear may surveil them. When organizations, like CAIR, that are supposed to help advocate for Muslims are also under surveillance, Muslims are left even more vulnerable, with little recourse for social justice. In many ways, it feels as if Muslims have nowhere to go.

Gendered Surveillance, Gendered Responses

Religion, race, ethnicity, and gender are organizing factors in the lives of Muslim Americans in post-9/11 society. Because religious symbols are gendered, the experiences of Muslim women and men with racialization do not mirror one another. It is therefore imperative to understand the locations where gender, religion, and race intersect. In addition to understanding how Muslims are racialized differentially, as I chronicle in the previous chapters, scholars should also recognize how responses to racialization are also gendered. Muslim women and men react to their racialized surveillance in unique ways because of their gender identities.

As Muslim surveillance continues to increase, Muslims in America also continue to alter their behavior to deal with this surveillance. While Muslim women's responses shift between resisting surveillance and conforming to it, Muslim men tend to focus on avoiding it. In this chapter, I described how Muslim women who wore the hijab participated in self-discipline. These women often participated in their own surveillance by carefully controlling their behaviors and actions in public spaces. They also controlled their dress and volunteered in schools to dispel myths about Islam and Muslims. These actions can be seen as both a form of self-discipline and a type of resistance to their surveillance. These women treated public spaces as a stage where they tried to invert negative associations of Islam through their actions and behaviors while under surveillance. They smiled more in public, chose to wear lighter-colored clothing and hijabs to make them appear less morbid, and volunteered their time speaking at schools—all in an attempt to dismantle the negative associations with Islam. They also admitted they experienced a psychological toll because of their racialization and hypersurveillance and the pressure to respond to it.

Because men are not easily identifiable as Muslim, they were not held accountable like Muslim women were in public spaces. They also did not express the same sentiments of collective responsibility echoed by Muslim women interviewed. Instead, they felt more keenly the repercussions of being associated with terrorism and diverted attention from their religious identity at work or in school to avoid this association. Because many were on TSA lists, they felt the power the state held over them. For this reason, Muslim men felt silenced and avoided bringing attention to their religious identity. This political disempowerment reflects how they are denied privileges associated with citizenship, such as the right to participate in political debate or discussions. For Muslim men, the fear of detention and deportation was real. This new era of hypersurveillance contributes to the racialization of Muslim men through the act of targeting their bodies for terror because of their religious identity.

5

Shifting Racial Terrain
for Muslim Americans

The Impact of
Racialized Surveillance

This sentiment that Muslims are acquiring a new racial identity in a post-9/11 society is gaining more steam as anti-Muslim attitudes continue to rise in America and Europe. In response to the terrorist shootings in San Bernardino, actor Samuel Jackson stated in an interview with the *Hollywood Reporter* that Muslims are becoming "the new black kids in America" (Cheney 2016). Jackson's comments reflect a growing belief that Muslims are increasingly experiencing racism, not just religious discrimination. The term *Islamophobia* is widely used to capture the anti-Muslim sentiments that have been on the rise since 9/11. But Islamophobia has not always been understood as a form of racism. Runnymede Trust defined the term in 1997 as a "fear of Islam" (Richardson 1997). Since 9/11, there has been a spike in studies on Islamophobia, with the majority of them treating Islamophobia and racism as distinct concepts (Garner and Selod 2015), but in the last few years, there has been a growing body of scholarship that situates Islamophobia as having everything to do with race and racism of Muslims (Meer and Modood 2010; Meer 2013; Tyrer 2013; Garner and Selod 2015; Love 2017). I further this argument by showing the processes of how a religious identity and a racial identity intersect, guided by gender, to resituate Arab and South Asian Muslims on the American racial hierarchy.

In the previous chapters, I described how racialized surveillance of Muslim Americans is one of the ways a Muslim identity is understood as racial. Because race in the United States has typically been understood as solely a black-and-white paradigm, there is a tendency to equate Muslim experiences as racial only if they can be compared neatly to black experiences in the United States. This way of thinking is reflected in Samuel Jackson's claim. But Jackson's statement is problematic because it relies on the assumption that Muslims are not already black. African Americans make up the largest American-born Muslim population in the United States (Pew Research Center 2011). For some scholars, the term *black* is used to refer to a racial classification or social location on the racial hierarchy (Bonilla-Silva 2002; Treitler 2013). Bonilla-Silva uses the term *collective black* to refer to the bottom of the tri-racial hierarchy that has white at the top and honorary white in the middle. Treitler argues African Americans have been situated on the bottom of the racial hierarchy as a result of antiblackness perpetuated by immigrants in an attempt to move to the top of the racial hierarchy, closer to whiteness. Treitler makes it clear that black is a social location rather than referring to actual pigmentation. For example, she shows how Afro-Caribbeans, who are phenotypically similar to African Americans, have been somewhat successful at distancing themselves from African Americans on the racial hierarchy. Their immigrant status protects them from some of the stereotypes that African Americans face.[1]

South Asian and Arab Muslims have also been able to distance themselves from the bottom of the racial hierarchy. They have enjoyed many of the privileges that socioeconomic status affords. The Muslim Americans I interviewed lived in suburban neighborhoods and had access to resourced public and private schools. They were middle- to upper-middle-class citizens who had access to resources that have historically been denied to many African Americans due to structural racism, like residential racial segregation and disparities in the American public education system. The Immigration and Nationality Act of 1965 opened the borders of the United States to professionals and highly educated immigrants from Pakistan, India, Jordan, Egypt, and Lebanon, and so South Asians and Arabs migrated to the United States after the Civil Rights Act of 1964 passed, which subjected housing and employment practices to legal action if they were discriminatory in practice. The Muslim men and women I interviewed were able to benefit from these civil rights policies, which also included the Equal Employment Act of 1972. Their unique histories also excluded them from experiencing the racism that African Americans have historically endured in the United States. Their history with racism has been unique, as detailed in chapter 1.

Some of the Arab Muslims I talked to told me there had been times in their lives they passed for white due to their skin pigmentation. Maryam's statement clearly highlights the impact the hijab has on one's racial identity: "Before

I started wearing the hijab, I never felt like a minority. It wasn't until after I started to wear the hijab that I realized what it was like to be a minority in this country." The hijab stripped her of her whiteness. It is important to realize that Arab and South Asian Americans' experiences with race are not uniform but diverse because of their differential histories of exclusion and inclusion in the United States. Consequently, they occupy different locations on the racial hierarchy. As chronicled in chapter 1, the location that Arabs and South Asians occupy on the racial hierarchy differs due to a myriad of factors including skin pigmentation, religious identity, and reasons for migration to the United States.

In the current era of the War on Terror, marked by hypersurveillance of Muslim bodies, I argue that South Asian and Arab Muslim Americans' racial experiences have once again changed due to the current sociopolitical climate. For Muslim Americans, their racial and ethnic identities intersect with their racialized religious identity to incite new experiences. We must continually reexamine the racial hierarchy because one's location on it is not static but fluctuates (Omi and Winant 2015). Because of the institutionalization of anti-Muslim sentiments in attitudes and policies, South Asian and Arab Muslim men and women have been shifted down the hierarchy away from whiteness. For Arab Muslims, the racial classification of white is no longer appropriate, while for South Asian Muslims, their status as a model minority or honorary whites no longer reflects their lived realities with racism.

Racialized Identities and the Loss of Citizenship

For Asians and South Asians living in the United States, their socioeconomic success and ability to live in predominantly white neighborhoods has led to the assumption they are whitening and the belief that their encounters with racism are minimal. Arabs and South Asians continue to experience discrimination in the form of social exclusion (such as being denied their status as Americans), hate crimes, and racial profiling (Kibria 1998; Kibria 2003; Purkayastha 2005; Naber 2006; Dhingra 2007; Cainkar 2009). There have been some cases where South Asian Indians identified with other communities of color because of their racialized experiences, specifically Blacks and Latinx, over whites, while in other instances, South Asian Indians perpetuated anti-blackness in order to access whiteness (Dhingra 2003). This belief that Asians are whitening ignores how they are denied social aspects of citizenship like never being perceived as authentic Americans but rather as *not American* (Kim 2008). The status of honorary whites is fragile for many racialized ethnic groups who experience some socioeconomic mobility yet also social exclusion because they are not treated or seen as real Americans (Tuan 1998). The loss of these privileges of citizenship is one of the impacts of a racialized identity.

Regardless of their ability to access resources, South Asians and Asians have always been made to feel as if they do not really belong because of their ethnic and religious identities. For Muslim Americans living in a society that is engaged in a War on Terror, not only is their status as Americans questioned; it is under attack.

After 9/11, the perceptions of Muslim Americans quickly shifted from being not quite American because of their religious and ethnic identity to being a threat to America. Religious signifiers such as names or religious clothing (the hijab or the jilbaab) mark Muslims as targets for surveillance because it incites the misperception that they are dangerous, violent, oppressed, and misogynists. Because these religious signifiers are racialized, Muslim bodies encounter interactions with both the state and their private citizens that are guided by racist assumptions rooted in stereotypes of Muslims. While one may experience social isolation or questions about one's American identity such as "Where are you really from?" because of an ethnic identity, a Muslim identity incites hostility like "Go back to where you came from!" As the previous chapters show, Muslim bodies are subjected to surveillance by both the state and their fellow private citizens.

In this era of hypersurveillance, South Asian and Arab Muslim Americans are under undue stress to prove they are American. Sunaina Maira's (2009) study reveals how South Asian Muslim immigrant youth living in the United States under the War on Terror had to negotiate several aspects of cultural citizenship, like feeling both connected and rejected from a transnational South Asian identity as well an American one. By studying cultural citizenship, Maira shows how South Asian Muslim youth make sense of their identities in relation to the power exerted over their bodies by a state engaged in empire building via racializing Muslims. Her most recent study examines how the 9/11 generation of Muslim youth respond to their surveillance in diverse ways (Maira 2016). I show that seven to ten years after the terrorist attacks on 9/11, South Asian and Arab Muslim Americans encountered racialized surveillance, revealing how their bodies were watched and monitored while others are protected. The distinction of which bodies should be watched and which ones should be protected exposes who is able to enjoy all the benefits citizenship affords. Muslim names and religious signifiers, like the hijab, incite suspicion of American citizens, and as a result, their bodies are under the watchful gazes of the state and their fellow private citizens. Muslims are constructed as individuals who are unable to assimilate into American society because their religious identity is seen as too culturally distinct from Western and American values.

The way the state exerts its power and discipline over some is by constructing the ideal citizen versus the undeserving citizen. According to Ong, it is "the cultural practices and beliefs produced out of negotiating the often ambivalent and contested relations with the state and its hegemonic forms that establish the criteria of belonging within a national population and territory" (1996: 738). In chapter 2, I showed how Muslims are made to feel they are not American when they are treated as if they will do harm to the state. The state uses ascriptive characteristics like race, gender, class, and religion to define who is an American and who is not an American. I have shown that the performance of security by TSA, where Muslim women who wear the hijab are publicly stopped and searched, produces and constructs which citizen is to be protected and which one should be surveilled. The placement of Muslim men on the Selectee List at airports lets Muslim men know they are being watched and surveilled by the state. The state actively participates in the association of Islam with terror, misogyny, and anti-American sentiments, creating the illusion that Muslim bodies require hypersurveillance. By perpetuating the "us" versus "them" narrative that surrounds national security, the state is defining the boundaries of citizenship. As a result, Muslims are the "them," and religious affiliation becomes a litmus test once again for who can access citizenship—this time its cultural benefits.

Glenn argues that it is not just the state who acts as a gatekeeper of citizenship but also private citizens. She states that formal citizenship pertains to the law and polity, while substantive citizenship encompasses the ability to act upon the rights citizenship entails: "Citizenship is not just a matter of formal legal status; it is a matter of belonging, including recognition by other members of the community. Formal law and legal rulings create a structure that legitimates the granting or denial of recognition . . . *the maintenance of boundaries relies on 'enforcement' not only by designated officials, but also by so-called members of the public*" (Glenn 2002: 196; emphasis added).

Glenn brings up one of the most important aspects of citizenship: the state and private citizens work together to protect the racial, ethnic, and religious boundaries of it. In chapter 3, I described in detail the ways that private citizens participate in surveillance of South Asian and Arab Muslim Americans, challenging their status as citizens. Muslim American women who wear the hijab are treated as if they are not American but foreigners. They are yelled at in public spaces because they symbolize the presence of Islam in America. Private citizens question Muslim men about their association with terror.

This act of denying Muslims their American identity is a racializing act and is accomplished through hypersurveillance. The belief that to be American is to be white is resurfacing as Muslims are made to feel they are incapable of being loyal to America because their bodies are equated with terror and their values are somehow antithetical to Western or American ones. In many ways, it feels as if America is revisiting its past: the early twentieth century, when South Asian men desperately fought for naturalization were denied it because their religious identity situated them as incapable of sharing

Western values.[2] The act of racialized surveillance is also an act that strips one of citizenship.

Slipping Down the Racial Hierarchy

Where do Muslims fit into the racial hierarchy? This is an impossible question to answer because Muslims are racially and ethnically diverse—they are already situated on the racial hierarchy. But we are not defined by just one identity but by our multiple intersecting identities, and the racial hierarchy is not static. Therefore, this book does not contend that Muslim has become a race but rather that South Asians and Arabs who are Muslims are moving down the racial hierarchy because of the racialization of their Muslim identity. The hypersurveillance of Muslim bodies is one of the processes where scholars are able to capture how a Muslim identity is racialized. The racial hierarchy is not static because social constructions around race are constantly shifting due to the social and political contexts (Omi and Winant 2015).[3] The vast majority of the Arab and South Asian Muslim Americans in this study were privileged economically, yet they were incapable of accessing all the privileges associated with citizenship. Purkayastha demonstrates the ways that boundaries are created between South Asian Americans and whites because of the ways their ethnicity has been racialized. While South Asians have been able to live in white suburban neighborhoods, attain professional degrees, and send their kids to affluent schools, they are still treated as if they are not quite American (Purkayastha 2005). In the War on Terror, not only are Muslims not quite American; they are perceived and treated as if they are a potential threat to national security. In addition to skin tone, their ethnic and cultural differences, including religion, act as a barrier to racial equity with whites. Several scholars have also noted that since 9/11, Arabs' visibility as minorities is intensifying because they are denied the privileges that would normally accompany their racial classification of white (Naber 2008; Shryock 2008; Tehranian 2010).

The term *invisible minority* reflects how many Arabs have been marginalized, yet their experiences with racism have largely been ignored because they are racially classified as white according to the U.S. Census (Tehranian 2010). Maghbouleh (2017) chronicles how Iranian Americans have experienced the limits of whiteness and become a racialized other, crossing the color line, in post-9/11 society. Many scholars examine how religion, particularly a Muslim identity, influences this process of racialization for both South Asians and Arabs living in the United States (Purkayastha 2005; Bayoumi 2006; Naber 2008; Cainkar 2009; Bayoumi 2015). I continue with this work by identifying how the racialization of a Muslim identity became institutionalized by the state and was maintained by private citizens and Muslims themselves.

When identified as Muslims, whether through the hijab or a Muslim name, the racial classification as white stops applying to Syrians, Lebanese, and Iraqi Americans. Whiteness comes with certain benefits, like being able to walk into a store without being stared at, monitored, or verbally harassed; boarding a flight in the airport without having your body searched several times, and not having to monitor what you say out of fear that someone will report you to law enforcement. It affords individuals these tangible material and social benefits (Harris 1993). Arabs who are Muslim are being ejected from the racial classification of white because their religious identity marks them as the other,[4] and South Asian Muslims are simultaneously losing their footing as honorary whites. The men and women I interviewed enjoyed class privilege, but in a society deeply invested in a war to combat and prevent terror, their socioeconomic status does not protect them from this differential treatment in society. In this new era of hypersurveillance, Arabs and South Asians who are Muslim are increasingly encountering racism in their daily lives. Although they have been allowed entry into white spaces, they are starting to recognize their marginalization within them due to their surveillance. They no longer feel safe or comfortable in public spaces because of the hostility they encounter. The state and private citizens participate in the process of defining and redefining who is allowed to claim a white identity when they actively racialize groups. Together, they act as gatekeepers of whiteness, rearticulating what it means to be white in America.

Racializing Muslims is not a partisan practice but rather one that is motivated by political gain. It is a shared act that occurs in what appear to be liberal cities like Chicago as well as more conservative cities like Dallas and Fort Worth. The Muslim Americans I interviewed had similar encounters in both cities. Many of the experiences I documented happened under the Obama administration—a Democratic one. Policies on national security that target Muslims have not been radically different under a Democratic president compare to a Republican one. Obama did not eliminate the USA PATRIOT Act or stop the hypersurveillance of Muslims; in fact, the surveillance of Muslims thrived under the Obama administration. Michael Rosino and Matthew Hughey (2015) argue that both Democrats and Republicans have historically and currently rely on racialized discourses to garner support from white voters. The racialized discourse against Muslims espoused by Donald Trump in the 2016 presidential elections exemplifies how this tactic is used by politicians to secure white votes. While Trump's rhetoric was overt, the Democratic presidential candidate Hillary Clinton relied on more subtle and nuanced ways to perpetuate the stereotype that Muslims are only understood as a threat to national security. Clinton said in her first presidential debate, "We need to be cooperating with Muslim nations and with the American Muslim community.

They're on the frontlines. They can provide information to us that we might not get anywhere else. They need to have close working cooperation with law enforcement in these communities, not be alienated and pushed away."[5] Although this language may seem inclusive, it only presents Muslims in relation to threats of terror. Muslims are represented as useful to society because they will help identify the potential terrorists. Thus the construction of whiteness and the rejection of Muslims from it is a shared ideology among liberal and conservative whites.[6]

Theories of race and ethnicity are strengthened when an intersectional approach is employed to understand the complexities of how race is structured into society and the impact it has on everyday interactions (Crenshaw 2009). For Muslim Americans, gender, race, and religion intersect in unique ways. I described the interactional processes that a Muslim identity is racialized through surveillance, which is guided by gender. The racialization of Muslim Americans is not a static process, but is constantly changing due to the sociopolitical climate. I avoid making the claim that the South Asian and Arab Muslims I interviewed are on the bottom of the racial hierarchy because they still enjoy many of the economic and social privileges that have been historically denied to African Americans. Referring back to Samuel Jackson's comment at the beginning of this chapter, Muslims are not the new black but are moving closer to the bottom of the racial hierarchy, further away from whiteness.

I believe this process of racialization is ongoing. While there have been cases of anti-Muslim racism prior to 9/11, its institutionalization is a relatively new phenomenon. I document the practices behind the racialized surveillance of South Asian and Arab Muslims and how it impacts their racial identity within the context of a surveillance society. There are many other forms of discrimination Muslims encounter that scholars should examine and uncover. Right now, the trajectory for Muslims in America appears to be bleak. Anytime a terrorist attack occurs, Muslims have to prepare themselves for increased anger from their fellow citizens as well as increased surveillance from the state.

We need to constantly reexamine where new immigrants and their offspring, like Arabs and South Asians, are located on the racial hierarchy. Their experiences with racism cannot be ignored and as the United States moves toward a multiracial and ethnic society, theories of race and ethnicity should reflect this new demographic. The black-and-white-only model of race can no longer explain all experiences of racism or a racialized society in America, and the racial classification of Asian does not accurately capture the racial experiences of South Asian Muslims. The campaign to add a Middle Eastern North African (MENA) racial category to the 2020 U.S. census reflects this changing racial demographic (Bahrampour 2016). Arab activists argue there is a need to collect data on this population, which is increasingly experiencing discrimination. But Ibrahim Cooper, a spokesperson for the Council on American

Islamic Relations, worries this information could be used to surveil that population: "Unfortunately in today's environment, we have to have concerns about the possible misuse of this data. We've had too many problems in the post-9/11 era when the American government singles out Arab Americans or Muslim Americans for profiling" (cited in Bahrampour 2016). This concern with collecting data on Arabs is not one that should be ignored. Surveillance that is guided by a racialized religious identity may continue to intensify, resulting in more severe abuses of civil liberties, including the arrests and detentions of innocent people. While chronicling Muslim experiences with racism is crucial to combatting discrimination in the courts and institutional practices, the anxiety that data collected on them could be used by the state to further surveil them is not unfounded, as I show in this book.

There are other forms of discrimination this population is encountering, like workplace discrimination, that would add to an understanding of the racialization of South Asian and Arab Muslims. But it is also important not to conflate all Muslim experiences. Future research will uncover the nuances in how ethnicity and race intersect with a religious identity. Although in this book I show that South Asians and Arabs encounter similar experiences because they are Muslim, African American Muslims' encounters with a racialized religious identity may differ because of their unique history with racism in the United States. The hijab may mark African Americans as foreigners like it does for South Asians and Arabs, altering the way their bodies are read and, subsequently, the way they are treated.

As I show in this book, racialized identities and experiences are constructed and created through social interactions with private citizens and state policies. There are political, economic, and social motivations behind the process of racialization. For example, the need to maintain a surveillance industry is driven by the idea that terrorism is one of the greatest threats to Americans. This surveillance industry needs bodies to watch and monitor; therefore racializing a Muslim body as a potential terrorist becomes a necessity to keep the surveillance industry well resourced. Through this process of racialized surveillance, South Asian and Arab Muslims are moving further away from whiteness on the racial hierarchy.

Conclusion

The Future for Muslims in the United States

The future for Muslims in America is one of the questions that keeps coming up as anti-Muslim sentiments continue to grow. Concerns about internment if another major terrorist attack occurs in the United States no longer feel implausible. President Trump discussed the possibility of a Muslim registry during his campaign. Noah Feldman, a law professor at Harvard, wrote an op-ed piece in the *New York Times* that while the law that made internment possible has never been overturned, it would be difficult, but not impossible, to see this practice reinstituted (Feldman 2016). Violence and hate crimes toward Muslims have risen significantly because Donald Trump perpetuated Islamophobic sentiments during his campaign for president.

On January 27, 2017, shortly after his inauguration, Trump signed Executive Order 13769, *Protecting the Nation from Foreign Terrorist Entry into the United States*, which banned noncitizens from seven countries from entering the United States. The countries were Yemen, Sudan, Somalia, Syria, Libya, Iraq, and Iran. This executive order was quickly dubbed a "Muslim ban" because the only common characteristic these countries shared was that they were all Muslim-majority. The very same evening the order was signed, chaos unfolded in U.S. airports. Refugees were banned from coming to the United States and sent back to countries where their lives were in danger. Travelers, many with valid visas, were stopped at the U.S. border and detained for hours. Some were mothers traveling with young children, while others were older adults coming to visit their kids who lived in the United States. Several passengers found themselves stranded in their country of origin because they were not allowed to board flights flying back to the United States. Thousands of protesters swarmed U.S. airports demanding the release of these passengers. The ACLU quickly mobilized and by late evening, a Brooklyn federal judge and a Virginia federal judge both placed a temporary halt to the order. Trump signed a revised ban, Executive Order 13780, which removed Iraq from the list. The ban was again blocked by several federal courts, citing the anti-Muslim rhetoric that he campaigned on as evidence that the motivation for the ban was religious discrimination.

This response has been in many ways surprising. While Muslims are more aggressively targeted, as I've shown, both President George W. Bush and President Barack Obama participated in surveillance of Muslims. Yet there were no protests at airports when Bush prevented Muslim noncitizens from twenty-four countries from entering the United States immediately after 9/11. The covert ways in which the Obama and Bush administrations implemented these policies did not incite protest. Both Bush and Obama utilized rhetoric that made it appear their policies were targeting not Muslims but terrorism. In his State of the Union address in 2002, George W. Bush said of Islam, "Let the skeptics look to Islam's own rich history—with its centuries of learning, and tolerance, and progress" (CNN 2015). Similarly, Obama avoided using the term *Islamic radical terrorism* in an attempt to distinguish Islam from terrorism. The rhetoric used by both presidents presented to the public the notion that Islam and Muslims were not targets of discrimination or racism by the state but rather that these policies were focused on terror. In contrast, the public today is more aware that Trump's overt anti-Muslim and Islamophobic rhetoric is racist toward Muslims. Undoubtedly, the efforts by civil rights organizations and Muslim advocacy groups like the Council on American Islamic Relations and the American Civil Liberties Union, which have increased substantially since 9/11, have also had some impact on awareness (Bakalian and Bozorgmehr 2009; Love 2017). We are at an interesting crossroads for Muslims in America. And while at this new crossroads there is more support for Muslims, they are also more vulnerable than ever to the punitive actions of the state and hate crimes.

As many scholars have shown, race and racism are structured into society (Bonilla-Silva 2010; Omi and Winant 2015). The racialization of Muslims is also tied to social structures and cannot be understood only as a product of the miseducation of the population about Islam. While it is important to educate the public about Islam and Muslims, this alone will not eliminate racism against them. As long as there is economic and political utility to racializing Muslims, it will continue. I have shown that the surveillance state is directly tied to racializing a Muslim body as worthy of surveillance. Companies will continue to invest in new technologies, like face recognition tools, for use at U.S. airports (Schlangenstein 2017). Investment in surveillance technologies is rooted in the ideology that these tools will make America safe from another terrorist attack. But these practices, as shown in this book, are not effective in reducing terrorism but instead create racial hierarchies. Statistics show that Americans have a 1 in 45,808 chance of being killed by a foreign terrorist attack, based on data collected from 1975 to 2015 (Nowrasteh 2016). Americans are more likely to die due to health issues, like heart attacks and cancer, or even an animal attack, than from foreign terrorism. Yet the fear of Muslims and terrorism drives support for increased surveillance.

The purpose of national security should be to keep the country and all of its citizens safe. The surveillance practices the state has engaged in against Muslim Americans reveals major flaws in the state's efforts to prevent another terrorist attack. The inefficient use of billions of dollars in resources toward surveillance that targets a whole population, the majority of whom are law-abiding citizens, based on racial stereotypes does not prevent terrorism. Instead, it strips citizens of their civil rights and the civil liberties they should be afforded through citizenship. When a society supports national security over civil liberties and expands the power of the state, freedom and democracy are weakened. But American history shows that freedom has always been denied to racialized groups like African Americans. While today it is Muslims, African Americans, and Latinx who may be the target of state surveillance, tomorrow it could be anyone.

We should all want to live in a safe and secure society. Ineffective practices take much-needed resources away from finding the root causes of violence in America and consequently addressing these issues to reduce violence. Having a Muslim name or wearing the hijab does not make one more likely to commit acts of terror. An individual's propensity to commit domestic violence and abuse may reveal who is more likely to commit acts of violence in the United States than who is not (Freeman 2017). According to a report on Countering Violent Extremism (CVE) by the Government Accountability Office, violence committed by white supremacists and alt-right groups has resulted in almost the same number of deaths of innocent Americans as those committed by Muslims (Government Accountability Office 2017). The main difference is that Muslim terrorists committed fewer attacks, while domestic white terrorists committed more attacks, killing fewer in each assault. And yet, even with this data, President Trump has said he would revamp the CVE program by only focusing on "radical Islamic terrorism" ignoring the increased violence that is perpetrated by white supremacists, white nationalists, and anti-government groups. By ignoring the violence committed by white nationalists, America will not be safer from domestic terrorism.

It is entirely possible to have a country that is committed to keeping its citizens safe without racially profiling an entire religious group. The either/ or of civil liberties versus national security is a dangerous one. It produces an ideology that it is OK to sacrifice the rights of some people over others. This way of thinking has led to some of the worst human rights abuses in history, including the internment of Japanese Americans. We should and can learn from the mistakes we have made in the past to ensure a better future.

Appendix

Methodology

I interviewed 48 South Asian and Arab American Muslim Americans between 2009 and 2012 about their lives since September 11th. The interviews ranged in length from forty-five minutes to three hours and took place in the greater Chicago area in Illinois and the Dallas/Fort Worth metropolitan area in Texas. The majority of the participants were South Asian (29) compared to Arab (19). Participants consisted of 15 South Asian American women (11 Pakistani and 4 Indian), 14 South Asian American men (9 Pakistani, 4 Indian, and 1 Bengali), 10 Arab American women (8 Palestinian, 1 Egyptian, and 1 Syrian), and 9 Arab American men (8 Palestinian and 1 Lebanese). Participants' ages ranged from twenty to seventy-one. The majority of the participants were native citizens or born in the United States (34), while a little under one-third (14) were foreign-born and were naturalized citizens. More than half were professionals with graduate degrees in medicine, law, and business.

A little more than half of the woman participants wore the hijab; therefore, I was able to compare the role of religious signifiers in the lives of Muslim women. Of the 14 women interviewed who wore the hijab, only 1 also wore the jilbaab (a coat-like garment Muslim women wear over their clothes to hide their figures). None of the men I interviewed wore religious symbols, like a beard. There is some debate about whether or not Islam requires Muslim men to grow a beard. Some argue it is better to do it because Prophet Muhammed had a beard, while others claim it is not necessary because it is not in the Quran.

The interviews consisted of a series of semistructured, open-ended questions about the everyday lives of the participants before and after 9/11 in order to assess the impact this event has had on the daily lives of Muslims. We discussed at length what their relationship was like with their neighbors, coworkers, and friends before 9/11 and if it changed after the terrorist attacks. I asked Muslim American men and women who they spent most of their time with and about their work/education experiences. I wanted to know how 9/11 changed their everyday lives. Because I was curious about how religiosity influenced experiences with anti-Muslim discrimination, I asked a series of questions about their participation and membership in religious organizations, such as mosques and Muslim organizations at schools they attended. I also asked about race and ethnicity and what role each played in their daily lives in order to understand which experiences should be attributed to their races or ethnicities and which were related to their religious identity.

According to the Pew Research Center in 2011, Muslims comprise just 0.8 percent of the U.S. population. As a result, I had to seek out Muslims for this study. Participants were recruited through snowball sampling—participants were asked to recommend another person to be interviewed. Snowball sampling is a reliable method when the population is hard to access (Gray et al. 2007). I had an easier time accessing Muslim woman participants than Muslim men; I had a difficult time getting Muslim American men to participate in the interviews. Because I am a woman, I knew it could be challenging for me to interview Muslim American men due to the gender dynamics of the religion. Although some Muslim Americans abide by gender segregation due to religious beliefs, as a Muslim American, I knew that there is diversity in the beliefs of the Muslim American community and that many men would be OK with being interviewed by a woman. I hoped my status as a Muslim American woman would grant me access to Muslim American men. It did not. Because of the difficulties I encountered in getting interviews with Muslim American men, I relied on the Muslim American women I interviewed to recommend a Muslim American man for me to interview. This resulted in only a handful of interviews. I explained to the first few male Muslim interviewees the difficulties I encountered getting Muslim men to participate in the study. These men then generously connected me to their friends and family members, who agreed to participate in the interviews. After conducting the interviews, I found the reason Muslim American men were opting out of participating had less to do with gender relationships and more to do with the fear of surveillance. I believe Muslim American men feared talking to a stranger about their experiences post-9/11 because of the hypersurveillance they have had to endure. Once I secured the trust of a few Muslim American men, they were able to vouch for me to their friends and family members, which is how I was able to incorporate men's voices in this book.

Many Muslim American men and women were harassed at work because of their religious identity and did not want to compromise their employment or bring any more negative attention onto themselves because of their religious identity. For these reasons, I changed the names of the participants I interviewed in order to protect their anonymity in this study.

Acknowledgments

This book would not have been possible without the guidance, mentorship, and support of so many people. I am indebted to those who read through the chapters and provided me with thoughtful and insightful critique. I also want to thank everyone who gave me invaluable advice throughout the process of publishing my first book. I am equally grateful to my friends and family for cheering me on and helping me make it to the finish line.

First, I am eternally indebted to the Muslim American men and women who took their time to speak with me about their experiences in the years since 9/11. I am grateful for their kindness in inviting me into their homes. I met with them in coffee shops and restaurants in Chicago, Dallas, and Fort Worth. It is their stories that shine in this book and highlight the injustices that Muslim Americans face. I want to thank them for their bravery and courage in speaking with me about their experiences, particularly at a time when their voices are increasingly being silenced.

I was fortunate to have stellar faculty at Loyola University Chicago, who gave me invaluable feedback on the dissertation that was the precursor to this book. Fred Kniss was a great mentor and source of support while he was at Loyola. Judy Wittner, Phil Nyden, David Embrick, and Rhys Williams provided me with insightful comments that helped me think through some difficult concepts. I am particularly appreciative that Rhys Williams joined my committee when he did. His careful eye on each chapter and expertise really strengthened my ideas. I was also lucky to be surrounded by smart and engaged graduate students at Loyola. Thank you Bhoomi Thakore, Kasey Henricks, Reuben Miller, Neil Holmgren, Dennis Watson, Grace Scrimgeour, Kim Fox, and Cortney Rowland King for the friendship, support, and scholarly debates during my time at Loyola. Not only did Patty Robertson and Rosa Negussie provide me with much-needed academic support; they both became dear friends by the time I left Loyola.

Nizam Arain and Mahruq Khan guided me in so many ways with this project when I hit some walls getting it off the ground. I cannot thank you both enough for the mentorship and friendship you provided me when I really needed it. Richard Shank read through drafts of chapters and helped me think through some concepts. While I was in Chicago I was lucky to be a part of a writing group that read through chapters and provided feedback. I greatly appreciate the lively discussions I had with Brian Sargent, Elizabeth Onasch, Juhi Verma, Armando Lara-Millan, Melissa Abad, Robert Vargas, and Mosi Ifatunji while we were all working on our dissertations. Our meetings helped me grow as a scholar and see the value in creating an intellectual community.

The book really began to take shape after I moved to Boston. I cannot thank Leslie Wang and Jennifer Musto enough for reading the book draft and giving me feedback. Although our research interests differ, their insights and intellectual engagement with several chapters of my book helped me frame the book. My meetings with these two brilliant scholars left me inspired. I am truly grateful for their support and friendship.

I have met so many colleagues along the way who have provided me with support in other ways. I am sincerely indebted to David Brunsma, Pawan Dhingra, Matthew Hughey, Sarah Babb, Silvia Dominguez, and Tiffany Joseph for their generosity with their time in advising me over the last five years. Their support helped me navigate the unfamiliar process of publishing a book. I have also greatly benefited from meeting and conversing with scholars whose work I deeply admire, who have laid down the intellectual groundwork for scholars like myself. Conversations with Moustafa Bayoumi, Nadine Naber, Louise Cainkar, Evelyn Alsultany, Nazli Kibria, Pawan Dhingra, Bandana Purkayastha, Vivek Bald, Erik Love, Neda Maghbouleh, Nasar Meer, Steve Garner, and Sahar Aziz, either in person or via email, have greatly enriched my work.

At Simmons College, I found the most supportive and inspiring colleagues in the sociology department. Becky Thompson, Shelley White, Dawna Thomas, Anima Adjepong, Donna Cole, Steve London, Valerie Leiter, and Jyoti Puri supported me in every way possible. Jyoti Puri read through an early draft of the book and gave me pointed critique, which helped me bring the book into focus. Becky Thompson guided me on the process of writing with her wisdom. Valerie Leiter's door was always open whenever I needed it. I am also thankful for the support of the dean's office. Thank you to Renee White and Leanne Doherty Mason for providing institutional support for this project. Tricia Elam Walker organized a writing retreat at Simmons College and provided insightful feedback on my chapters. Judah Axe, Deron Graves, and Kristin Nicole Dukes also provided thoughtful insights on my work in our helpful, if short-lived, writing group at Simmons.

I am indebted to Jessica Cobb for helping me develop the manuscript into a book. Her critique and insights, along with her edits, helped formulate many of the ideas and concepts. A very special thank-you to my editor at Rutgers University Press, Peter Mickulas, who has given me a tremendous amount of support and advice throughout the publishing process. A special debt of gratitude goes to William Varner for allowing me to use his image for the cover of the book. I am also indebted to several people for bringing me out to give talks at their colleges and universities. The feedback at each of these institutions provided me with so much food for thought intellectually. To those who provided feedback at LaMoyne College, the University of Wisconsin La Crosse, Wright State University, Bentley University, Virginia Tech, the National Scientific Research Institute at the University of Quebec, the University of Michigan's Racism Lab, the Sociology Department at Boston College, and the Workshop on Race and Racial Ideology at the University of Chicago, your comments, questions, and thoughts were instrumental to my ability to think through so many ideas presented in this book.

I would also like to thank Helen Marrow and Theda Skocpol for the invitation to be a part of the Scholars Strategy Network and for disseminating this research to a larger audience. I am also grateful to Hatem Bazian for including me in the Islamophobia Studies project at the University of California, Berkeley.

Several graduate students helped along the way. Thanks to Calista Ross, Kaitlyn Collins, and Stephanie Orman for their work on the manuscript at different phases while they were graduate student in the Gender and Cultural Studies program at Simmons College. Thank you to Bianca Gonzalez-Lesser and Devon Gross for their feedback on my work. There are also several graduate students whom I have been in conversation with about their work, which has made me think about my research in new ways. Thanks to Maheen Haider, Juliette Galonnier, Inaash Islam, Patrick Casey, Bilal Hussain, and Meghan Tinsley for your exciting and insightful work.

Kristen Schilt, Robert Vargas, and Kimberly Hoang have been there for me whenever I needed advice. I am lucky to have such amazing friends who are also scholars I truly admire. I also want to thank all the academics who are part of the New England Workshop on Racial and Ethnic Scholars, who provided both professional and emotional support throughout the last four years.

There are a few individuals who have gone above and beyond for me. These are the advisors who everyone needs to be successful in academia. Steve Garner has been an incredible mentor over the last few years. He has supported my work in so many ways. I am incredibly honored to have collaborated with such an excellent scholar who is also an incredible human being. Not only has Nazli Kibria been a great source of knowledge; she has also been incredibly supportive since I came to Boston. Collaborating with her has made me a better scholar. I owe so much to her mentorship, for which I hope I can one day repay. Finally, there was a point in graduate school when I thought I was going to sink rather than swim. If it were not for the support and advice of David Embrick, I would have sunk. He has continued to be an incredible mentor since graduate school and is also now a dear friend. He has shown me the value of mentorship in academia. I will always be indebted to him for his guidance, his amazing sense of humor, and his belief in me at a time when I needed it the most.

Finally, I have to thank my friends and family who have supported me since I started this journey. Heather Kenny and Arlene Tee have been solid and reliable friends for the last twenty years. I am grateful for their continued friendship and support. My brother, Omar, and his wife, Roshan, and my three amazing nieces have always been there when needed. My sister Samira and my two nephews have shown me what strength really looks like. My brother-in-law and his wife—Jess and Loni—and their two sons have provided me with much needed rest and relaxation over the last few years. Thanks to my wonderful and amazing in-laws, Jay and Sheila, for providing free summer camp for my daughter so I could write over the summers. To my parents, I owe everything. Sayeeda and Farooq Selod were my inspiration for this book. Your courage after 9/11 motivated me to go to graduate school and study Muslims. You also taught me to stand up for what is right. This book is the result of your continued support and influence. To my daughter, Isra English, your presence in this world makes me want to make it a better place for you. I know you are going to be part of the light that brings us out of the dark. My partner, Eben English, has been my rock. I cannot thank him enough for parenting solo on countless weekends, editing my work, indexing the book, talking through difficult concepts with me, and believing in me. You always encourage and inspire me to push myself beyond where I think I can go.

Notes

Introduction

1   See the White House press release on May 1, 2006, titled "Vice President's Remarks at the World Affairs Council of Philadelphia Luncheon Honoring Professor Bernard Lewis," at The White House: President George W. Bush, accessed June 20, 2014, http://georgewbush-whitehouse.archives.gov/news/releases/2006/05/20060501-3.html.

2   It restricted access to medical care for women, brutally enforced a restrictive dress code, and limited the ability of women to move about the city.

3   According to an article published in *Foreign Policy* by John Arquilla, Ronald Reagan began a war on terror in response to the bombing of marine barracks in Lebanon in 1983.

4   There have been concerns about safety issues surrounding body scanners. Several stories have surfaced questioning what the impact of exposure to radiation from the body scanners could have on the larger population. Some scientists have argued that the radiation is a carcinogen, and therefore they think there is a possibility that it could make individuals more susceptible to cancer.

5   A mass killing is defined as occurring when there are four or more victims. According to the FBI, the statistics on mass killings are inaccurate because there is underreporting by police departments. For example, Florida does not report homicide data to the FBI. See Overberg et al. (2013) for a report on mass shootings.

6   These examples may be outdated at the time of publication due to the frequency of gun violence in the United States.

7   The Department of Homeland Security's website changes periodically, particularly with a change in administration. This video was accessed under the Obama administration.

8   Under the Obama administration, CVE focused on extreme right wing groups as well as Muslims and terrorism. There is concern under the Trump administration that CVE will only focus on Muslims and terrorism. See Patel's (2017) blog post "The Trump Administration Provides One More Reason to Discontinue CVE."

9   The stereotype of black women as unfit mothers can be seen through the contrasting experiences of two women, Lenore Skenazy and Debra Harrell. In July 2014,

Debra Harrell, a black working mother, was arrested and her nine-year-old daughter was taken away from her by the state because she sent her daughter to the park to play alone while she worked at McDonalds. She gave her daughter a cell phone but did not want to leave her alone in their home because of a recent burglary that happened in her building (CBS/AP 2014). In 2008, a few years earlier, Lenore Skenazy, a white middle-class mother and author, wrote a story about how she allowed her nine-year-old son to ride the train in New York City alone. While both mothers were criticized for their parenting, Debra Harrell was criminalized while Lenore Skenazy was credited with starting a new parenting philosophy, free-range parenting (Skenazy 2015).

Chapter 1   Moving from South Asian and Arab Identities to a Muslim Identity

1   See Khandelwal's *Becoming American, Becoming Indian: An Immigrant Community in New York City* (2002) about how prior to laws passed in the 1980s, South Asians were classified as white according to the U.S. Census Bureau.

2   Individuals who claim Algerian, Bahraini, Egyptian, Emirati, Iraqi, Jordanian, Kuwaiti, Lebanese, Libyan, Moroccan, Omani, Palestinian, Qatari, Saudi Arabian, Syrian, Tunisian, and/or Yemeni ancestry are considered Arab according to the U.S. census.

3   According to Cainkar (2009), Arabs living in Detroit, Buffalo, Cincinnati, and St. Louis faced challenges in the courts regarding their naturalization.

4   Although Syrian Christians were able to have some success accessing whiteness, particularly through naturalization, they were also not treated as fully white in the United States. Sarah Gualtieri (2009) chronicles the experiences of Syrian immigrants and their status as Syrians and Americans in the early twentieth century in *Between Arab and White: Race and Ethnicity in the Early Syrian American Diaspora*.

5   See Cainkar 2009.

6   President Trump signed two executive orders (known as the "Muslim ban") that attempted to deny refugees and noncitizens from first seven, then six Muslim-majority countries entry to the United States.

7   This prediction by Pew may now be inaccurate in light of President Trump's executive orders and policies that seek to reduce immigration to the United States from Muslim-majority countries.

8   Because there is a large Palestinian presence in Chicago, the Palestinian Muslims I interviewed socialized amongst themselves. The same was true for the Pakistani and Indian Muslim communities in both Chicago and the Dallas/Fort Worth area. While Pakistanis and Indians would mix, most of the people I talked to were married to someone who was also from their ethnic background. The "Muslim first" classification in some ways could be seen as a response to the racialization of a Muslim identity, but socioeconomic status and migratory patterns still matter in terms of whether or not South Asian and Arab Muslims are integrated.

9   Ground Zero is where the Twin Towers were once located prior to the September 11th terrorist attacks. See Bail 2015.

10   This anti-sharia fear is one that is being used to garner fear of Muslims in America. The belief is that Muslims are trying to institute Islamic law in America, which is not the case. Anti-Muslim activists like Gabriel Brigitte from ACT for America promotes the idea that Muslims are trying to Islamicize America through

sharia law. Politicians, like the mayor of Irving, have introduced anti-sharia bills to legislator partially for political support from their constituents who fear Muslims in America.

11 It should be noted that Sikhs have continued to be mislabeled as Muslims since 9/11 and have therefore been consistent targets of Islamophobia. Individuals with darker skin tones may experience anti-Muslim harassment after a terrorist attack or during a politically charged election cycle. In the *Politics of Islamophobia: Race, Power and Fantasy*, David Tyrer argues this just confirms how Muslims are raced, because the visual religious cues worn by Sikhs are misinterpreted as Muslim. Also see Erik Love's book (2017).

12 In "Muslim First, Arab Second: A Strategic Politics of Race and Gender" (2005), Nadine Naber discusses how college is where many Muslim youth experience a stronger identification with their religious identity.

Chapter 2   Flying while Muslim

1 The TSA website changes as the administration changes. I accessed it during the Obama administration. The language and content changed once Trump became president.

2 One of the issues is that body scanners show naked images of passengers as they pass through them.

3 I have no way of substantiating if the individuals I interviewed were or were not on the list. Some told me they were told by TSA agents they were on a list and others said they were told their name was like someone else's on the list.

4 Interviews were done before the implementation of body scanners at airports. These testimonies reflect Muslim American men's and women's experiences with metal detectors and body searches by TSA agents.

5 None of the Muslim women I interviewed mentioned they were on a list and the majority traveled with Muslim men, indicating this may have been an anomaly.

6 Now TSA agents perform a chemical swipe of their hands and have them pat down their heads and necks to test for dangerous weapons. This was not done at the time of the interviews.

Chapter 3   Citizen Surveillance

1 See the *Huffington Post* article "Anti-Islam Bus Ads OK'd by Judge: Pamela Geller Wins Preliminary Ruling to Call Enemies of Israel 'Savages'" reported by the Associated Press (Huffington Post/AP 2012).

2 Immediately after a crisis, like a terrorist attack, darker-skinned men are targeted by the public as threats. This is best exemplified in the cases of Indian men who were attacked after 9/11 because they were mistaken for Muslims or Arabs. The misidentification of Sikhs is another example of this, which both Erik Love (2017) and David Tyrer (2013) note in their books. Because Sikhs wear the turban, they are often misrecognized as Muslim. While I do not mean to downplay their experiences, in the time period I examined, Muslim men were not targeted by strangers in the same way that women who wear the hijab were. Strangers did not consistently harass them in public because of their skin tone.

3 A website titled the Islamophobia Network has listed Ayaan Hirsi Ali as an Islamophobic activist. She argues that Islam is a religion of violence and argues for

the West to defeat Islam. The Southern Poverty Law Center has labeled her an anti-Muslim extremist.

4 It is common for Pakistanis to be misidentified for Indian.

5 In the *New York Times* article, Tierney says that people who live in New York wear black for a multitude of reasons, including its practicality (hides dirt), its effect of making people look thinner, and how it is seen as elegant (Tierney 1994). Muslim women who wear the hijab felt they were perceived as morbid for wearing a black hijab even though in a big city like Chicago, it is viewed as fashionable to wear black. In other words, they are held to different standards of fashion and beauty.

6 The USA PATRIOT Act has given more power to the state to use secret evidence and participate in surveillance without warrants.

7 Acquisti and Fong (2015) show that online job candidates who were identifiable as Muslim were less likely to get a callback than those who had a Christian-sounding name.

8 Sahar Aziz (2012) argues that the hijab has shifted from symbolizing oppression to symbolizing terror.

Chapter 4   Self-Discipline or Resistance?

1 It should be noted that online forums such as Reddit falsely identified one of the brothers as Sunil Tripathi, a Brown student who was missing and had committed suicide.

2 According to an article by Hunter Stuart in the *Huffington Post*, a Palestinian doctor named Heba Abolaban, who wears the hijab, was punched in the shoulder by a white man who yelled, "Fuck you Muslims!" (Stuart 2013).

3 Christopher Bail (2015) in *Terrified: How Anti-Muslim Fringe Organizations Became Mainstream* shows how in the weeks immediately after 9/11, there was a spike in vandalism and threats made at U.S. mosques.

4 The Stop Islamization of America campaign organized by Pamela Geller and Robert Spencer rallied around preventing the building of the Park 51 Islamic center near the World Trade Center site. They have been classified as a hate group that perpetuates Islamophobia in the United States by the Southern Poverty Law Center.

5 Muslim American women are no different than the women interviewed by Arlie Hochschild and Anne Machung in the late 1990s in their book *The Second Shift* (2003). These women also do more of the childcare and housework even if they are employed. There is a gender component to the type of volunteer work that Muslim women take on.

6 There were two back-to-back terrorist attacks in England in 2017. On May 22, 2017, a suicide bomber attacked outside of an Arianna Grande concert, killing twenty-two concert goers. On June 3, 2017, three men drove a van into a crowd on London Bridge, killing eight pedestrians. Terrorist attacks in Europe have been used by anti-Muslim politicians and hate groups in the United States to justify banning Muslims, bring back internment camps, and deport and detain them.

7 While Will Smith coined the term to discuss African American males' experiences on predominantly white college campuses, the term is useful to understand how Muslims too experience stress as a result of their racialization.

8 David Embrick, Silvia Dominguez, and Baran Karsak (2017) argue that racial microaggressions should be understood structurally. This concept is also useful in

understanding how Muslim encounters with racial micro- and macroaggressions stem from state policies that target and racialize Muslims.

Chapter 5   Shifting Racial Terrain for Muslim Americans

1   Afro-Caribbeans are viewed as docile and reliable workers compared to African Americans (Treitler 2013).

2   See chapter 1 for a history of how some South Asian immigrants were denied citizenship because of their religious and cultural identities.

3   See Khandewal's *Becoming American, Becoming Indian: An Immigrant Community in New York City* (2002) about how prior to laws passed in the 1980s, South Asians were classified as white according to the U.S. Census Bureau.

4   I want to make clear that I am not arguing that Arab Christians may not also experience this exclusion from whiteness. Skin tone and pigmentation as well as other factors, like nation of origin, can also produce the same effect.

5   See the transcript published from the first presidential debate in the *Washington Post* (Blake 2016).

6   Hughey (2012) shows how groups with what would appear to be opposing political viewpoints, like white nationalists and white anti-racists, actually make meaning of whiteness via similar ideologies on race. It is important to draw on this work because it can be used to show that anti-Muslim sentiments are pervasive and not limited to white Southern Republicans.

References

Abdelkader, Engy. 2016. *When Islamophobia Turns Violent: The 2016 US Presidential Elections*. The Bridge Initiative, Georgetown University Center for Muslim-Christian Understanding. Washington, D.C. http://bridge.georgetown.edu/wp-content/uploads/2016/05/When-Islamophobia-Turns-Violent.pdf.

Abu-Lughod, Lila. 2013. *Do Muslim Women Need Saving?* 1st ed. Cambridge, Mass.: Harvard University Press.

Abu-Raiya, Hisham, Kenneth I. Pargament, and Annette Mahoney. 2011. "Examining Coping Methods with Stressful Interpersonal Events Experienced by Muslims Living in the United States following the 9/11 Attacks." *Psychology of Religion and Spirituality* 3 (1): 1–14. doi:10.1037/a0020034.

Acquisti, Alessandro, and Christina M. Fong. 2015. "An Experiment in Hiring Discrimination via Online Social Networks." *SSRN Electronic Journal.* doi:10.2139/ssrn.2031979.

Ahmed, Leila. 1992. *Women and Gender in Islam.* New Haven, Conn.: Yale University Press.

Alexander, Michelle. 2012 *The New Jim Crow: Mass Incarceration in the Age of Colorblindness.* New York, N.Y.: New Press.

Al-Saji, A. 2010. "The Racialization of Muslim Veils: A Philosophical Analysis." *Philosophy & Social Criticism* 36 (8): 875–902. doi:10.1177/0191453710375589.

Alsultany, Evelyn. 2012. *Arabs and Muslims in the Media.* 1st ed. New York: New York University Press.

American Civil Liberties Union. n.d.(a). "Factsheet: The NYPD Muslim Surveillance Program." Accessed on December 10, 2014, at https://www.aclu.org/other/factsheet-nypd-muslim-surveillance-program?redirect=factsheet-nypd-muslim-surveillance-program.

American Civil Liberties Union. n.d.(b). "The Five Problems with CAPPS II." Accessed on July 10, 2015, at https://www.aclu.org/other/five-problems-capps-ii?redirect=five-problems-capps-ii.

American Civil Liberties Union. n.d.(c). "Nationwide Anti-Mosque Activity." Last modified February 2018. Accessed May 9, 2017, at https://www.aclu.org/map/nationwide-anti-mosque-activity.

American Civil Liberties Union. n.d.(d). "Racial Profiling Definition." Accessed March 24, 2015, at https://www.aclu.org/other/racial-profiling-definition?redirect=racial-profiling-definition.

American Civil Liberties Union of Massachusetts. n.d. "'Countering Violent Extremism' a Flawed Approach to Law Enforcement." Accessed December 5, 2017, at https://aclum .org/our-work/aclum-issues/freedom-of-expression-and-association/countering-violent -extremism-a-flawed-approach-to-law-enforcement/.

Arab American Institute. 2014. "Demographics—Arab American Institute." Accessed May 14, 2016, at http://www.aaiusa.org/demographics.

Arab American Institute. 2015. "State Profiles: Arab American Populations in 50 States." Accessed May 14, 2016, at http://www.aaiusa.org/state-profiles.

Arquilla, John. 2012. "Three Wars on Terror Ronald Reagan and the Battle for Obama's Strategic Soul." *Foreign Policy*. September 12, 2012. http://foreignpolicy.com/2012/09/10/ three-wars-on-terror/.

Aziz, Sahar. 2012. "From the Oppressed to the Terrorist: Muslim American Women in the Crosshairs of Intersectionality." *Race & Poverty L.J.*: 191–264. http://scholarship.law .tamu.edu/cgi/viewcontent.cgi?article=1099&context=facscholar.

Bagby, Ihsan. 2012. "The American Mosque 2011." *Council on American-Islamic Relations: US Mosque Study 2011*.

Bahrampour, Tara. 2016. "A U.S. Census Proposal to Add Category for People of Middle Eastern Descent Makes Some Uneasy." *Washington Post*. October 21, 2016. https://www .washingtonpost.com/local/social-issues/a-proposal-to-add-a-us-census-category-for -people-of-middle-eastern-descent-makes-some-uneasy/2016/10/20/8e9847a0-960e -11e6-bb29-bf2701dbe0a3_story.html?utm_term=.9d763da37304.

Bail, Christopher A. 2015. *Terrified: How Anti-Muslim Fringe Organizations Became Mainstream*. 1st ed. Princeton, N.J.: Princeton University Pres.

Bakalian, Anny P., and Mehdi Bozorgmehr. 2009. *Backlash 9/11: Middle Eastern and Muslim Americans Respond*. Berkeley: University of California Press.

Bald, Vivek. 2015. *Bengali Harlem and the Lost Stories of South Asian America*. Cambridge, Mass.: Harvard University Press.

Batalova, Jeanne, and Jie Zong. 2018. "Middle Eastern and North African Immigrants in the United States." http://www.migrationpolicy.org/article/middle-eastern-and-north -african-immigrants-united-states.

Bayoumi, Moustafa. 2006. "Racing Religion." *CR: The New Centennial Review* 6 (2): 267–293. doi:10.1353/ncr.2007.0000.

Bayoumi, Moustafa. 2015. *This American Muslim Life: Dispatches from the War on Terror*. New York: New York University Press.

Beinart, Peter. 2016. "Bill Clinton's Lapse into Trumpism: In His Convention Speech, He Suggested That Muslims Need to Earn the Rights That All Other Americans Enjoy." *Atlantic*. July 27, 2016. https://www.theatlantic.com/politics/archive/2016/07/bill -clintons-lapse-into-trumpism/493175/.

Bellah, Robert N., Richard Mansen, William M. Sullivan, Ann Swidler, and Steven M. Tipton. 2007. *Habits of the Heart*. 1st ed. Berkeley: University of California Press.

Bender, Bryan. 2015. "Local Islam Leader Rips Antiterror Plan: Says Youth Focus Targets Muslims." *Boston Globe*, February 19, 2015, A:1.

Blackburn, Yasmina. 2014. "Illinois Mosque Faces an Increasingly Common Zoning Problem." *Al Jazeera*. June 14, 2014. http://america.aljazeera.com/articles/2014/6/14/illinois -mosque-nomadic.html.

Blake, Aaron. 2016. "The First Trump-Clinton Presidential Debate Transcript, Annotated." *Washington Post*. September 26, 2016. https://www.washingtonpost.com/news/the-fix/ wp/2016/09/26/the-first-trump-clinton-presidential-debate-transcript-annotated/?utm _term=.acc92f4f5cf9.

Bonikowski, Bart. 2005. "Flying while Arab (Or Was It Muslim? Or Middle Eastern?): A Theoretical Analysis of Racial Profiling after September 11th." *Discourse of Sociological Practice* 7: 315–328.

Bonilla-Silva, Eduardo. 2001. *White Supremacy and Racism in the Post-Civil Rights Era.* 1st ed. Boulder, Colo.: Lynne Rienner.

Bonilla-Silva, Eduardo. 2002. "We Are All Americans!: The Latin Americanization of Racial Stratification in the USA." *Race and Society* 5 (1): 3–16. doi:10.1016/j.racsoc.2003.12.008.

Bonilla-Silva, Eduardo. 2010. *Racism without Racists.* 3rd ed. Lanham, Md.: Rowman & Littlefield.

Boyette, Chris. 2012. "Poll: Majority of New Yorkers Approve of NYPD Surveillance of Muslims." CNN. March 3, 2012. http://www.cnn.com/2012/03/13/justice/new-york -police-muslims-poll/.

Brayne, Sarah. 2014. "Surveillance and System Avoidance." *American Sociological Review* 79 (3): 367–391. doi:10.1177/0003122414530398.

Cainkar, Louise. 2004. "Palestinians." In *Encyclopedia of Chicago.* Chicago: Chicago Historical Society.

Cainkar, Louise. 2009. *Homeland Insecurity: The Arab American and Muslim American Experience after 9/11.* 1st ed. New York: Russell Sage Foundation.

Callimachi, Rakmini. 2015. "ISIS Enshrines a Theology of Rape." *New York Times.* August 13, 2015. https://www.nytimes.com/2015/08/14/world/middleeast/isis-enshrines-a -theology-of-rape.html?mcubz=0&_r=0.

Carafano, James, Robert Poole, and James Roberts. 2006. *Time to Rethink Airport Security.* Backgrounder. Heritage Foundation. https://www.heritage.org/homeland-security/ report/time-rethink-airport-security.

CBS/AP. 2014. "S.C. Mom's Arrest over Daughter Alone in Park Sparks Debate." *CBS News.* July 28, 2014. https://www.cbsnews.com/news/south-carolina-moms-arrest-over -daughter-alone-in-park-sparks-debate/.

Cheney, Alexandra. 2016. "Samuel L. Jackson on #OscarsSoWhite and How 'Muslim Americans Are the New Black Kids.'" December 10, 2016. https://www.hollywoodreporter.com/ news/samuel-l-jackson-oscarssowhite-how-muslim-americas-are-new-black-kids-955015.

Chua-Eoan, Howard. 2010. "Park51: The 'Ground Zero Mosque.'" *Time.* December 9, 2010. http://content.time.com/time/specials/packages/article/0,28804,2035319_2034971 _2034944,00.html.

Cole, David D. 2003. *Enemy Aliens: Double Standards and Constitutional Freedoms in the War on Terrorism.* New York: New Press.

Crenshaw, Kimberle. 2009. "Demarginalizing the Intersection of Race and Sex: A Black Feminist Critique of Antidiscrimination Doctrine, Feminist Theory, and Antiracist Politics [1989]." In *Feminist Legal Studies.* Edited by Joanne Conaghan. New York: Routledge, 57–80.

Deleuze, Gilles. 1992. "Postscript on the Societies of Control." *October* 59: 3–7.

Dhingra, Pawan H. 2003. "Being American between Black and White: Second-Generation Asian American Professionals' Racial Identities." *Journal of Asian American Studies* 6 (2): 117–147.

Dhingra, Pawan. 2007. *Managing Multicultural Lives.* 1st ed. Stanford, Calif.: Stanford University Press.

Dhingra, Pawan. 2012. *Life behind the Lobby.* Stanford, Calif.: Stanford University Press.

Ellis, Ralph, and Darius Johnson. 2016. "Muslim Family Seeks Apology from United Airlines." CNN. April 2, 2016. http://www.cnn.com/2016/04/02/us/muslim-family-united -airlines/.

El-Sayed, Abdulrahman M., and Sandro Galea. 2009. "The Health of Arab-Americans Living in the United States: A Systematic Review of the Literature." *BMC Public Health* 9 (1). doi:10.1186/1471-2458-9-272.

Embrick, David G., Silvia Domínguez, and Baran Karsak. 2017. "More than Just Insults: Rethinking Sociology's Contribution to Scholarship on Racial Microaggressions." *Sociological Inquiry* 87 (2): 193–206. doi:10.1111/soin.12184.

Etehad, Melissa. 2016. "After Nice, Newt Gingrich Wants to 'Test' Every Muslim in the U.S. and Deport Sharia Believers." *Washington Post*. July 15, 2016. https://www .washingtonpost.com/news/morning-mix/wp/2016/07/15/after-nice-newt-gingrich -wants-to-test-every-american-muslim-and-deport-those-who-believe-in-sharia/?utm _term=.9b2fd30ccc80.

Fantz, Ashley, Steve Almasy, and Anne Claire Stapleton. 2015. "Muslim Teen Ahmed Mohamed Creates Clock, Shows Teachers, Gets Arrested." CNN. September 16, 2015. http://www.cnn.com/2015/09/16/us/texas-student-ahmed-muslim-clock-bomb/.

Federal Bureau of Investigation. n.d. Terrorist Screening Center—FAQs. Accessed March 7, 2018, at https://www.fbi.gov/file-repository/terrorist-screening-center-frequently-asked -questions.pdf/view.

Feldman, Noah. 2016. "Why Korematsu Is Not a Precedent." *New York Times*. November 18, 2016. https://www.nytimes.com/2016/11/21/opinion/why-korematsu-is-not-a-precedent .html?_r=0.

Foucault, Michel. 1995. *Discipline and Punish*. 1st ed. New York: Vintage Books.

Freeman, Hadley. 2017. "What Do Many Lone Attackers Have in Common? Domestic Violence." *Guardian*. March 28, 2017. https://www.theguardian.com/commentisfree/ 2017/mar/28/lone-attackers-domestic-violence-khalid-masood-westminster-attacks -terrorism.

Fuchs, Chris. 2017. "Judge Approves Settlement over Post 9/11 NYPD Surveillance." *NBC News*. March 22, 2017. https://www.nbcnews.com/news/asian-america/judge-approves -settlement-over-post-9-11-nypd-muslim-surveillance-n737101.

Gaines, Lee V. 2014. "Des Plaines Approves Permit for More Mosque Parking." *Chicago Tribune*. November 19, 2014. http://www.chicagotribune.com/suburbs/des-plaines/ct -des-plaines-mosque-traffic-1120-20141119-story.html.

Galonnier, Juliette. 2015. "When White Devils Join the Deen: White Americans Converts to Islam and the Experience of Non-normative Whiteness." *Sciences Po/CNRS: 1–46*.

Garner, Steve. 2006. "The Uses of Whiteness: What Sociologists Working on Europe Can Draw from US Research on Whiteness." *Sociology* 40 (2): 257–275. doi:10.1177/0038038506062032.

Garner, Steve, and Saher Selod. 2015. "The Racialization of Muslims: Empirical Studies of Islamophobia." *Critical Sociology* 41 (1): 9–19. doi:10.1177/0896920514531606.

Gibb, Lindsay. 2016. "Man Rips Off Woman's Hijab during Flight, Yells 'This Is America!'" *Think Progress*. May 14, 2016. https://thinkprogress.org/man-rips-off-womans-hijab -during-flight-yells-this-is-america-4e6425e1eb88.

Giddens, Anthony. 1990. *The Consequences of Modernity*. 1st ed. Cambridge: Polity Press in association with Blackwell.

Gjelten, Tom. 2016. On "American Muslim Women Explain Why They Do—Or Don't—Cover." NPR: *Codeswitch*. Hosted by Gene Demby and Shereen Marisol. February 2, 2016. https://www.npr.org/sections/codeswitch/2016/02/02/465180930/ american-muslim-women-explain-why-they-do-or-dont-cover.

Glenn, Evelyn Nakano. 2002. *Unequal Freedom*. 1st ed. Cambridge, Mass.: Harvard University Press.

Glenn, Evelyn Nakano. 2009. "Consuming Lightness: Segmented Markets and Global Capital in the Skin-Whitening Trade." In *Shades of Difference: Why Skin Color Matters*. Stanford, Calif.: Stanford University Press.

Golash-Boza, Tanya. 2006. "Dropping the Hyphen? Becoming Latino(A)-American through Racialized Assimilation." *Social Forces* 85 (1): 27–55. doi:10.1353/sof.2006.0124.

Golash-Boza, Tanya Maria. 2012. *Immigration Nation*. New York: Routledge.

Golash-Boza, Tanya, and Pierrette Hondagneu-Sotelo. 2013. "Latino Immigrant Men and the Deportation Crisis: A Gendered Racial Removal Program." *Latino Studies* 11 (3): 271–292. doi:10.1057/lst.2013.14.

Goldsborough, Bob. 2011. "Mosque Controversies Prompt Zoning Change in Dupage." *Chicago Tribune*. October 11, 2011. http://articles.chicagotribune.com/2011-10-11/news/chi-dupage-board-places-new-restrictions-on-new-houses-of-worship-20111011_1_zoning-change-jim-zay-jeff-redick.

Grabell, Michael. 2012. "TSA Finally Investigating Cancer Risk of X-ray Body Scanners: Lingering Questions on the Safety of Backscatters Have Forced the TSA to Commission an Independent Study." *Mother Jones*. December 19, 2012. http://www.motherjones.com/politics/2012/12/tsa-investigation-cancer-risk-x-ray-body-scanners/.

Gray, Paul S., John B. Williamson, David A. Karp, and John R. Dalphin. 2007. *The Research Imagination: An Introduction to Qualitative and Quantitative Methods*. New York: Cambridge University Press.

Greenwald, Glenn, and Murtaza Hussain. 2014. "Meet the Muslim-American Leaders the FBI and NSA Have Been Spying On." *Intercept*. June 9, 2014. https://theintercept.com/2014/07/09/under-surveillance/.

Grewal, Zareena. 2014. *Islam Is a Foreign Country: American Muslims and the Global Crisis Of Authority (Nation of Nations)*. New York: New York University Press.

Gualtieri, Sarah M. A. 2009. *Between Arab and White: Race and Ethnicity in the Early Syrian American Diaspora*. Berkeley: University of California Press.

Haggerty, Kevin D., and Richard V. Ericson. 2000. "The Surveillant Assemblage." *British Journal of Sociology* 51 (4): 605–622. doi:10.1080/00071310020015280.

Handeyside, Hugh. 2014. "Numbers Tell the Story of Our Government's Watchlisting Binge." Blog. American Civil Liberties Union. Accessed October 1, 2016, at https://www.aclu.org/blog/numbers-tell-story-our-governments-watchlisting-binge?redirect=blog/national-security-technology-and-liberty/numbers-tell-story-our-governments-watchlisting-binge.

Harris, Cheryl I. 1993. "Whiteness as Property." *Harvard Law Review* 106 (8): 1707. doi:10.2307/1341787.

Hing, Bill Ong. 2006. "Misusing Immigration Policies in the Name of Homeland Security." *CR: The New Centennial Review* 6 (1): 195–224. doi:10.1353/ncr.2006.0018.

Hirschkind, Charles, and Saba Mahmood. 2002. "Feminism, the Taliban, and Politics of Counter-Insurgency." *Anthropological Quarterly* 75 (2): 339–354. doi:10.1353/anq.2002.0031.

Hochschild, Arlie. 2001. *Time Bind: When Work Becomes Home and Home Becomes Work*. 2nd ed. New York: Holt Paperbacks.

Hochschild, Arlie Russell, and Anne Machung. 2003. *The Second Shift*. 2nd ed. London: Penguin.

Hoeffel, Elizabeth M., Sonya Rastogi, Myoung Ouk Kim, and Shahid Hasan. 2012. *The Asian Population: 2010*. U.S. Department of Commerce, Economics and Statistics Administration, U.S. Census Bureau.

hooks, bell. 1992. *Black Looks*. Boston: South End Press.

Hoover, J. Nicholas. 2009. "TSA Awards $493 Million Contract to CSC." *Information Week*. September 30, 2009. http://www.informationweek.com/architecture/tsa-awards-$493-million-contract-to-csc/d/d-id/1083560?.

Huffington Post/AP. 2012. "Anti-Islam Bus Ads OK'd by Judge: Pamela Geller Wins Preliminary Ruling to Call Enemies of Israel 'Savages.'" July 20, 2012. http://www.huffingtonpost.com/2012/07/20/anti-islam-bus-ad-judge-pamela-geller-israel-savage-mta_n_1689813.html.

Hughey, Matthew W. 2012. *White Bound: Nationalists, Antiracists, and the Shared Meanings Of Race*. 1st ed. Stanford, Calif.: Stanford University Press.

Hunter, Margaret L. 2011. "Buying Racial Capital: Skin-Bleaching and Cosmetic Surgery in a Globalized World." *Journal of Pan African Studies* 4 (4): 142–164.

Huntington, Samuel P. 1993. "The Clash of Civilizations?" *Foreign Affairs* 72 (3): 22. doi:10.2307/20045621.

Jamal, Amaney. 2005. "The Political Participation and Engagement of Muslim Americans: Mosque Involvement and Group Consciousness." *American Politics Research* 33 (4): 521–544. doi:10.1177/1532673X04271385.

Jansen, Bart. 2015. "Lawsuit: TSA Needs Formal Regulations for Full-Body Scanners." *USA Today*. July 15, 2015. https://www.usatoday.com/story/news/2015/07/15/tsa-lawsuit-full-body-scanners-cei-transgender-equality-rutherford/30193799/.

Jones, Jeffrey. 2010. "Americans Back Profiling Air Travelers to Combat Terrorism." Gallup. January 15, 2010. http://www.gallup.com/poll/125078/americans-back-profiling-air-travelers-combat-terrorism.aspx.

Khandelwal, Madhulika. 2002. *Becoming American, Becoming Indian: An Immigrant Community in New York City*. New York: New York University Press.

Kibria, Nazli. 1998. "The Contested Meanings of 'Asian American': Racial Dilemmas in the Contemporary US." *Ethnic and Racial Studies* 21 (5): 939–958. doi:10.1080/014198798329739.

Kibria, Nazli. 2003. *Becoming Asian American: Second-Generation Chinese and Korean American Identities*. Baltimore: John Hopkins University Press.

Kibria, Nazli. 2011. *Muslims in Motion: Islam and Nationality in Bangladeshi Diaspora*. New Brunswick, N.J.: Rutgers University Press.

Kibria, Nazli, Cara Bowman, and Megan O'Leary. 2014. *Race and Immigration*. 1st ed. Cambridge: Polity Press.

Kim, Nadia Y. 2008. *Imperial Citizens: Koreans and Race from Seoul to LA*. Stanford, Calif.: Stanford University Press.

Kleiner, Yevgenia. 2010. "Racial Profiling in the Name Of National Security: Protecting Minority Travelers' Civil Liberties in the Age of Terrorism." *Boston College Third World Law Journal* 30 (1): 103–144.

Kumar, Deepa. 2012. *Islamophobia and The Politics of Empire*. 1st ed. Chicago: Haymarket.

Kundnani, Arun. 2012. "Radicalisation: The Journey of a Concept." *Race & Class* 54 (2): 3–25.

Kundnani, Arun. 2014. *The Muslims Are Coming! Islamophobia, Extremism, and the Domestic War on Terror*. 1st ed. London: Verso.

Lafree, Gary, Laura Dugan, and Erin Miller. 2012. "Integrated United States Security Database (IUSSD): Data on the Terrorist Attacks in the United States Homeland, 1970 to 2011: Final Report to Resilient Systems Division, DHS Science and Technology Directorate." National Consortium for the Study of Terrorism and Responses to Terrorism. December 2012. https://www.start.umd.edu/sites/default/files/files/publications/START_IUSSDDataTerroristAttacksUS_1970-2011.pdf.

Lal, Vinay. 2004. "Indians." In *Encyclopedia of Chicago*. Chicago: Chicago Historical Society. Accessed May 26, 2015, at http://www.encyclopedia.chicagohistory.org/pages/635.html.

Lewis, Bernard. 1990. "The Roots of Muslim Rage." September 1990. *Atlantic Monthly*.

Lipton, Eric. 2006. "Faces, Too, Are Searched at U.S. Airports." *New York Times*. August 17, 2006. http://www.nytimes.com/2006/08/17/washington/17screeners.html?pagewanted=all.

Logan, John R. 2003. "America's Newcomers." Accessed July 8, 2016, at https://eric.ed.gov/?id=ED479961.

Lopez, Haney. 2006. *White by Law: The Social Construction of Race*. New York: New York University Press.

Love, Erik. 2017. *Islamophobia and Racism in America*. 1st ed. New York: New York University Press.

Lyon, David. 1994. *The Electronic Eye*. 1st ed. Minneapolis: University of Minnesota Press.

Lyon, David. 2001. *Surveillance Society: Monitoring Everyday Life*. 1st ed. Buckingham: Open University Press.

Lyon, David. 2003. *Surveillance after September 11*. 1st ed. Malden, Mass.: Polity Press.

Maghbouleh, Neda. 2017. *The Limits of Whiteness*. 1st ed. Stanford, Calif.: Stanford University Press.

Maira, Sunaina. 2009. *Missing*. 1st ed. Durham, N.C.: Duke University Press.

Maira, Sunaina. 2016. *9/11 Generation: Youth, Rights, and Solidarity in the War on Terror*. New York: NYU Press.

Mamdani, Mahmood. 2004. *Good Muslim, Bad Muslim: America, the Cold War, and the Roots of Terror*. 1st ed. New York: Pantheon Books.

Marx, Gary T., and Glenn W. Muschert. 2007. "Personal Information, Borders, and the New Surveillance Studies." *Annual Review of Law and Social Science* 3 (1): 375–395. doi:10.1146/annurev.lawsocsci.3.081806.112824.

Meer, Nasar. 2013. "Racialization and Religion: Race, Culture and Difference in the Study of Antisemitism and Islamophobia." *Ethnic and Racial Studies* 36 (3): 385–398.

Meer, Nasar, and Tariq Modood. 2010. "The Racialization of Muslims." In *Thinking Through Islamophobia: Global Perspectives*. Edited by S. Sayid and A. Vakil. New York: Columbia University Press, 69–84.

Mehrotra, Ajay K. 2004. "Pakistanis." In *Encyclopedia of Chicago*. Chicago: Chicago Historical Society. Accessed May 26, 2015, at http://www.encyclopedia.chicagohistory.org/pages/944.html.

Mogahed, Dalia, and Youssef Chouhoud. 2017. *American Muslim Poll 2017: Muslims at the Crossroads*. Institute for Social Policy and Understanding. Accessed June 5, 2015, at http://www.ispu.org/wp-content/uploads/2017/05/AMP-2017_Full-Report.pdf.

Mohamed, Besheer. 2016. *A New Estimate of the U.S. Muslim Population*. Pew Research Center. January 6, 2016. http://www.pewresearch.org/fact-tank/2016/01/06/a-new-estimate-of-the-u-s-muslim-population/.

Moore, Peter. 2016. "Divide on Muslim Neighborhood Patrols but Majority Now Back Muslim Travel Ban." *YouGov*. March 28, 2016. https://today.yougov.com/news/2016/03/28/divide-muslim-neighborhood-patrols/.

Moosavi, Leon. 2015. "The Racialization of Muslim Converts in Britain and Their Experiences of Islamophobia." *Critical Sociology* 41 (1): 41–56. doi:10.1177/0896920513504601.

Moradi, Bonnie, and Nadia Talal Hasan. 2004. "Arab American Persons' Reported Experiences of Discrimination and Mental Health: The Mediating Role of Personal Control." *Journal of Counseling Psychology* 51 (4): 418–428. doi:10.1037/0022-0167.51.4.418.

Naber, Nadine. 2000. "Ambiguous Insiders: An Investigation of Arab American Invisibility." *Ethnic and Racial Studies* 23 (1): 37–61. doi:10.1080/014198700329123.

Naber, Nadine. 2005. "Muslim First, Arab Second: A Strategic Politics of Race and Gender." *The Muslim World* 95 (4): 479–495. doi:10.1111/j.1478-1913.2005.00107.x.

Naber, Nadine. 2006. "The Rules of Forced Engagement: Race, Gender, and the Culture of Fear Among Arab Immigrants in San Francisco Post-9/11." *Cultural Dynamics* 18 (3): 235–267. doi:10.1177/0921374006071614.

Naber, Nadine. 2007. "Introduction: Arab Americans and U.S. Racial Formations." In *Race and Arab Americans Before and After 9/11: From Invisible Citizens to Visible Subjects*. Syracuse, N.Y.: Syracuse University Press.

Nagel, Joane. 1998. "Masculinity and Nationalism: Gender and Sexuality in the Making of Nations." *Ethnic and Racial Studies* 21 (2): 242–269. doi:10.1080/014198798330007.

Nakashima, Ellen, and Alec Klein. 2007. "U.S. Agency Tries to Fix No-Fly List Mistakes." *Washington Post*. January 20, 2007. January 20, 2007. http://www.washingtonpost.com/wp-dyn/content/article/2007/01/19/AR2007011901649.html.

National Center for Counterterrorism. 2017. "Terrorist Identities Datamart Environment." Accessed March 8, 2018, at https://www.dni.gov/index.php/nctc-newsroom/nctc-resources/item/1718-terrorist-identities-datamart-environment-tide-fact-sheet-current-as-of-30-june-2016.

New York Civil Liberties Union. 2013. "Rights Groups File Lawsuit Challenging NYPD's Muslim Surveillance Program as Unconstitutional." Accessed June 10, 2016, at https://www.nyclu.org/en/press-releases/rights-groups-file-lawsuit-challenging-nypds-muslim-surveillance-program.

Nguyen, Rosa. 2015. "Civil Rights Groups Protest Federal Program to Combat Extremism, Saying It Targets Muslims." *Boston Globe*. August 7, 2015. http://www.bostonglobe.com/metro/2015/08/06/civil-rights-groups-protest-federal-program-combat-extremism-saying-targets-muslims/XefStmtvTuJAyBr8Z8XWLJ/story.html.

Nowrasteh, Alex. 2016. "Terrorism and Immigration: A Risk Analysis." CATO Institute. September 13, 2016. Number 798. https://object.cato.org/sites/cato.org/files/pubs/pdf/pa798_1_1.pdf.

Numrich, Paul D., and Elfriede Wedam. 2015. *Religion and Community in the New Urban America*. London: Oxford University Press.

Office of Inspector General. 2008. *TSA's Administration and Coordination of Mass Transit Security Programs*. OIG-08-66. June 2008. https://web.archive.org/web/20100528125853/https://www.dhs.gov/xoig/assets/mgmtrpts/OIG_08-66_Jun08.pdf.

O'Harrow, Robert, Jr. 2005. "In Age of Security, Firm Mines Wealth of Personal Data." *Washington Post*. January 20, 2005. http://www.washingtonpost.com/wp-dyn/articles/A22269-2005Jan19.html.

Omi, Michael, and Howard Winant. 2015. *Racial Formation in the United States*. 3rd ed. New York: Routledge.

Ong, Aihwa. 1996. "Cultural Citizenship as Subject-Making: Immigrants Negotiate Racial and Cultural Boundaries in the United States." *Current Anthropology* 37 (5): 737–762. doi:10.1086/204560.

Overberg, Paul, Meghan Hoyer, and Jodi Upton. 2013. "Behind the Bloodshed: The Untold Story of America's Mass Killings." *USA Today*. December 3, 2013. http://www.gannett-cdn.com/GDContent/mass-killings/index.html.

Pasquarella, Jennie. 2013. "Muslims Need Not Apply: How USCIS Secretly Mandates the Discriminatory Delay and Denial of Citizenship and Immigration Benefits to Aspiring Americans." *Los Angeles: American Civil Liberties Union of Southern California*. August. Accessed May 20, 2017, at https://www.aclusocal.org/en/publications/muslims-need-not-apply.

Patel, Faiza. 2017. "The Trump Administration Provides One More Reason to Discontinue CVE." Brennan Center for Justice. July 12, 2017. https://www.brennancenter.org/blog/trump-administration-provides-one-more-reason-discontinue-cve.

Paul, Jeff. 2015. "Police Up Security at Irving Mosque after Threats." CBS DSW. April 9, 2015. http://dfw.cbslocal.com/2015/04/09/police-step-up-security-at-irving-mosque-after-threats/.

Peek, Lori A. 2012. *Behind the Backlash*. Philadelphia: Temple University Press.

Penzenstadler, Nick, and Russ Ptacek. 2015. "Lost, Stolen, Broken: TSA Pays Millions for Bag Claims, USA TODAY Investigation Finds." *USA Today*. July 1, 2015. https://www.usatoday.com/story/news/2015/07/02/tsa-damage-tops-3m/29353815/.

Pew Research Center. 2011. *Muslim Americans: No Signs of Growth in Alienation or Support for Extremism Mainstream and Moderate Attitudes*. August 30, 2011. http://www.pewforum.org/2011/08/30/muslim-americans-no-signs-of-growth-in-alienation-or-support-for-extremism/.

Pew Research Center. 2015. *U.S. Public Becoming Less Religious: Modest Drop in Overall Rates of Belief and Practice, but Religiously Affiliated Americans Are as Observant as Before*. November 3, 2015. http://www.pewforum.org/2015/11/03/u-s-public-becoming-less-religious/.

Pew Research Center. 2017. *US Muslims Concerned about Their Place in Society, but Continue to Believe in the American Dream*. July 26, 2017. http://www.pewforum.org/2017/07/26/demographic-portrait-of-muslim-americans/.

Pilkington, Ed. 2014. "Federal Judge Tosses Out Legal Challenge Over NYPD Surveillance of Muslims." *Guardian*. February 21, 2014. https://www.theguardian.com/world/2014/feb/21/nypd-muslim-surveillance-legal-challenge-judge.

Prashad, Vijay. 2001. *The Karma of Brown Folk*. Minneapolis: University of Minnesota Press.

Puar, Jasbir K. 2007. *Terrorist Assemblages: Homonationalism in Queer Times*. Durham, N.C.: Duke University Press.

Purkayastha, Bandana. 2005. *Negotiating Ethnicity*. New Brunswick, N.J.: Rutgers University Press.

Quraishi, Jen. 2011. "Southwest Kicks Another Muslim Off Flight." *Mother Jones*. March 17, 2011. http://www.motherjones.com/politics/2011/03/southwest-discrimination-muslim-woman-kicked-off-plane-fml/.

Rahman, Shahzia. On "Muslim Women Who Wear Hijabs Are Fearful of Backlash after Attacks." NPR: *Morning Edition*. Hosted by David Greene. December 11, 2015. https://www.npr.org/2015/12/11/459313073/muslim-women-who-wear-hijabs-are-fearful-of-backlash-after-attacks.

Ramirez, Deborah, Jennifer Hoopes, and Tara Lan Quinlan. 2011. "Defining Racial Profiling in a Post-September 11 World." *American Criminal Law Review* 40: 1195.

Rampell, Catherine. 2016. "Ivy League Economist Ethnically Profiled, Interrogated for Doing Math on American Airlines Flight." *Washington Post*. May 7, 2016. https://www.washingtonpost.com/news/rampage/wp/2016/05/07/ivy-league-economist-interrogated-for-doing-math-on-american-airlines-flight/?tid=sm_fb&utm_term=.b708bc956aa8.

Rana, Junaid Akram. 2011. *Terrifying Muslims*. Durham, N.C.: Duke University Press.

Rao, Sameer. 2015. "Muslim Girl Reportedly Attacked, Called 'ISIS' at Bronx Public School a Spokesman for the Council on American-Islamic Relations Says Muslim Youth 'Have Been Experiencing This for Quite Some Time.'" *Colorlines*. December 8, 2015. http://www.colorlines.com/articles/muslim-girl-reportedly-attacked-called-isis-bronx-public-school.

Razack, Sherene. 2008. *Casting Out*. Toronto: University of Toronto Press.

Reid, Tim. 2015. "America's Muslims Object to Obama's Push for More Self-Surveillance." *Yahoo News*. December 8, 2015. https://www.yahoo.com/news/americas-muslims-object -obamas-push-more-self-surveillance-212033281.html.

Richardson, Robin, and Gordon Conway. 1997. *Islamophobia: A Challenge for Us All*. London: Runnymede Trust, Commission on British Muslims and Islamophobia.

Roberts, Dorothy E. 2004. "Welfare Reform and Economic Freedom: Low-Income Mothers' Decisions about Work at Home and in the Market." *Faculty Scholarship*. Paper 584: 1029–1064.

Roots, Roger. 2003. "Terrorized into Absurdity the Creation of the Transportation Security Administration." *Independent Review* 7 (4): 503–517.

Rosino, Michael L., and Matthew W. Hughey. 2015. "Who's Invited to the (Political) Party: Race and Party Politics in the USA." *Ethnic and Racial Studies* 39 (3): 325–332. doi:10.108 0/01419870.2016.1096413.

Said, Edward W. 2014. *Orientalism*. London: Knopf Doubleday.

Salcido, Olivia, and Cecilia Menjívar. 2012. "Gendered Paths to Legal Citizenship: The Case of Latin-American Immigrants in Phoenix, Arizona." *Law & Society Review* 46 (2): 335–368. doi:10.1111/j.1540-5893.2012.00491.x.

Sander, Libby. 2006. "6 Imams Removed from Flight for Behavior Deemed Suspicious." *New York Times*. November 22, 2006. http://www.nytimes.com/2006/11/22/us/22muslim .html?_r=0.

Sanghani, Rhadika. 2016. "Gender Segregation: The Truth about Muslim Women 'Forced' to Sit Away from Men." *Telegraph*. January 19, 2016. http://www.telegraph.co.uk/women/ life/gender-segregation-the-truth-about-muslim-women-forced-to-sit-aw/.

Scahill, Jeremy, and Ryan Devereaux. 2014. "Watch Commander: Barack Obama's Secret Terrorist-Tracking System, by the Numbers." *Intercept*. August 5, 2014. https:// theintercept.com/2014/08/05/watch-commander/.

Schlangenstein, Mary. 2017. "JetBlue and Delta Test Biometric Scanning to Replace Boarding Passes." *Bloomberg*. May 31, 2017. https://www.bloomberg.com/news/articles/2017-05 -31/jetblue-tests-using-face-recognition-to-scrap-boarding-passes.

Shaheen, Jack G. 2008. *Guilty: Hollywood's Verdict on Arabs after 9/11*. Northampton, Mass.: Olive Branch.

Shaheen, Jack G. 2014. *Reel Bad Arabs*. 3rd ed. Northampton, Mass.: Olive Branch.

Shane, Scott. 2011. "Congressional Hearing Puts Muslim Civil Rights Group in the Hot Seat Again." *New York Times*. March 11, 2011. http://www.nytimes.com/2011/03/12/us/ politics/12muslims.html?mcubz=0.

Shehata, Dina Samir. 2015. "Anti-Sharia Bill Dead, but Sentiment Alive Third Time Not a Charm for Foreign Law Ban in Texas." *Austin Chronicle*. May 22, 2015. https://www .austinchronicle.com/news/2015-05-22/anti-sharia-bill-dead-but-sentiment-alive/.

Shryock, Andrew. 2008. "The Moral Analogies of Race." In *Race and Arab Americans before and after 9/11: From Invisible Citizens to Visible Subjects*. Syracuse, N.Y.: Syracuse University Press.

Shryock, Andrew. 2010. *Islamophobia/Islamophilia*. Bloomington: Indiana University Press.

Siddiqui, Sabrina. 2014. "Americans' Attitudes Toward Muslims and Arabs Are Getting Worse, Poll Finds." *Huffington Post*. July 29, 2014. http://www.huffingtonpost.com/ 2014/07/29/arab-muslim-poll_n_5628919.html.

Skenazy, Lenore. 2015. "I Let My Son Ride the Subway Alone. I Got Labeled 'The World's Worst Mom.'" *Washington Post*. January 16, 2015. https://www.washingtonpost.com/ posteverything/wp/2015/01/16/i-let-my-9-year-old-ride-the-subway-alone-i-got-labeled -the-worlds-worst-mom/?utm_term=.13587d322304.

Smith, Jane I. 1999. *Islam in America*. New York: Columbia University Press.

Smith, W. A., W. R. Allen, and L. L. Danley. 2007. "'Assume the Position ... You Fit the Description': Psychosocial Experiences and Racial Battle Fatigue among African American Male College Students." *American Behavioral Scientist* 51 (4): 551–578. doi:10.1177/0002764207307742.

Southern Poverty Law Center. 2017. "Update: 1,094 Bias-Related Incidents in the Month Following the Election." https://www.splcenter.org/hatewatch/2016/12/16/update-1094 -bias-related-incidents-month-following-election.

Stampnitzky, Lisa. 2013. *Disciplining Terror*. 1st ed. Cambridge: Cambridge University Press.

Stoller, Gary. 2005. "Airport Screening Rules Change Dec. 22." *USA Today*. December 13, 2005. https://usatoday30.usatoday.com/travel/news/2005-12-12-screening-usat_x.htm.

Stuart, Hunter. 2013. "Heba Abolaban, Muslim Woman, Says She Was Attacked Over Boston Bombings." *Huffington Post*. April 18, 2013. http://www.huffingtonpost.com/2013/ 04/18/heba-abolaban-muslim-woman-attacked-boston_n_3112065.html.

Suleiman, Michael W. 1999. *Arabs in America*. Philadelphia: Temple University Press.

Sullivan, John L., and Henriët Hendriks. 2009. "Public Support for Civil Liberties Pre- and Post-9/11." *Annual Review of Law And Social Science* 5 (1): 375–391. doi:10.1146/annurev .lawsocsci.093008.131525.

Susskind, Yifat. 2014. "Under Isis, Iraqi Women Again Face an Old Nightmare: Violence and Repression." *Guardian*. July 3, 2014. https://www.theguardian.com/global -development/poverty-matters/2014/jul/03/isis-iraqi-women-rape-violence-repression.

Tehranian, John. 2010. *Whitewashed: America's Invisible Middle Eastern Minority*. 1st ed. New York: New York University Press.

Tierney, John. 1994. "The Big City; Color Blind." *New York Times*. Accessed March 5, 2014, at http://www.nytimes.com/1994/09/18/magazine/the-big-city-color-blind.html.

Toaldo, Mattia. 2012. "The Reagan Administration and the Origins of the War on Terror: Lebanon and Libya as Case Studies." *New Middle Eastern Studies* (2): 1–17.

Tranchin, Rob. 2010. "Arlington Muslims Report Continued Harassment." *KERA News*. Accessed March 20, 2014, at http://keranews.org/post/arlington-muslims-report -continued-harassment.

Transportation Security Administration. n.d. "Security Screening." Accessed March 7, 2018, at https://www.tsa.gov/travel/security-screening.

Treitler, Vilna Bashi. 2013. *The Ethnic Project: Transforming Racial Fiction into Ethnic Factions*. Stanford, Calif.: Stanford University Press.

Tsuda, Takeyuki. 2014. "'I'm American, Not Japanese!': The Struggle for Racial Citizenship among Later-Generation Japanese Americans." *Ethnic and Racial Studies* 37 (3): 405–424. doi:10.1080/01419870.2012.681675.

Tuan, Mia. 1998. *Forever Foreigners or Honorary Whites?: The Asian Ethnic Experience Today*. New Brunswick, N.J.: Rutgers University Press, 1998.

Tyrer, David. 2013. *The Politics of Islamophobia: Race, Power and Fantasy*. London: Pluto Press.

U.S. Census Bureau. n.d. "American Fact Finder." Accessed on November 10, 2016, at https:// factfinder.census.gov/faces/tableservices/jsf/pages/productview.xhtml?pid=DEC_10 _PL_QTPL&prodType=table.

U.S. Department of Homeland Security. 2008. *Screening of Passengers by Observation Techniques (SPOT) Program*. https://www.dhs.gov/xlibrary/assets/privacy/privacy_pia_tsa _spot.pdf.

U.S. Department of Homeland Security. 2017. "If You See Something, Say Something™ | Homeland Security." Accessed on July 5, 2017, at https://www.dhs.gov/see-something-say -something.

U.S. Department of Justice. 2013. *A Study of Active Shooter Incidents in the United States between 2000 and 2013*. FBI Report. September 16, 2013.

U.S. Department of State. 2001. "The Taliban's War against Women." 2001–2009 Archive. November 20, 2001. https://2001-2009.state.gov/g/drl/rls/6185.htm.

U.S. Government Accountability Office. 2013. *TSA Should Limit Future Funding for Behavior Detection Activities*. Government Accountability Report. November 2013.

U.S. Government Accountability Office. 2017. *Countering Violent Extremism: Actions Needed to Define Strategy and Assess Progress of Federal Efforts*. Government Accountability Office Report. April 2017.

Vasquez, Jessica M. 2010. "Blurred Borders for Some but Not 'Others': Racialization, 'Flexible Ethnicity,' Gender, and Third-Generation Mexican American Identity." *Sociological Perspectives* 53 (1): 45–72. doi:10.1525/sop.2010.53.1.45.

Volpp, Leti. 2003. "The Citizen and the Terrorist." In *September 11 in History: A Watershed Moment?* Durham, N.C.: Duke University Press.

Wacquant, Loïc. 2014. "Marginality, Ethnicity and Penality in the Neo-liberal City: An Analytic Cartography." *Ethnic and Racial Studies* 37 (10): 1687–1711. doi:10.1080/01419870 .2014.931991.

Weissman, Cale Guthrie. 2015. "These Are the Insane New Technologies Airports Are Using to Learn Everything about You." *Business Insider*. June 19, 2015. http://www .businessinsider.com/new-airport-tracking-technologies-can-learn-everything-about-you -2015-6.

Williams, Rhys, and G. Vashi. 2007. "Hijab and American Muslim Women: Creating the Space for Autonomous Selves." *Sociology of Religion* 68 (3): 269–287. doi:10.1093/ socrel/68.3.269.

Winter, Jana, and Cora Currier. 2015. "Exclusive: TSA's Secret Behavior Checklist to Spot Terrorists." *Intercept*. March 27, 2105. https://theintercept.com/2015/03/27/revealed-tsas -closely-held-behavior-checklist-spot-terrorists/.

Index

Tierney, John, 88, 150n5 (chap. 3)
Transportation Security Administration
(TSA): creation of, 51; criticism of,
54–55; Muslim experiences with agents
of, 3, 64–68, 72; and screening programs,
16–17, 51–55, 149n6; technologies used,
14, 51
travel ban. *See* Muslim ban
Treitler, Vilna, 126
Trump, Donald: and anti-Muslim rhetoric,
3, 10, 131; Muslim ban proposed by, 18, 29,
37, 114, 134–135, 148n6; Muslim registration proposed by, 21, 114
Tyrer, David, 41, 149n11, 149n2 (chap. 3)

Unisys, 13
United States v. Balsara, 32
United States v. Bhagat Singh Thind, 32
United States v. Dolla, 32
United States v. Dow, 33
U.S. Airways, 49
USA PATRIOT Act. *See* PATRIOT Act
U.S. Census: racial categorizations used by,
32, 45, 130, 132, 148nn1–2, 151n3
U.S. Department of State: reports on Tali-
ban by, 9

U.S. Government Accountability Office, 52,
55, 136

Van Duye, Beth, 41
volunteering. *See* civic engagement

War on Drugs, 122
War on Terror: academic foundations of, 7;
origins of, 13; and Reagan administration,
13; and surveillance, 4
welfare, 25
*When Islamophobia Turns Violent: The 2016
US Presidential Elections* (Abdelkader), 10
whiteness, 151n6; and beauty, 87–88; and
citizenship, 33, 88, 118; construction of, 31,
131–132; and hijab, 45–47, 79, 127; Muslims' self-identification as, 38; privileges
of, 35, 88, 131; and racial hierarchy, 127,
132–133
white supremacists, 136, 147n8, 151n6
Winant, Howard, 21–22
World Trade Center: 9/11 attacks on, 1; 1993
bombing of, 7

YouGov, 21

Zogby Analytics, 21

About the Author

SAHER SELOD is an assistant professor of sociology at Simmons College. She has published widely on the racialization of Muslims.

CPSIA information can be obtained
at www.ICGtesting.com
Printed in the USA
LVHW090924150121
676550LV00016B/151